Praise for the B-

Michael is a valued friend, and I r̶____ ____ ..u understanding of our complicated political enviro. ____ ume of much cynicism, this book examines those who represent t̶.̶ pest of what makes our political system work and underscores that good character is good politics. From my more than fifty-five years in the public relations business, I couldn't agree more.

—*Howard J. Rubenstein, Public Relations Executive, New York, NY*

Today public cynicism about government officials is very high. Michael Kerrigan's well-done analysis of several people who have served with distinction reminds us that public service remains our highest calling and that it can and should be done well.

—*Joel Klein, Chancellor, New York City Schools, New York, NY*

Michael Kerrigan is a highly principled and deeply religious man. In *Politics with Principle: Ten Characters with Character*, he finds these same qualities in ten of his "pals in politics." Because his probing questions are directed to close friends, the reader will discover, in their verbatim responses, some interesting nuggets about public figures that would never be found in a "Who's Who."

—*Charles S. Robb, former Governor and United States Senator, Virginia*

I have known Mike for many years, both socially and professionally. His insight into how government works and the people that make it work are the best in Washington. I know many of the characters in his book and share his assessments of their characters and abilities. The book will be a refreshing read at a time when the American people are questioning our political institutions and its leaders.

—*Thomas Hale Boggs, Jr., Esq., Patton Boggs LLP, Washington, D.C.*

Michael Kerrigan is a longtime friend and has great insight into the functioning of government, history, and our leaders. He has great appreciation for the need of moral, disciplined leadership not only to lead but also to set examples for generations to come. It is in stark contrast to the comment "they are all crooks" and the cynicism that is so prevalent today. Many of our leaders are individuals with outstanding principles and character, which is seldom reported but greatly needed for our country to excel. Thanks to Michael we can gain insight and learn from some of them.

—*Don Nickles, former United States Senator, Oklahoma*

Michael Kerrigan's *Politics with Principle: Ten Characters with Character*... is a refreshing and timely showcase of the virtue and humility of men and women in service to others. In these tumultuous times, it is critical we light more candles and do less cursing the darkness. It's about time we shine the light on the good guys.

—*Mary Matalin, former assistant to President George W. Bush and former counselor to Vice President Dick Cheney*

These individuals are the kind of role models this nation needs, and Mike Kerrigan has done all of us a service in drawing attention to the integrity, the decency, and the strength of character their lives reflect in all they do.

—*Bill Brock, former United States Senator, Tennessee*

Mike Kerrigan has done a masterful job of isolating and focusing on the elements of character that lead to principled and correct decision making. A solid read!

—*Frank Fahrenkopf, Co-Chairman of the Commission on Presidential Debates and former Chairman of the Republican National Committee*

Politics with Principle is a beacon of hope. America still has public servants that have made truth, integrity, and strong values the centerpiece of their lives. The role models in this book are not historic figures, but real people who have struggled daily in their quest to live in an honorable manner.

—*Robert Porter Lynch, author of* Business Alliances: The Hidden Competitive Weapon

Politics with Principle

Ten Characters with Character

Michael J. Kerrigan

Published by Wheatmark®
610 East Delano Street, Suite 104, Tucson, Arizona 85705 U.S.A.
www.wheatmark.com

William M. Bulger cover photo is by Michael Naimo. The copyright was purchased by William M. Bulger in 2010.

Paperback ISBN: 978-1-60494-447-1
Hardcover ISBN: 978-1-60494-448-8

LCCN: 2010930439

"It is not the critic who counts; not the man who points out how the strong man stumbles, or where the doer of deeds could have done them better. The credit belongs to the man who is actually in the arena, whose face is marred by dust and sweat and blood; who strives valiantly; who errs, who comes short again and again, because there is no effort without error and shortcoming; but who does actually strive to do the deeds; who knows great enthusiasms, the great devotions; who spends himself in a worthy cause; who at the best knows in the end the triumph of high achievement, and who at the worst, if he fails, at least fails while daring greatly, so that his place shall never be with those cold and timid souls who neither know victory nor defeat."

—*"The Man in the Arena,"*
speech at the Sorbonne
Paris, France
April 23, 1910
Theodore Roosevelt, 26th U.S. President

Dedication

A 46-star American flag dates this Ellis Island photo of the Great Hall between 1907–1912. Photo credit: National Park Service.

To my parents and all of my Irish Catholic ancestors, who built new lives in America while preserving their good character and their unwavering faith in God, family, and country. I stand on their shoulders.

I also dedicate this book to all who have worked in public service and served others without lying, cheating, or stealing.

Acknowledgements

A few important individuals deserve acknowledgement for helping me to bring this book to completion:

Mattias Caro, a longtime family friend and young lawyer, has provided indispensable assistance as a researcher and collaborator on this project.

Donna Kerrigan, the love of my life, my wife of forty-two years, a professional science writer and editor, lent her skills to this project and brought clarity to my thinking.

Each of the political characters chosen for this book deserves acknowledgement. Each person graciously donated time and provided thoughtful reflections and substantial edits that enriched the final product.

Author disclaimer: Michael J. Kerrigan received no compensation, incentives, or gratuities whatsoever for producing this book.

Contents

Introduction

Recently, my ten-year-old grandson, Kaelan James Kerrigan, in preparation for Grandfather's Day at his elementary school, asked me what kind of work I did. I responded that I was a lobbyist in Washington, working with Congress and federal agencies. Kaelan looked puzzled, and he further probed whether that was a good thing, whether I worked with good people.

Our conversation triggered a flashback to my childhood. When I was Kaelan's age, the lines of right and wrong, good and bad, were still hazy to me. Such concepts boiled down to whether or not my actions would get me thrown out of Catholic grammar school. Concerning politics, these lines of good versus bad got even hazier. Thanks to the *Chicago Tribune*, I was bombarded with examples of local politicians who put self-interest first, even at a cost to others. I wondered whether working in politics precluded being good. So when I was ten, Kaelan's age, I wrote to Mayor Richard J. Daley, asking him to explain just how politics worked in Chicago. His office sent a generic letter that did not answer my question.

Much later in life, I told Mark Elliott, a friend of many years, that I was going to write a book about political operatives I have known who demonstrated good character in their public and personal lives. Mark immediately quipped, "That's going to be a very short book! I bet you can't find ten." Challenged by Mark, I felt a bit like Abraham in Genesis. Like Abraham, I had to find ten good persons. If Abraham failed, the cities of Sodom and Gomorrah would be destroyed. In my case, I would lose a bet with a friend and have a disillusioned grandson.

Daley never gave me a straight answer, but I will give one to Kaelan. This book will answer my grandson's question and Mark's challenge. The pages that follow will show that there are indeed good people in politics. With admiration for their achievement and good character, I will present ten principled politicos—nine men and one woman. They will answer my questions about their personal and professional lives and their value systems, about how their formative years prepared them for being in politics and still being good. In short, they will answer the question that Mayor Richard J. Daley ignored.

I hope that Kaelan and others interested in politics, history, government, or ethics will find it interesting to discover the virtues that were important in the lives of these successful political players. By reading the biographies and interviews that follow, they will see what strengths these leaders brought to bear when their character was tested. They will see how they handled public pressure during adversity, how they were their own honest critics when that was necessary. Finally, readers will also see the joy that all ten have experienced during public service because they did not compromise their values in the process.

A Perennial Struggle: Good vs. Evil

Diogenes searches for an honest man.

"What was, will be again, what has been done, will be done again, and there is nothing new under the sun!"

—*Ecclesiastes 1:9*

Wasn't it just yesterday that the new administration promising hope and change in Washington had problems confirming cabinet officials because of irregularities in their tax returns? Didn't we just hear about Senator Max

Baucus securing a plum administration job for his girlfriend? Who can forget about former Senator John Edwards's adulterous escapades on the Presidential campaign trail, or the money Congressman Jefferson was hoarding in his freezer? What about the wild actions of the early '90s that started off with tales of post office and banking schemes sprouting up right in Congress's back yard? Mark Sanford has almost lost the governorship of South Carolina (and certainly a shot at the White House in 2012) because of his philandering and subsequent cover-up.

But it's not just the politicians. One name in the lobbying industry sums it up: Jack Abramoff, master of Congressional "pay to play."

Business isn't doing any better either. Who can ignore the idea of greed and corruption that seems to crop up every time we mention certain names, from Dennis Kozlowski to "Kenny Boy" Lay? Tyco, Enron, Lehman Brothers, Bear-Stearns, and AIG? Wall Street and greed are virtual synonyms in the public mind, as Congress bails out the bankers but leaves ordinary people on Main Street to fend for themselves.

And the military is not exempt from evil. What about Tailhook '91? Abu Ghraib? Our soldiers struggle on, facing divorce and suicide rates that have skyrocketed over the past twenty years.

Sports fans enjoy watching athletes compete and excel. Nothing seemed better than the summer of 1998, when Mark McGuire and Sammy Sosa pursued Roger Maris's magical record for home runs. Oh yeah. Steroids. It was too good to be true. Our heroes on the juice. Even Tiger Woods has joined the ranks of athletes who deliver disillusionment.

Enough certainly has happened to make one wonder, "Can I find virtuous people at all? If so, are any to be found in politics?"

It might comfort the reader to know that rampant as poor character is today, it is not a new problem. One of the great sages of the ancient world, Marcus Tullius Cicero, was a Roman statesman and philosopher in the first century BC. He had the courage and good judgment, the control and sense of right and wrong, to ferret out the corruption of his time. His memorable speech against Cataline denounces that man's machinations to overthrow the Roman government. "Oh what times! Oh what customs!" Cicero famously begins. The words he uses against Cataline could be applied to any corrupt figure today:

> How long, O Cataline, will you abuse our patience? How long is that madness of yours still to mock us? When is there to be an end of that unbridled audacity of yours?

Although more legend than history, the epic founder of Rome, Aeneas, faced numerous challenges to his character at the hands of corrupt and foolish figures. Aeneas was seduced and tempted by the Queen of Carthage. Many others challenged him militarily in order to see who would rule. All the while Aeneas remained faithful to his duty and his destiny to found Rome. The Romans of Cicero's time knew the *Aeneid* well. But even in the ancient world, this story was only the ideal, an inspirational myth that omitted much of the ancient world's corruption.

Indeed, shortly after Cicero's own lifetime, the Roman Republic ceased. Julius Caesar ascended the throne. The Roman Empire began. The height of Roman civilization, the Republic, gave way to increasing centralizing power and a loss of that Roman ideal of duty before power, of service and honor before self-glory and self-aggrandizement. It had not been too long ago in Rome's past that a farmer named Cincinnatus had taken the reigns of power to guide Rome through a dark period, only to lay down that power and return to farming once his mission was accomplished. Cincinnatus. Aeneas. Cicero. These men seemed more the exception to the rule than prototypes of Roman citizens.

The book of Ecclesiastes puts it most simply: "there is nothing new under the sun." The quest to identify and eliminate bad character in public life has preoccupied all peoples at all times.

Even in ancient Greece, good character was a concern. There was a man by the name of Diogenes, sometimes called Diogenes the Cynic. He was an eccentric philosopher. One famous story says that Diogenes carried a lantern around Athens. When he was asked what he was looking for, he quipped, "An honest man."

It's an ironic story. Greece, in most people's minds today, was the birthplace of democracy, of the virtuous citizen. It was the home of Socrates, Plato, Aristotle, Homer, Herodotus, and Thucydides. Yet Diogenes felt the need to literally light a lamp in order to find an honest man. If his experience and his good judgment led him to an honest man, all was not lost. Civilization would survive.

Whether in the era of Abraham, that of Diogenes, or the current time, the situation is the same. In all times, citizens wander, looking for the honest man. Our continual search keeps the situation from turning bleak.

Like Diogenes, modern citizens still search for good character. They may search for an honest person for two entirely different reasons. Cynics seek to prove that character simply does not exist in today's politics. For them, society is nothing more than an amalgamation of self-interests, and character is negotiable. Rules and laws are made merely to restrain these passions because people are, fundamentally, unable to govern themselves. A cynical Diogenes may believe that the world could only succeed through tyranny, absolute control.

History tells us that the possibility of such a cynical worldview is very real. Recall Hitler, Stalin, and Mao. Robespierre and Napoleon in France; Calvin in Geneva; Tsar Ivan in Russia; Saladin in the Holy Land; and even the despotic emperors like Nero and Diocletian in ancient Rome. This solution appeals to humanity precisely because it is simplistic, and it requires very little of citizens except one thing: submission.

The second possible worldview, however, is that of a realistic Diogenes. These citizens look for good character because they know that it needs to exist. They do not believe that the path of character and virtue has been tried and found wanting, but rather that it has been tried and achieved among a few in every new generation of citizens. These realists know that good character is the key to successful self-government, and an important deterrent from radical self-interest among our country's people of privilege: politicians, lobbyists, business leaders, as well as media and sports celebrities.

Benjamin Franklin famously quipped at our country's founding, "You have a Republic, if you can keep it." Unlike despotism, a Republic relies upon a citizenry that is temperate, prudent, courageous, and just. It needs people to rise above their narrow self-interests in pursuit of a common good. It needs to cultivate leaders who honor that as well. A commitment to virtue is the necessary and fundamental prerequisite to liberty. Without a person's own passions and selfish pursuits being subsumed by the virtuous life, liberty is nothing more than the pursuit of whatever makes us feel good. A selfish vision is limited; it must be. It is only concerned with the here and now.

History tells us, however, that we get the government that we deserve. We get the leaders that we deserve. If we do not care about virtue and character, our leaders will not either. Our common good is connected. Our character, as Heraclitus once said, "becomes our destiny." Looking for ten virtuous men and women, as Abraham once did, isn't some quest to placate God or simply a chance to pat ourselves on the back. It is a search for hope. If these people exist, then we know that, despite all the failings that repeatedly come up in human history, our society can make it. We will make it, as will our next generation if they recommit to developing good character and the practice of virtue.

Ten Characters with Character

Their Lives

Many inspiring stories in both cinema and literature share the common trait of dynamic and vivid personalities thrown into difficult situations. Similarly, the ten characters profiled here have been thrown into the often shallow and sometimes shark-infested waters of American politics. They demonstrate that exceptional men and women in public life are that way, in large part, because of the principles and moral values they bring—and do not betray—in their public service careers. As their personal and political roles have evolved and emerged, each enriching the other, these ten have had a positive impact on the nation's landscape. They have successfully navigated the seas of power between the shoals of what is right and proper and what is wrong and expedient. How they act when they get into these situations reveals their true character.

Our cast of characters includes five Republicans and five Democrats. They have practiced politics as members of Congress and state legislators, ambassadors, a Navy admiral, lawyers, lobbyists, president of a university, superintendent of the United States Naval Academy, and the head of the Antitrust Division of the Department of Justice. They hail from all parts of the country, from Massachusetts to California, from North Carolina to New Mexico, to states as near to our nation's capital as Maryland and Pennsylvania.

The lives of these characters span forty years of American political history. Each has been a leader at some time during this period. All value working with others of differing ideologies. As you read about each character, note the associations they formed, the peers they chose, the mentors they sought, and the organizations with which they affiliated themselves, all of which have helped to define their characters. Observe the role of family in the development of their characters. Study the wise choices they have made in their careers.

Please meet ten characters with good character:

- **Anne Bingaman** is a lawyer and entrepreneur originally from the very small town of Jerome, Arizona, who served in the Clinton administration as the head of the Antitrust Division of the Department of Justice.

- **Charlie Black** is a GOP political operative who worked closely with the Reagan and George H. W. Bush administrations and now works hard to train the next generation of political leaders.

- **Tom Bliley** began his career running his family's funeral business before serving as the Mayor of Richmond and then as a Congressman representing the Commonwealth of Virginia.

- **William Bulger** is a lifelong resident of Massachusetts. His tough-as-nails roots helped him endure as the longest-standing President of the Massachusetts State Senate in the history of the Commonwealth. He later served as President of the University of Massachusetts.

- **Ben Cardin** is a Maryland native who has served as Speaker of the House of Delegates, Congressman from the Third District, and currently as junior Senator from Maryland in the United States Senate.

- **Richard Carlson** headed the Voice of America during the late Cold War and served as an Ambassador during the first Bush administration. Orphaned by a teenage mother, he also worked as a journalist, TV news anchor, sailor, and president of King World Productions.

- **Paul Eckstein** is a prominent litigator from Arizona, who has successfully prosecuted a Governor in a state impeachment proceeding as well as built a substantial law practice with Perkins Coie Brown & Bain, PA.

- **Admiral Tom Lynch** served as Superintendent of the Naval Academy as well as captaining the "almost" 1963 National Champion Navy football team. He currently works as a venture capitalist.

- **Chuck Manatt** is a longtime lawyer and political operative in the Democratic Party, who, as National Party Chairman, rebuilt the DNC after Carter's defeat in 1980. He is a former Ambassador to the Dominican Republic and a dedicated farmer in his home state of Iowa.

- **Rick Santorum** is a former United States Congressman and two-term Senator from Pennsylvania, who is contemplating a run for the 2012 Presidency.

The Honorable Anne K. Bingaman

*"It takes the most character in appointive government jobs—
and it is actually easy if you don't want another job."*
—*Anne Bingaman*

In a marvelous essay tracing the course of his life, Mark Twain recounted how getting the measles at age twelve contributed greatly to making him an excellent author. He attributes the path of his life and career to seizing circumstances as they came. Anne Bingaman, lawyer, businesswoman, and entrepreneur, believes that such a thing—what she calls serendipity, or opportunities coming from unexpected events—has similarly shaped her life.

As with Mark Twain and measles, Anne sees her serendipitous life beginning with a trip she took with her parents to San Francisco when she was nine years old. On that trip, they saw the Stanford campus. While they were there, her parents said strictly and quietly to each other, "This is where very smart people go to school." Anne never forgot that day at Stanford and her parents' comment. At some point not long thereafter, Anne formed the conscious goal of going to Stanford. She did it, admitted from Central High School in Phoenix to the Stanford Class of 1965. While there, she lived on the Stanford Row, in a former sorority house, on the very street where her family had driven so many years before.

After graduating from Stanford in 1965, Anne enrolled in the Stanford Law School that fall. The next year, because there were seating charts in law school, Anne was assigned a seat—by chance—right next to a very handsome and outrageously funny man in the class, Jeff Bingaman by name. What Anne chose to do with that chance event was to buy tickets to the San Francisco Opera and ever so casually ask him to go. He did, events took their course, and a few years later, shortly after the bar exam, they married in Phoenix.

Marrying Jeff led inexorably to life in New Mexico, a state that, very honestly, Anne had associated only with Highway Route 66 prior to moving there. But she immediately loved it, and had the great good fortune to practice law there for almost fifteen years before moving to Washington, D.C. At the time of the Bingamans' move to New Mexico in the spring of 1969, there were few lawyers there. Only 800 members of the New Mexico Bar practiced law, including ten (yes, ten) women. Today, 800 lawyers probably could be found in a single building in downtown Washington.

Shortly after her arrival, the second-largest firm in the state hired Anne, making her the first woman in New Mexico to be hired by a major firm. In 1972, at the request of all twenty women who comprised the total female student population at the University of New Mexico Law School, Anne became the school's first female law professor. Again, Anne's talent was in the right place at the right time, Anne received tenure within three years, taught nine courses, and wrote a book and several law review articles.

Ultimately, Anne decided that she did not want to spend the next thirty years teaching and writing. She resigned as a faculty member in 1976, an unheard-of move at the time. She had no real plan as to what she would do because law firms in Santa Fe were still not hiring women. Although she was offered a job by her former firm in Albuquerque, Anne did not want to commute two and a half hours a day, every day.

At that point Anne's father intervened. He came from a long line of small business owners, and he had always told Anne and her brother to start their own businesses. This was a turning point in Anne's life. "Try it for a year. See what happens," her father said; "I'll pay your rent." Anne seized this opportunity and opened her own law office: Anne K. Bingaman, Attorney at Law, Santa Fe, New Mexico. She sent out announcements to the

Santa Fe bar, all 120 of them, and three days later got a call from Judge Donnan Stephenson, who had retired from the New Mexico Supreme Court to help Judge Harry L. Bigbee prepare and try the United Nuclear case against General Atomic and Gulf. Again, by serendipitous timing, Anne was opening her firm just as a prestigious judge in her state was retiring, bringing her the opportunity to work with him on a multinational lawsuit.

Anne met with Judge Stephenson. After describing the facts of a complicated billion-dollar case for several hours, Judge Stephenson, over Anne's heated objections, told her that she would be on the antitrust case for United Nuclear against General Atomic and its partner, Gulf Oil. Anne was horrified. She spent several days and weeks arguing with the judge and finding qualified antitrust firms to take this part of the case. He adamantly refused. Finally, she decided it was either do probate and real estate closings in Santa Fe, or give this a try.

As it turned out, Gulf was the only U.S. company in an international uranium cartel that it had operated until at least 1973. It had bought up all of United Nuclear's New Mexico uranium production while secretly a cartel member. Gulf had bought the uranium to keep competing supply off the market, because competitors would undercut the cartel price. Very clean, very straightforward, very legally correct. Again good fortune was Anne's when she hired two paralegals to help her prepare her case, only to discover that they were exceptionally bright and, in effect, able to act as her law partners as they dug into the facts of the uranium cartel and Gulf's role in it.

Over time, after pouring over the facts, Anne's strategy became clear: move for sanctions under Rule 37 for failure to answer the Cartel Interrogatories and failure to produce any Canadian Cartel Documents, which United Nuclear had requested before a Canadian secrecy law was passed, but which GAC/Gulf had neither revealed nor produced. On March 2, 1978, the trial court entered findings of fact and conclusions of law and granted Bingaman's motion for default judgment and other sanctions under Rule 37. The default judgment was valued at $1 billion based on uranium prices at the time it was entered. The New Mexico Supreme Court upheld the ruling in its entirety, with certiorari denied by the U.S. Supreme Court.

By the spring of 1978, Anne and two new law partners had been hired by several other companies who were plaintiffs against Gulf and GAC, because their uranium also had been bought by Gulf while secretly part of the cartel, just as United Nuclear's had been. Over the next several years, Bingaman's law firm represented Ranchers/Houston Natural Gas, Exxon Nuclear, and Sohio/Reserve, all in cases alleging the same antitrust cartel violations that United Nuclear had originally pursued, and other cases as well.

Looking back, Anne recalls those years in Santa Fe as the most wonderful years of her professional life. She had a truly great law firm, with outstanding lawyers, brilliant paralegals (thirty-two in total—Santa Fe turned out to be the best market on the planet for hiring paralegals). This could only have happened to a solo practitioner in the sparsely populated state of New Mexico, where, by 1977, Anne knew and was known by many lawyers, including Donnan Stephenson and Judge Bigbee—who had given her the biggest chance in her professional life, the one that shaped her entire future career.

As Anne describes it:

> It totally changed my self-image. It changed my own view of myself. I saw myself as heading a law firm, being in charge. Women in those days had a very different self-image than this. When I got out of law school, I didn't have an image that I was going to start a law firm. It just never crossed my mind. It wasn't that I dismissed it. It just didn't occur to me. Anyway, marrying Jeff, moving to New Mexico, and starting my own law firm were the really key things from which everything else flowed.

The Santa Fe years were wonderful, not just professionally but also personally: Anne's son John was born in Santa Fe in 1979. Her son's birth profoundly changed her personal life. During John's childhood, largely spent in Washington, D.C., he was Anne's boon companion. Just as Anne had the strength of character to open the first woman-owned law practice in Santa Fe, she also had the good judgment to make time for her son when she was blessed with a child. She knew how to keep the balance, to keep her family a priority in principle and in practice.

After Jeff won the United States Senate race in 1982, and the family moved to Washington, D.C., Anne's courage in agreeing to help Judges Stephenson and Bigbee fight Gulf brought still more good luck. It defined for her a field of law to practice in the Federal City that was important, relevant, and understandable to that town's law firms. Anne joined the Washington office of an Atlanta law firm, which Stu Eizenstat headed, continued to do antitrust litigation for nine years, and then had the immense honor and good fortune to be appointed by President Clinton as Assistant Attorney General for Antitrust in the Department of Justice.

Ann enjoys family time with her son John and husband Jeff.

Anne served as Assistant Attorney General for Antitrust for three and a half years, from 1993 to 1996, under Janet Reno, and again, a serendipitous event occurred—this time in the form of the Telecom Act, which Anne had never even heard of when she was sworn in as Assistant Attorney General in June of 1993. The Antitrust Division's ranks had grown to include as many as fifty lawyers devoted solely to administering the AT&T Consent Decree, the 1984 ruling that had broken up AT&T and prohibited the Bell Operating Companies from entering into the long-distance market. The Telecom Act, which was considered by Congress in heated debates and even more heated lobbying for almost two years, from January 1994 to the fall of 1995, turned out to heavily involve the expert views of the Consent Decree lawyers within the Antitrust Division, since it was the AT&T Consent Decree that would be replaced by the Telecom Act. Because Anne was the then head of the Antitrust Division, she was honored to be the Administration's witness in eight Congressional hearings about the effects of various permutations of the Telecom Act, and to represent the Administration in meetings with Senators and Congressmen who wanted to discuss the Administration's views on the proposed Act.

Anne describes the test of character that one faces in public service, the constant bombardment of people trying to sway one's efforts to faithfully execute one's duty:

> It takes the most character in appointive government jobs—and it is actually easy if you don't want another job. Antitrust was what I was qualified to do, I had done it for twenty years, and I thought I could honestly offer myself to the President of the United States as a candidate for that job, and I could do it. I never thought I could do another job, and I never wanted to do another job. And in interagency fights—there are plenty of them, over trade issues, over all types of stuff—there are myriad opportunities to cave and to sell out the best interest of the very agency you are sworn to protect and defend, and whose laws you are to faithfully execute (in my case, antitrust law), in order not to anger important people at another agency and get a reputation as a pain in the neck and unreasonable.
>
> Basically people are looking for a reason to roll you, right and left. But I didn't have any trouble with that. But where it would be hard, very hard, is if you were bucking for a higher job. Because with every promotion comes a whole new round of input about what is this person like: do they have good judgment? How do they work with others? Because if you've been fighting people—not that I always fought them, sometimes we agreed—but things just come up where antitrust is opposed to other interests, to trade interests, to another agency's view, and you just have to be willing to go to the mat and let the chips fall. It doesn't mean you are always going to win. But you've got to fight as hard as you can for the interests that you are charged with protecting.
>
> To do your appointive job well, you can't be seeking your subsequent government job. That's the truth. Because you would be personally conflicted between your own ambition and protecting the interests that you are charged with protecting.

Through the Antitrust Division and Anne's involvement in the Telecom Act, she became absolutely fascinated by the telecommunications industry. So much so that, rather than go the traditional route of joining a law firm after leaving government service, she decided that twenty-eight years of law practice had been wonderful, but that it was time to do something else. She decided to seek a business job instead.

Brian Thompson, CEO of LCI International and the nation's fourth-largest long-distance company hired Anne as president of the Local Services Division, competing against the Bell Companies for local customers.

Anne had a marvelous time and worked with wonderful people. But, even for Anne, luck is a fickle mistress, and in early March 1998, only fourteen months into the job, Anne found out that LCI had been sold over the weekend to Qwest, based in Denver. Anne had nothing against Qwest, but she wanted to be at company headquarters, not flying to Denver every couple of weeks for a one-hour meeting with the CEO and other executives. And so Anne did not take Qwest's offer, but left the merged company on July 1, 1998—again with no idea what she would do next.

Anne decided to turn her attention to the rural telephone company business. Again her timing was incredibly lucky. That fall, GTE announced the sale at auction of 1.4 million rural lines. Anne qualified in the GTE auction, along with two friends of hers from LCI, and a new company was formed. Anne focused on four states, did due diligence, hired consultants, raised money on Wall Street from private equity companies, and, with a group of prominent Hispanic investors, won at auction all of GTE's lines in New Mexico, Oklahoma, Texarkana, and 300,000 lines in Texas, for a total of 550,000 lines, in a $1.7 billion transaction. The deal was signed with GTE on September 4, 1999. They hired a COO, opened corporate offices in Dallas, and went from eight employees in January 2000 to 1,750 on September 1, 2000. Perhaps 800 of those were former GTE employees, but the rest were new hires. It was an incredibly exciting experience, and Anne served as the company's first CEO and Chair of the Board from September 1999 to the end of 2001.

In January 2002, the company had grown from a pure startup to full-fledged and well-functioning rural telephone enterprise, so it was time for Anne to go home. She returned to Washington, now the non-executive Chair of the Board of her company, Valor Telecom—but it was far from a full-time job. That spring, Anne decided to start another company.

Anne settled on an audio conferencing business for major law firms, with an emphasis on software that linked to law firms' billing systems, to avoid manual re-entry of charges on client bills, and several other software features. They went to market on February 1, 2003. It was slow at first, because as it turned out, IT staff at many law firms did not have audio conferencing high on their list. But Anne and her employees persevered, and by 2008, Anne had as clients all the lawyers in 40 percent of the top law firms in the U.S.

At that point, at the urging of her son John, who now works in private equity in New York, Anne decided, with great reluctance, to sell the company. Anne did so on August 12, 2008—just thirty-three days before bad subprime lending ultimately paralyzed Wall Street, producing a massive exodus of clients, drastic losses in stocks, and devaluation of assets by credit rating agencies. Since that infamous September day, when Lehman Brothers investment firm filed the largest bankruptcy in U.S. history, few are selling anything. Anne had been saved once more by her good fortune.

Anne had originally planned to start another business after selling her conferencing company, but as events have unfolded since September 2008, she realized that this is not the time nor environment to start another business. She now spends much of her time with her old friends from Central High in Phoenix, and with friends in D.C. and New York, working out with regularity and planning family trips, including a rafting trip with twenty friends down the Grand Canyon in 2010.

Like Mark Twain, Anne sees her life as marked by good fortune flowing from seemingly insignificant events such as Twain's getting the measles. Also like Twain, Anne was quick to seize opportunity out of each unexpected turn of fortune.

Charlie R. Black, Esquire

"I've walked away from candidates for huge violations of principle."

—Charlie Black

Charlie Black has dedicated a lifetime of work to politics, campaign management, public affairs, and government relations. Throughout his life, Charlie has used the opportunities earned and given to him to become one of the top political strategists for the Republican Party. He has been involved with almost every major Presidential campaign of the last thirty years. That life of politics has brought Charlie into contact with friends and professionals all of whom have profoundly shaped his life. Charlie's key to success in life is simple—never stop learning, and learn from great people:

> I have had many opportunities for great jobs, but just as importantly, [I've had] the chance to work for and with great people from whom I learned a lot. One must never stop learning, to be successful in life.

Charlie's political involvement began in college. At the University of Florida in the late 1960s, he joined the Young Republicans and the prominent conservative youth organization Young Americans for Freedom. This political engagement at the state and national levels brought Charlie into contact with David R. Jones, one of the most important leaders of the conservative wing of the Republican Party from the 1960s through the '90s. It was David who taught Charlie the importance of leadership skills: how to read the character and motivation of people; pick the right people for the right jobs; find the good and avoid saying negative things about people, friend or foe; and understand that today's enemy might be tomorrow's friend, so don't burn bridges. Jones's creed required that a man's word be his bond, and his loyalty to his friends be unwavering. Most importantly, David Jones applied his leadership skills not for personal gain but on behalf of his patriotic, conservative, anti-Communist philosophy. Jones emphasized to Black a very realistic and practical philosophy:

> To be effective, to implement conservative political philosophy, you've got to work through the two-party system. That applies to the Republican Party. If you're going to be a leader in the Republican Party, you're going to have to support non-conservative people and occasionally you're going to have to compromise on an issue. So I bought into that, and I've always stuck to it.

What Charlie took from Dave's tutelage was one goal, integrity. As Charlie says:

> What I respect most in a person is integrity—it is a threshold requirement for someone to get a lot of respect from me. But also, unselfishness, the ability to follow the Golden Rule, the most important of Christ's teachings: "Do unto others as you would have them do unto you." Which means, to do that—no one can do it perfectly—you have to sacrifice and put someone else's interests ahead of yours.

Out of college, Randal C. Teague brought Charlie to Washington to work on the national staff of Young Americans for Freedom—Charlie's first full-time job and also his entry into the political profession at the national level. Randy taught Charlie that the business of the conservative movement was just that, a business—so they had to run YAF in an organized way, with attention to detail and clear priorities. Randy taught Charlie a work ethic and determination to get that day's job done before leaving the office.

Following his work with Randy, Charlie went to work with Jesse Helms. Because of Charlie's involvement with Young Americans for Freedom, he was given the opportunity to work in Jesse's first campaign for the U.S. Senate. He learned political organizational skills in on-the-job training in Helms's 1972 campaign. More importantly, Charlie learned, through what would become a thirty-year association with Helms, never to compromise integrity for any purpose, especially not for a political purpose. The Jesse Helms Charlie knew was a straightforward man: "Tell people where you stand, marshal the arguments for your case, communicate clearly and effectively, and never back down." Helms also insisted this was possible to do while keeping a sense of humor.

Charlie got the biggest break of his professional career a few years later. In 1975, John P. Sears hired Charlie to work in Ronald Reagan's presidential campaign. John was a brilliant and creative political strategist. Charlie now reflects that he learned more about politics from John than from all the other political minds he has known in his life, put together. John taught Charlie that to understand current political trends and the desires of the electorate, one had to understand history and the political culture and traditions of every state. One had to see into the future about where each political leader would take the country. John taught Charlie that it takes this understanding, plus a lot of disciplined thought, to be creative in politics or public policy. He taught Charlie to have the courage to be creative, too. He gave Charlie confidence that he could perform at the highest levels of American politics by showing him how to do it.

John also was a great persuader when promoting political strategies and public policies. Creating a good idea is meaningless unless its creator can persuade the candidate and colleagues in the campaign to do it—and then persuade the news media that it is a plausible idea. John was the best salesman in politics. Through John's introduction to the national political scene, and through hard work and lessons learned, Charlie created his own chance to know and assist great national leaders over the past thirty-four years. This relationship lead to numerous opportunities because of both the doors John opened for Charlie and the growth Charlie experienced under John's tutelage:

When John Sears hired me in 1975 to work for Ronald Reagan's first campaign, that set in motion the entire career path that I have [followed] ever since. That period gave me the self-confidence that I could perform and be successful on a national level in politics and public affairs.

Charlie's association with John Sears soon led to several more prominent roles. Bill Brock hired Charlie as political director of the Republican National Committee when Brock was Chairman. Bill taught Charlie that intellectual and policy content are essential elements of a winning political party. Brock also taught Charlie that one could be a tough competitor in campaigns without engaging in personal attacks. Brock knew where to draw the line to maintain civility.

When Charlie's work brought him to help with the Reagan Administration in 1980, he took the rare chance to learn from Ronald and Nancy Reagan personally. Ronald taught him how critical it was for political leaders to devote themselves to improving their nation and the world, and not just sustaining it. Nancy taught him that some rare individuals, by offering selfless devotion to a leader, make it possible for that leader to achieve great dreams for the country. Together these insights captured for Charlie the political brilliance that characterized the Reagan years in the White House. In particular, Charlie admired Reagan's ability to pick the right people for the right job and then to delegate. But such delegation only worked because Reagan had a clear idea of his priorities. And with clear priorities, together with trust for the people working under him, Reagan could provide effective and strong leadership. Charlie recalls:

> Reagan wanted to defeat Communism, cut taxes, and reduce the size of government. But in order to get the military buildup he needed to defeat Communism, he had to compromise with Tip O'Neil. Because he was able to work with the Democrats in other areas, thanks to Reagan, the world was better, the wall came down.

Charlie continued to play an active role in Republican Party politics. His contact with George H. W. Bush (41st President) as an outside advisor taught Charlie that a political leader should always rise above self-interest and do the honorable thing. Bush (41) did what he thought was right, regardless of the political consequences.

Of course, Charlie had supported and worked for Jack Kemp leading up to the race against Bush in 1988. It was Kemp, one of Charlie's best friends in politics, who taught Charlie that conservatism could not and

Charlie lays out possible political scenarios.

should not succeed if it did not address the needs of every American. The original compassionate conservative, Jack thought about the poor and disadvantaged of society every day. He reached out to them privately and in his creative conservative public policies.

Another wonderful opportunity in Charlie's life has been to know a star of the "greatest generation," Bob Dole. A living testimony to the need for service and sacrifice for one's country, Dole also showed Charlie the importance of working across party lines through civil relationships. When Charlie first worked for him in 1976, he was surprised to learn that Dole was a close friend of George McGovern! Dole was one of the great legislative leaders of the last century because he got things done and didn't care who got the credit.

Yet another privilege of Charlie's life has been a personal friendship with John McCain for over thirty years. McCain taught Charlie a long time ago not to complain about any bad break. Charlie admired McCain's courage to be completely fearless in doing what he thinks is right, and his high standard of loyalty in friendship. Most of all, Charlie learned from McCain a personal demonstration of Churchill's admonition, "Never, ever, ever give up!"

The sum total of these professional and political contacts is a deep sense of gratitude for the United States, shown through Charlie's desire to serve:

> I believe the United States is the greatest country on Earth. And the key
> to that, as de Tocqueville identified when the Republic was new, is citizen

participation and service to community, state, and country. I have been able to spend a majority of my adult life in politics and make a living doing it. And I have spent many, many hours in politics and helping others in volunteer work. There is an obligation for American citizens to do that to keep the country great.

Charlie's early years growing up in the Black family shaped his work ethic and his values. His parents, Ray and Lorraine, taught and showed him the importance of honesty, hard work, humility, good citizenship, and belief in Christ. Charlie remains close to several Baptist pastors, but Jay Wolf deserves mention for his particularly important role in Charlie's life because he taught him about witnessing his faith and reaching out to non-believers. He also taught Charlie the need to study the Bible in order to be a good witness. Doug Coe, another great lay Christian leader, also influenced Charlie. Doug taught Charlie, and countless others, how to work with non-Christians to achieve world peace and cooperation by putting into action the principles of Jesus Christ—practicing patience, extending mercy, giving generously—without necessarily preaching.

In Charlie's early thirties, he saw the need to create a stable business in government relations and public affairs, rather than just bouncing from campaign to campaign for the rest of his life. Bill Timmons, Sr., showed Charlie how to do this—how to translate political experience into professional services for large businesses. And Timmons welcomed his new competitor into his field by mentoring Charlie for many years. Charlie has always tried to return this favor by mentoring young people in business. That's an obligation that Charlie has taken seriously throughout his life:

> Part of our obligation, for those of us who have been around in politics and government for a long time, is to teach and train young people and the people that we work with, sometimes even older people. I usually summarize it for young people in politics, that there are two essential rules: that your word is good and that you are loyal to your friends. There are other things that they need to be taught, but if they get those two right, then that's a pretty good path to character development.
>
> For those of us who are involved in campaigns and government and those of us involved in the spin-offs of campaigns from government, like public affairs, we must pick people of good character to support for elective office or for the executive branch or even for our government-related businesses. Sometimes, somebody is very effective in politics, or in a government

job, or in a private-sector job, whose character is marginal. We must still hold out for integrity. We need not and should not reward bad character in or around politics.

His ability to work with the other side of the aisle has been part of Charlie's success, especially with Peter Kelly, Jim Healey, and Scott Pastrick, Charlie's main Democratic partners. They had the courage to join forces with this young conservative Republican, and showed Charlie how to create an effective bipartisan professional firm. These men are not just examples of how Charlie can work across party lines; they have been among his best personal friends for over twenty-five years.

Another profound influence on Charlie's life is his wife, Judy Black. Together they have learned that God's greatest gift is the unconditional love of a good marriage. Judy taught Charlie that politics and business are fine, but that one's faith, spouse, and family must always be given priority. She convinced Charlie that amid his life as a successful operative in Washington, he could still take the time to help those in need. Judy's example causes Charlie to never let a day go by that he doesn't try to help, or mentor, another person.

Many other good friends have contributed lessons as well. Taken collectively, all the people mentioned in this profile are the reason Charlie feels that he has led a charmed and blessed life. He thinks that he may not have yet lived up to the example provided by some of the great leaders he has known, but their good character remains in his memory, and he emulates their virtues as his aspiration. For Charlie Black, imitation of the good character he witnessed in his training forms the basis of his own principled political practice.

The Honorable Thomas J. Bliley, Jr.

"Too often, I think, people come to Washington and get carried away with the trappings of office. Stick with what got you here."

—Tom Bliley

Thomas J. Bliley, Jr., is a longtime public servant, most prominently representing Virginia in the U.S. House of Representatives from 1981 to 2001. Today, after three decades in public service, Tom serves as a senior government affairs advisor in the Washington office of Steptoe & Johnson, LLP. His career is a classic among Washington stories.

Tom is a lifelong Virginian. Born in Chesterfield, Virginia, during the Great Depression, Tom attended Catholic schools growing up. Faith was important to the Bliley family. Tom grew up with many heroic relatives who unselfishly gave their entire lives to God's service within the Catholic Church: Tom's uncle as Prior of a Benedictine Abbey and two of his aunts as nuns, one a Benedictine, and the other a Sister of Charity.

Following high school, Tom received his Bachelor of Arts degree from Georgetown University in 1952, and then he chose to give himself unselfishly to public service and took a commission with the United States Navy for several years, rising to the rank of Lieutenant. In 1955, Tom married Mary Virginia. Together they have two children and four grandchildren.

Upon his return from naval service, Tom joined his family business, working in the funeral home that his father had established. Eventually, he became its president. In 1968, Tom made the most important professional decision of his life: he again entered public service, as the Vice Mayor of Richmond, Virginia. After just two years, he was elected Mayor of Richmond, and went on to serve in that capacity for seven years. His term encountered significant character-testing challenges, including the desegregation of Richmond's school system. While keeping taxes low and preventing onerous regulation on business during his term, Tom navigated tough political waters. His good character and willingness to listen to his constituents helped the city thrive.

In 1980, Tom's call to public service came again. Perhaps to the chagrin of Mary, his wife of now over fifty years, Tom ran for the seat in the Seventh District of Virginia in the U.S. House of Representatives. Tom's win was historic: he was the first Republican to win his district outright since Reconstruction. He won convincingly and has been a stalwart Washington supporter of conservative values ever since. Indeed, Tom's principles and his district's preferences have not always lined up. Tom is pro-life, while more than 65 percent of his district remains staunchly in favor of abortion rights. Nevertheless, Tom has always followed Edmund Burke's sage advice for representatives:

> As your Member of Parliament, I owe you my industry, but if I sacrifice my judgment for your opinion, I have not served you well.

Tom started and ended in historic ways in the House. He was known for his pleasant demeanor and his gentlemanly manners. He also stood out by wearing his trademark bow ties. In Congress, he quickly gained a reputation for his abilities as a legislator. While still a Republican freshman, he was appointed to the powerful Energy and Commerce Committee, which exercises jurisdiction over energy, health care, telecommunications, consumer protection, and the environment. Tom was soon to make his mark in all these areas.

After a dozen years of service as a backbench Republican under

Democratic rule, Tom joined forces with Newt Gingrich and other conservatives to become architects of the Republican takeover of the House in
1994. The historic election in that year could not have been possible without the perseverance of Tom and his colleagues.

The shift from Democratic to Republican control had a big impact on
Tom's life. He was named Chairman of the Commerce Committee, the oldest committee in the House. The ensuing six years brought a whirlwind of
legislative achievement. This era occurred under a Democratic president—
Bill Clinton—offering more evidence of Tom's excellent talent at teamwork
and bipartisanship. Here are some examples of what Tom accomplished by
practicing principled politics:

- The Telecommunications Act of 1996. Tom's vision to unleash the
  market forces of the nation's telecommunications industry is widely
  heralded as one of the key boosts to the economy in the late 1990s
  and an essential force in promoting the Internet as an everyday
  experience for most Americans.
- The State Children's Health Insurance Program (SCHIP). In 1998,
  Tom played a critical role in ensuring that all children were provided
  health insurance. As a father of adopted children, he has a special
  sensitivity to the needs of uninsured, needy children. SCHIP reauthorization was one of the first public laws that President Obama
  signed into law in 2009.
- The Gramm-Leach-Bliley Act. After over six decades of stifling
  regulation, particularly in light of new technological developments,
  Tom led the fight to repeal and replace the Glass-Steagall Act that
  separated commercial from investment banking with a more com-
  monsense, modern regulation. Upon passage, Tom was an outspoken advocate for robust enforcement of banking oversight by ap-
  propriate regulatory authorities.
- Electronic Signatures in Global and National Commerce Act (ES-
  IGN). Tom's leadership led to the enactment of the ESIGN Act in
  June 2000. ESIGN brought interstate commerce into the Internet
  age, allowing vendors and financial services companies to conduct
  business efficiently and reliably.

Tom left Congress in 2001. He had agreed to a House rule limiting him
to six years as Chairman. One of his former staff members, Eric Cantor,
succeeded him; Cantor now serves as Minority Whip in the House, and is

Bliley and his cosponsors move their Bill on the House floor.

a rising star in the Republican Party. Tom leaves a legacy of integrity, which has at its foundation his absolute commitment to truthfulness. Tom has always felt that this was his strength in serving his constituents. Once at a meeting back in Tom's district, a constituent came up to him and remarked, "I have supported you on every vote for ten years, but you voted for [a particular bill], and I will never support you again." With a bit of disarming humor, Tom replied, "Sir, if you disagreed with only one vote in ten years, I think I have served you well. By the way, I see you have a wedding band. Have you agreed with your wife on everything for ten years?"

Since his departure from the House, Tom has served as a government relations advisor for a vast array of clients. He continues to play a significant role in the public policy process—on Capitol Hill, in the Federal Communications Commission, and in other regulatory agencies. Tom remains active in Richmond community affairs, including numerous board and commission memberships. He enjoys time with his family, a good golf game, and a well-deserved martini from time to time.

The Honorable William M. Bulger

"Integrity without knowledge is weak and useless, and knowledge without integrity is dangerous and dreadful."
—*Samuel Johnson,* Rasselas

Wilyiam Bulger looms large in Boston politics. Bill was first elected to the Massachusetts House of Representatives as a Democrat in 1960. He took his seat a few weeks before John F. Kennedy's inauguration. Bill heeded JFK's stirring call to be people of courage, judgment, integrity, and dedication—a call proposing these traits as ideals of public service. This was JFK's famous "City on a Hill" speech. While today's generation of politicians may find it impossible to appreciate the zeal and optimism JFK kindled in 1960, Bill did not. By 1970, he was elected to the State Senate. Soon after, Bulger served as that body's President for eighteen years. Finally, Bill led the University of Massachusetts for almost eight years as its President, having been invited by the Board of Trustees and formally receiving his appointment from a Republican governor.

Bill's life began in South Boston. Early in life, he seized the reins of his own destiny. In his 1996 political memoir, *While the Music Lasts: My Life in Politics*, Bill recalls how as a ninth-grader in catechism class, he overheard two boys from Catholic college preparatory schools talking about books, schoolwork, and ideas in a way that was totally foreign to him at the time. He knew then and there that his own education was inadequate. Initiative led him to march into Boston College High and ask what it would take to apply there. Realizing his own educational deficiencies, Bill offered to repeat the ninth grade. BC High accepted his offer. A part-time job at John's Meat Market and some help from his sister, Jean, helped Bill meet the $150 annual tuition. It was a momentous decision, one that placed him on the academic path to Boston College and Boston College Law School.

BC High was but the first of many great influences on Bill's young life. Books brought Bill beyond the projects of South Boston. At seventeen, he says, "Books came like storms whirling through my mind, leaving me uncomfortably embarrassed when normality returned." His intellectual influences are Dr. Samuel Johnson and Father Carl Thayer. Johnson's insight on character profoundly impressed Bill, as he warned that knowledge without integrity could be dangerous. And Bill's teacher, Father Carl Thayer, was Johnson's equal in judging men's character: "Show me what a man does when no one else is around, when no one knows what he is doing, and I'll tell you what kind of person he is."

It was Father Thayer who introduced Bulger, the college student, to the ancient Greeks and Romans. That course began for Bill a relationship with Father Thayer that would last until the end of Thayer's life in 1990. Father Thayer most admired men of action: Demosthenes, Thucydides, and Cicero. He used these ancients to teach Bill the skill of political persuasion while preserving personal integrity.

After studying "Oration on the Crown," a speech Demosthenes delivered in the face of his own defeat, Bulger chose to write his college paper about James Michael Curley's 1946 trial and 1947 imprisonment for mail fraud during his last term as Mayor of Boston. What intrigued Bill about the prosecution of Curley was that in order to get someone who was deemed "bad," the prosecutors themselves felt free to behave badly, even illegally.

When he reached voting age, Bulger supported Curley during one of his many successful runs for Mayor. Under the slogan, "Curly Gets Things Done," James Michael was reelected for a fourth term in spite of being under indictment. Much of Bill's political career was modeled after the best of Curley. In Bulger's 2009 biography of Curley, he captures their mutual view of politics:

I think, if I understand Curley correctly, that he was not so much interested in the power as he was in what the power enabled him to accomplish.

It is men like Curley and Bulger, men of dedication and talent, who do,
in fact, make sacrifices by devoting themselves to public service, who are
essential for the survival of our democracy. As Bulger explains again in the
Curly biography:

> Why do they stay at it? Why do they choose public service in the first
> place?
>
> I think there is a basic recognition that this kind of service is worth-
> while no matter what the cost. And this sense of its value grows with
> experience.
>
> Others may think the politician is on an ego trip, or the politician has
> base motives, psychological or otherwise, for selfish gain or enrichment
> in some way. But the politician who stays the course soon realizes that it
> will just have to be enough that he himself knows what good he has done.

In Bulger's view, the life of James Michael Curley affirms the idea that
a life in politics remains worth undertaking even though it often includes
some rough periods.

But what motivates Bill Bulger to withstand the slings and arrows of
outrageous fortune in politics? Bill's first motivation for his own career in
politics was to improve tomorrow for his family. A lucky excursion-boat trip
to the picturesque community of Steel Pier, on the tip of Cape Cod, led Bill
to a dance with Mary Foley. That friendship led to a marriage of fifty years,
producing nine children and thirty-two grandchildren. His second motivation was his love of his neighborhood, South Boston, his childhood home
and his family home since 1966. In politics, Bill could also build a better
tomorrow for his neighborhood. Throughout Bill's career, the national media has trashed the reputation of South Boston. This cruel and false portrait
comes, as Bill surmises, because "the rootless have always had contempt for
the rooted, which may explain why social engineers chose South Boston for
their disruptive forced busing experimentation."

Bulger well understood that attacks and lies are common in the political
arena. In Bill's first race for the Massachusetts House of Representatives, his
opponents attacked him personally, referring to him as "Same-Suit Bulger,"
because Bill's blue suit was the only one he owned. Bill never responded in
kind. Although possessing a quick wit, Bill never used it to disparage an

opponent personally, but he often used it to decry unacceptable political actions. For example, when describing Judge W. Arthur Garrity's steward-ship of forced busing in Boston, Bill said, "this most important case... was handled with the sensitivity of a chainsaw and the foresight of a mackerel."

One provocation constant in most of Bill's future campaigns also came in his first one. The *Boston Globe* frequently whipped it up. Bob Dineen, an opponent's "horse holder," tried to tar Bill with the image of Bill's brother Jim: "You belong in prison with your brother." Bill's father had been ap-prehensive that Jim (aka a fugitive called Whitey) Bulger's problems would hurt Bill's political prospects.

Loyalty has been a prime virtue in Bill's life. Take Ted Kennedy's first race for Senate. Jack was President of the United States, Bobby the Attorney General, and the campaign was supported by the large war chest of Ambas-sador Joe Kennedy. One premise of Ted's campaign was that he was rich and needed nothing. Unfortunately this implied that candidates without wealth—Abraham Lincoln comes to mind—are inherently larcenists and fundamentally without character.

Bill had already publicly announced his support for Teddy's primary opponent, Bill's South Boston neighbor Eddie McCormack. The Kennedy campaign organized and invited several prominent Massachusetts poli-ticians to luncheon at the famous Boston restaurant Locke-Ober, whose most famous dish was lobster Savannah. Bill ordered the lobster Savannah. While Bill was eating the succulent lobster, campaign staffers began count-ing heads, going around the table asking who would be with Ted. Everyone was eagerly pledging support.

When it came to Bill, he said, "I can't be with you, Ted. The McCor-macks are my neighbors."

Ted was unhappy and responded, "I don't know whether we should try to persuade him. I don't think we can afford to feed him."

"Well," Bill replied, "I just came to be sociable."

Another example of Bill's loyalty is evident in his support of Paul Ma-honey for a district court judgeship. Mahoney, Bill's administrative assis-tant, was appointed subject to the approval of the Executive Council, as Massachusetts's law requires. Bill appeared before the Council to testify in Paul's support. Two enemies of Bill's, the controversial Harvard professor Alan Dershowitz and Harvey Silvergate, were there to oppose. The two had wrongly predicted to the Council, in advance of the hearing, that Ma-honey would be indicted. Further, Dershowitz had publicly attacked Bulger and Mahoney as "thugs," "henchmen," "crooks," etc. Bulger knew that

Mahoney's reputation was about to be savaged, which prompted him to preempt the attack.

Echoes indeed of the Crown Oration! When the Chairman tried to silence Bill, Bulger quoted Edmund Burke's admonition that there comes a time when forbearance ceases to be a virtue. "We have reached that time with this pair," he said. "These two are murderers," Bill told the Council, "murderers of reputations. Too many have put up with them too long."

Bill then recited a list of points in Paul's favor. Knowing Paul's character allowed Bill to say with assurance that neither Dershowitz nor Silvergate could offer a single fact that argued against Mahoney's approval:

> These men have no grievance against Paul Mahoney. All you will hear from them is their antipathy toward me. With that in mind, consider their credibility. They are crafty men, vindictive men, manipulative men, true connivers.

As anticipated they offered no evidence damaging to Mahoney. The Council approved the appointment. Paul has served faithfully and competently on the bench for twenty years. Much more than a judgeship was at stake: since then Dershowitz has dropped his attacks on Mahoney but continues to attack Bulger personally by trying to link him to his brother's activities, calling him "head of the mob" or "the real Godfather."

These battles with antagonists and the press have occurred repeatedly throughout Bill's career. The issue comes down simply to the integrity of a man's reputation. Bill and James Michael Curley shared a common antipathy for the press when it oversteps its role in relation to politicians:

> If the press would rule, then let it stand for election, rather than rule through intimidation of those who are in fact chosen by the electorate.

Unfortunately, the press has one tool Bill feels strongly it should not wield: the ability to tarnish a man's good name without consequences. It comes from what Bill sees as that "shifty and dishonest decision" of the Supreme Court in *Sullivan v. The New York Times* (1964). For most of the existence of our Republic, like any other citizen, a public office holder could sue a publisher for libel, unless the publisher could prove the truth of his statements. This liability for false defamation fostered responsibility on the part of the press. But the Supreme Court held in *Sullivan* that persons in public office could not sue for libel unless they could prove actual malice.

The court simply made it virtually impossible for the victim to do anything about libelous publications. The media, granted such immunity, were given a license to lie.

Principled politicians take stands, even against what is perceived as popular wisdom. Bill saw the forced busing decree of W. Arthur Garrity as unjust and unwise, and always insisted that it would prove counterproductive. He understood the issue as being not about race but about misuse of the state's power. The forced busing of South Boston's children was a danger to them and to the community. Even if busing could rescue black children from schools they did not want to attend, which was doubtful, would it not drive white children of the poor into schools they did not want to attend? And would it not do so on the basis of their skin color? The goal, after all, was to rescue children from undesirable schools, not to evict them from desirable schools.

Forced busing was popular with unaffected proponents including politicians from Ted Kennedy to Mayor Marian Barry of Washington, D.C., as well as reporters Robert Turner of the *Boston Globe* and Tom Wicker of the *New York Times*. These proponents of forced busing would not put their own children at the disposition of Garrity, but would insist otherwise for the parents of children in South Boston.

Dr. Coleman was a sociologist who initially fostered the busing idea, but then opposed it. He described the unintended result as aligning aggrieved black parents against the School Department and the "innocent third party," namely South Boston.

Bill opposed forced busing based upon the natural right of parents to supervise the education of their children. Black parents, Bill believed, should have been encouraged and assisted in choosing any school for their own children. It should have been the same for all: maximum choice. The forced-busing decree proved counterproductive, as he warned. The school population dropped from 94,000 to about 55,000 students in only a couple of years. The children of South Boston attended schools with black children with no problem; it was the uprooting of children from South Boston neighborhood schools and shipping them all over the city on the basis of skin color that was the basis of the community's objection. South Boston people were the innocent third party in the drama.

Dr. Coleman told Bill that the most segregated of acts is the choice of the racial isolation of suburbia. Bill gently needled a State Senator, asking whether there might be some guilty feeling on the part of the folks from Wellesley (Judge Garrity's home) or Hyannis Port. The proponents of this

Bill joins Pavarotti at the microphone.

terribly ill-advised policy, especially the *Globe*, pitted black people and white people against each other unnecessarily. The *Globe* thought of itself as a heroic proponent of Civil Rights. But in fact, by their encouragement of the judge, they were foisting an impossible burden upon the city. The *Globe's* writers lived in the suburbs, as did the *Globe's* owners. Few today can envision the plight of a South Boston parent with children in public school. Bill blamed the social planners who were willing to oppose the natural right of parents to educate their children. South Boston families had no alternative, unless they had the money to afford private schools.

That was not Bill's last brush with controversy. His Presidency of the University of Massachusetts's system ended abruptly. He had prepared himself for the possibility that his differences with the Republican Governor could force him to leave his post prematurely. He remains grateful for the time he served UMass. It was always a struggle, but a good one on behalf of a broader educational opportunity for the people of the Commonwealth. Few goals are more worthwhile. Bill comforted himself by recalling Demosthenes:

> Demosthenes was a man who meant what he said and said what he meant.
> When fortune was unkind, he knew that he had done his best and had

done it unselfishly. I admired his manner of using his power of persuasion. The power of persuasion had worked for me through eighteen years and ten elections for the Presidency of the Senate and seven years as President of UMass.

An abrupt end may make a task feel thankless, but it does not make it meaningless. Bill also thought of his friend Congressman Joe Moakley, whose timely phone call one evening had forever enriched Bill's perspective on politics:

> We had been friends since childhood. One day in 1991 Joe phoned to inform me that the doctors could do no more for him. He asked me to prepare remarks for his funeral. He went on to explain how he was putting things in order. "I'm just seeing things as they really are, Bill," were his words. As we were reviewing his many political milestones, it struck me that one accomplishment that had no political gain attached, Moakley's charitable work to successfully pursue the murderers of six Jesuit priests and their housekeepers in El Salvador, gave him the greatest comfort and meaning at the end.

His friend Moakley had discovered what the ancient Pericles had already declared: "It is by honor and not by gold that the helpless end of life is cheered." Like Moakley, at the close of his political career, Bill Bulger was cheered by knowing he had behaved honorably and served his fellow citizens.

The Honorable Benjamin L. Cardin

"When I first started in the legislature, I saw a lot of marriages that were destroyed in Annapolis. Just go home at night. Pick your own priorities. If you want to go home to your family every night, you can."

—*Ben Cardin*

Senator Ben Cardin is a lifelong public servant of Maryland. Ben was elected to Maryland's House of Delegates at twenty-three. He served as its speaker for eight years, starting at age thirty-five. He has spent the last twenty years representing Maryland in Congress: from 1987 onward in the House, and since 2006 in the Senate.

It might seem strange, at first, to refer to the Senator by his first name, but regardless of who you are, a tourist in Washington, D.C., or a Senate colleague, Ben wants you to call him by his first name. He doesn't believe in titles, and he explains why:

Our founders got it right when they didn't want Americans to have titles or to become royalty. I know that titles—whether you're a doctor, a manager, or a legislator—focus on demanding respect. I really do think it is inhibiting, and that you're better off talking to people as equals. I have a rule at my office: "Call me by my first name; don't call me Senator." In a way, it's because I want to be able to communicate with all as equals. I want to be able to get their talent, their information, and their expertise. If it becomes too formal, then I think something is lost in that.

Following history and tradition is a core part of Ben's life. Ben was born on October 5, 1943, the third generation of a Jewish-Russian immigrant family in Maryland. From an early age, his family instilled in Cardin the importance of ethics, responsibility, and public service, as his grandfather built up his own business in Baltimore and his father served in the Maryland House of Delegates and sat on the Supreme Bench of Baltimore City.

Ethics were instilled in Ben by his environment, too. Since its early days as a colony, Maryland has been a haven for religious freedom; the Maryland Toleration Act of 1649 was the great forerunner to the First Amendment's Free Exercise clause. This fact is not lost on the Cardin family—nor are the memories of times when the state did not live up to the good character established in its legislation:

My grandparents wanted their children to grow up in a country where they were able to practice their Jewish faith and fully participate in their community and government. My father, one of their sons, became a lawyer, state legislator, circuit court judge, and president of the synagogue, and now his son serves in the United States Senate.

While our founding fathers made freedom of religion a priority, equal protection for all races took longer to achieve. I attended Liberty School No. 64, a public elementary school in Baltimore City. It was part of a segregated public school system that, under law, denied every student in Baltimore the opportunity to learn in a classroom that represented the diversity of our community.

I remember with great sadness how discrimination was not only condoned, but also more often than not, actually encouraged against blacks, Jews, Catholics, and other minorities in the community. There were neighborhoods that my parents warned me to avoid for [...] safety, because I was Jewish.

The local movie theater denied admissions to African-Americans. Community swimming pools had signs that said "No Jews, no blacks allowed." Even Baltimore's amusement parks and sports clubs were segregated by race.

In 1964, Ben married Myrna Edelman and graduated from the University of Pittsburgh with a BA in economics. Ringing in Ben's ear, though, was John Kennedy's iconic call to the youth of America: "Ask not what your country can do for you, but ask what you can do for your country." This triggered Ben's strong belief in the difference one person can make, the good one person can accomplish, when his or her actions are based upon a commitment to ethics and service. Three years later he received a law degree from the University of Maryland, graduating first in his class. That same year, 1967, at the age of twenty-three, Ben answered Kennedy's call to service and was elected to the Maryland House of Delegates. Ben's strength of character drives his desire to serve and has not waned. He describes himself today:

> I am an optimist, and I strongly believe that government can be a force for good in improving the lives of people. I also am a realist who sets priorities about what I can accomplish. I would say that honesty, a strong moral compass, and the ability to listen are very important to me. I try to be honest with myself—about what I want to accomplish and why. I also believe it's important to listen to others, even to those with whom I may disagree.

From a very early moment, Ben realized the enormous power he wielded as a public servant—a power suffused with responsibility:

> My first major victory in life as an elected official was getting a backstop in a high school field so that the Little League could have a place to play. I always remembered that the Northwest Little League was looking for a place to play. Northwest High School had a field, but they couldn't play there because they didn't have a backstop. A ball would go out of the field, and retrieving it was not safe. They were really desperate. I picked up the phone, and I called the mayor of Baltimore, and he took my call. I said I had this problem and needed a backstop to be put up. Then the new backstop appeared at Northwest.
>
> It just showed me the power I had in the Maryland General Assembly

at age twenty-three. It taught me a very valuable lesson that first I had power; second, I could get things done; and third, I should use [that power] properly. Suppose there shouldn't have been a backstop there. The mayor was taking my word for it, and it was a real lesson to me. And it also told me that I could get things done, and I could make a difference in people's lives. These children would have a place to play, and it was important to them.

Ben's political philosophy is that government can be a force for good when dedicated public servants, with a strong moral compass, step forward to prioritize necessary reforms and programs to help all citizens. This requires patience and an ability to listen to those with whom you disagree. It requires a strong ethical norm that calls out and stands up for injustice wherever it is seen. These themes have defined Ben's legislative career.

Ben was an active member of many committees of the State Legislature. Well aware of his ethics and his understanding of how to wield power, his colleagues elected him the youngest Speaker of the House for Maryland in over a hundred years. The year was 1979, and Ben was thirty-five years of age, Presented with a unique opportunity to guide the state's legislative agenda, Ben worked diligently to reform the House's ethics rules. To this day, Ben still involves himself in this cause, teaching ethics at the Johns Hopkins University and working with the ethics program at the U.S. Naval Academy. Additionally, he guided key reforms of school finance and property tax, both of which improved conditions for Maryland residents.

In 1987, Ben left the House of Delegates and was elected to Congress for Maryland's Third Congressional District. Originally a Baltimore-based district, the Third Congressional District now includes portions of Anne Arundel County as well as the city of Annapolis, following the 2000 census. Nevertheless, Ben won reelection nine times, winning by margins of at least twenty points in each election.

Cardin's signature work came in expanding Medicare benefits, first to include preventative exams for diseases such as colon, prostate, and breast cancer, as well as osteoporosis. He also secured expanded prescription drug coverage for chronic diseases, and authored bills to reform and expand welfare services, the childcare tax credit, and the welfare-to-work program.

Ben also authorized legislation enacted in 2001 that expanded the amount Americans could save for retirement. *Worth Magazine* cited Cardin as among the top "One hundred people who have influenced the way Americans think about money." The publication lauded his work on fiscal

Ben shares a story with tomorrow's talent.

policy, as well as in other areas. He has also written legislation to help fund graduate medical education and guarantee coverage for emergency health services—and worked to hold fathers accountable for child support.

Ben continued his role as a respected leader, begun at the state-level legislature, among his colleagues in the U.S. House of Representatives, where he served as Senior Democratic Whip. Ben also chaired for the minority in the Organization, Study, and Review Committee and in the Steering Committee of the Democratic Caucus. Furthering his work on bipartisan ethics reform, he chaired the Bipartisan Ethics Task Force in 1997 in order to review House ethics procedures. Additionally, in the House, he served on committees ranging from Ways and Means, and Budget, to Public Works and Transportation, Judiciary, Ethics, House Administration, and Homeland Security. He was also the senior Democrat on the Trade Subcommittee and the Human Resources Subcommittee of Ways and Means.

His signature leadership efforts, however, came following fellow Marylander, Representative Steny Hoyer, as a Commissioner of the U.S. Helsinki Commission—a committee that advocates for human rights globally. Ben has carried over his service on this committee since being elected to the

Senate, and he currently chairs the Commission. His role in the Commission has allowed Ben to travel worldwide and apply his vision for public service to international issues in need of leadership and moral clarity.

In 2006, Ben won an open-seat Senate race against Republican challenger Michael Steele. Since moving across the Capitol, Ben has continued his active role in the Senate's affairs. Ben currently sits on the Committees for Environment and Public Works, the Judiciary, Foreign Relations, Budget, and Small Business and Entrepreneurship. This is in addition to his continuing work with the Helsinki Commission.

Ben has used his experience to quickly advance a strong legislative agenda. He secured a dental benefit program in the reauthorization of the Children's Health Insurance Program, as well as a first-time tax credit for homebuyers and a higher surety cap for small businesses in the American Recovery and Reinvestment Act. Ben continues diligently working for his constituents today. He works hard to ensure that the foundations upon which our Republic stands will be there for future generations.

A free press is one of many traditions that Ben considers important for securing democracy. He has recently taken up the fight to ensure that an open and vibrant press continues for many generations:

> Our country depends on an open and free press to monitor what happens in our communities so that Americans can make sound judgments about their lives and leaders. Thomas Jefferson, a man who was frequently vilified by newspapers, summed it up best when he said: "If I had to choose between government without newspapers, and newspapers without government, I wouldn't hesitate to choose the latter."
>
> Like Jefferson, I believe that a well-informed public is the core of our democracy. How can we forget the role newspapers played in uncovering the Watergate and Enron scandals or the AIG bonus debacle? News stories, reported by journalists, often bring to public attention decisions and actions that affect all of us.

Ben also believes that strong families are integral to strong nations, since most other traditions—both civic and religious—are handed on most directly through the family. So it comes as no surprise that Ben's home life is important to him. He's been married for over forty-five years, with two children. Amid all his accomplishments, putting his family first—above even work and ambition—was the right choice in life for him:

You set your own priorities. When I first started in the legislature, I saw a lot of marriages that were destroyed in Annapolis. I was just really worried about that. Maybe it's inconsistent, family life with public life, and it really challenged me in the beginning. It was not at all inconsistent. Pick your own priorities: if you want to go drinking every night, you can; if you want to go home to your family every night, you can. And the person who goes drinking every night doesn't get any more bills passed than the person who goes home at night. That's true. I got more bills passed than a lot of the drinkers. I became speaker; they didn't. And I went home every night to my family. I felt that was the right thing to do, and I wanted to do that.

Ben's strong family has known both joys and sorrows. Living life in the public eye can make a family tragedy even harder to bear, but that was not the case for the Cardins. In 1998, when Ben and Myrna tragically lost their thirty-year-old-son, Michael, family friend and fellow-Congressman Steny Hoyer offered comfort from the floor of the Congress. Despite all the pain Ben and Myrna were facing, it speaks volumes about them that they permitted these words to be placed in the Congressional Record:

> There were two characteristics, Mr. Speaker, which I remember most about Michael. He cared more for others than for himself, and he was an intelligent young man whose greatest concern was for those less fortunate...
>
> In 1993, Michael graduated from the University of Maryland School of Law. With his grandfather in attendance, Michael received his Juris Doctorate degree after hearing his father deliver the commencement address...This past winter, Michael was admitted to the Maryland bar; a bright future lay ahead. After passing the bar, he worked in Baltimore for the special counsel and volunteered at the Hamden Family Center, working with children and families.
>
> At the service this past Sunday, his father rose and said that there were many instances of which he and Myrna had no knowledge, incidents that demonstrated with individual people, homeless, children, people in trouble, Michael repeatedly showed the character that he had, which I suspect was in his genes, because it was consistent with the Cardin contribution...I do not know any family that I have ever met, Mr. Speaker, that is more supportive, closer, more giving, more respectful of one another than the family headed by Ben and Myrna Cardin. They are wonderful human beings, good and decent people who loved and nurtured their son

without reservation. Michael, for the thirty years that he had, got the best that there was in the Cardin family.

Steny and Ben have enjoyed a close professional and personal relationship throughout their careers. In many respects, Steny has been a mentor for Ben as a Congressman, and as Chair of the Helsinki Commission, Steny has enabled Ben to continue making a difference globally, regardless of reward. As Ben says:

> A lot of things I've done—and this is really following another person I admire greatly, Steny Hoyer—Steny Hoyer used the power of the Chairman of the Helsinki Commission to really help human rights around the world [. ...He] did it because it was the right thing to do...I try to follow his example (as current Chairman) and really try to make a difference for a lot of minority communities. I know people back home don't know what I'm doing there, but it really is helping others. I have a selfless role model to follow in Steny Hoyer.

Throughout his career, Ben has achieved numerous honors and distinctions in his pursuit of selfless service. As a legislator, he has received a grade of "A" from the NAACP, a score of 100 from the Human Rights Campaign, and a 100 percent rating from the League of Conservation Voters. He holds honorary degrees from the University of Baltimore School of Law, the University of Maryland at Baltimore, the Baltimore Hebrew University, Goucher College, and Villa Julie College. He has sat on numerous boards and received honors from a myriad of civic organizations.

As Ben continues his public service, he remains animated by the same melding of optimism and realism with which he began his career. Ben's work remains grounded in his belief that there is more that unites people than divides them, and that the same basic morals and principles should guide all people. A proper public good includes the ability to live free of oppression, to earn a decent living, and to raise children in safety and security. Every person, whether legislator or citizen, can impact society. This is the legacy Ben Cardin hopes to leave.

Ambassador Richard Carlson (Ret.)

"So manners bring you outside yourself and keep you from drowning in the sea of "me," and force you to acknowledge other people."

—*Dick Carlson*

When a man has done so much in a lifetime, it is prosaic to sum up that life in one sentence. Name a job, and Dick Carlson has mastered it. He's been a magazine writer for *Time* and *Look*, a newspaper columnist and reporter for United Press International, a law clerk, a private detective, a TV anchorman, an organized crime expert, a TV network documentary filmmaker, a merchant seaman (and member of one of the smallest and toughest unions in America), an international radio show host and counter-terrorism expert. He even ran for mayor of San Diego—and almost won. And yet his most enduring legacies, he says, are his two sons, Tucker and Buckley, his grandchildren, and his wife, Patricia. Who, then, is Dick Carlson?

A voracious reader with a personal library of more than 10,000 books.

Dick has never passed on an opportunity that presented adventure or interest. Once he even attempted to read in preparation for the California bar, without bothering to attend law school!

Dick has a perpetually open mind, open in such a way that he is always seeking to add to his rich inner life. As his son Tucker remarks:

> He's an intellectual and a very deep person. He is the best-read person I've ever met. My father reads a book a day, every day. That's not an exaggeration. His library is so large that you think it is not real. You can walk through it and he's read everything. He brings a book with him everywhere.

Dick's life, at its beginning was neither simple nor easy. Dick was an orphan. His mother was a pretty blonde girl from a small town near Boston. In the snowy winter of 1941, when Dick was six weeks old and she was sixteen years old, she dropped him off at an orphanage called the Home for Little Wanderers, in Boston, and disappeared from his life. Only many decades later did he track down his mother, Dorothy Anderson, and find information about his father, Richard Boynton, after combing through old records in Boston.

For the first few years of his life, farmed out from the orphanage as an infant, Dick lived as a foster child with a close-knit family in Malden, near Boston. Although he didn't leave their home until he was almost three, Dick has no memory of those years. He found out about them in 1979, when the elderly foster parents, carrying an album of photos of Dick as a baby, tracked him down in San Diego, where he had been anchoring the news on the CBS television station.

Dick was taken from his foster home by the orphanage to be adopted by the Carlson family. His new parents were in their mid-thirties and childless. They lived a few miles from Boston in the small town of Norwood, with a population at the time of 16,000 people. Dick's father was an executive at the Winslow Brothers & Smith Tannery of Norwood, the oldest tannery in America, run by former Massachusetts Governor Frank Allen and owned by the same family since 1776. The Carlson family lived in a house on Vernon Street in Norwood, built around World War I by his mother's father, a successful Norwood builder. The Carlsons were conventional upper-middle-class New Englanders, who provided a good life for Dick, even when the tannery closed in 1949 after a bitter strike and Dick's father was thrown out of work. The Carlson family gave Dick affection, good manners, and a dog and cat as pets, which prompted Dick's lifelong love of animals.

Dick's parents never mentioned his adoption. No one ever spoke of it to Dick—neither the neighbors in Norwood nor the Carlsons' many relatives. The culture of the time, or at least the culture of his family, dictated taciturnity about events or situations considered too personal for conversation. People in his family could never say the word "cancer," for instance, or "divorce." They had euphemisms for them, if they mentioned their existence at all. It wasn't until Dick's adoptive mother died many years later that Dick learned factually that he had been adopted.

In some respect, he didn't have to be told. He already knew it. He knew in his gut, for reasons he still can't explain, that he wasn't fully the son of his parents. He loved them; they loved him. Yet he never felt completely connected to them. Perhaps he had lived too long, too formatively, with his forgotten foster parents.

Conditions changed for the worse for Dick's adoptive family at Christmas 1953, when his forty-four-year-old father died of a heart attack. In the ensuing weeks, twelve-year-old Dick consciously knew that he would now be responsible for making his own way in life. He prayed at night that he could do that. He never thought to pray that things would be easier, but he prayed that God would make him strong enough to build successfully on the life he had been given. This began his path of self-sustained employment, learning, and adventure.

Dick's jobs were typical of any young man: working in a Christmas tree lot, mowing lawns, bagging groceries in a store, working on a produce truck early in the morning before school. But something else made Dick different. He was wild at times, aggressive and quick to fight, particularly after the death of his father, but he was usually polite to everyone. He treated every person in the same respectful manner, unless they purposefully crossed him. Tucker describes it best, in reflecting on the lessons his father taught to him and his brother:

> Manners set you apart. Manners do two things, according to my father. Manners are something that people can instantly recognize in you. Decent people have good manners, and that's how you know them. Decent people walking down the street know each other by their manners. Instantly you know someone by his or her manners. Also, manners put the world into perspective. All manners are about thinking about other people, acknowledging the existence of other people and their desires. So manners bring

you outside yourself and keep you from drowning in the sea of "me," and force you to acknowledge other people. They make you less selfish, bottom line.

Geography, serendipity, and friendships played a large role in Dick's destiny. He wanted to go to Brown University, in Providence. At sixteen, in his senior year of high school, he had an older girlfriend at Pembroke College (then the female counterpart to Brown), and he spent a lot of time with her on campus. But his mother was forced to go to work after his adoptive father died, and there wasn't enough money for Dick's tuition at Brown— not that Brown would have taken him if he had been rolling in cash. Dick was expelled from high school that year for frequent truancy and general delinquency.

He recalls being completely bored:

I seldom went to class. I missed weeks at a stretch. The truant officer, Mr. Hopkins, was always looking for me. I was either at the library reading or in a saloon drinking beer and eating clam cakes with my Pembroke friend. I was definitely a juvenile delinquent. But, I want you to know that obstacles related to past behavior can be overcome. For example, this year [2010], I was inducted into my high school's Hall of Fame. These were the people who expelled me fifty-two years before. I went to the ceremonial lunch, and there were four or five inductees and a hundred or so people. Nobody mentioned that I had been booted from the school. I wanted to say something about it, but they asked me not to. I think they were a little embarrassed, though I wasn't.

Dick joined the military at age seventeen, one step ahead of the law and two steps ahead of the draft. It straightened him out immediately. Later, Dick tested himself physically, becoming a deep-water SCUBA diver and a sport parachutist and skydiver.

Dick became a reporter for United Press International at age twenty-two, after working as a copy boy for the night city editor of the *Los Angeles Times*, Glen Binford, who boosted Dick's career by sending him out to report news stories for the *Times*. Over the years, Dick's jobs brought him into frequent contact with political figures like a young Ronald Reagan and Bobby Kennedy, and show-business stars like Doris Day and Rosalind Russell—he lived in her guest house in Beverly Hills—Jimmy Stewart, Jack Warner of Warner Brothers, Cary Grant, Frank Sinatra, and Mia Farrow, with whom he was very friendly. Dick once flew to Las Vegas on Sinatra's plane with Farrow and Tina Sinatra to join Sinatra at his weekend opening at the Sands Hotel in 1965.

Dick worked often with Jake Ehrlich, the famous criminal lawyer and prolific writer upon whom the character of Perry Mason was based. He was friendly for years with famed San Francisco businessman Louis Lurie, owner of the Mark Hopkins Hotel, around whose lunch table he rubbed elbows with the famous men of the time. Working then as a UPI reporter, Lurie remarked to the young Carlson that lunches like this are a "good way to meet interesting people." And they were.

As a young man Dick moonlighted as a private eye for Hal Lipset, America's greatest gumshoe and wireman, the fellow who invented the bug in a martini olive. For many years Dick was a dues-paying member of the Sailor's Union of the Pacific, a small, very tough San Francisco union, and he sailed, with a Coast Guard Merchant Marine permit as an Ordinary Seaman on a Pacific Far East Line tramp freighter in South Asia for much of a year, taking a leave from UPI.

Dick had a lot of jobs. In fact, he may sound like a book-jacket blurb from the 1950s, about the diverse occupations of the author. Find the interesting in life. Never hoard an opportunity. Those are part of the life philosophies that Dick lived by and passed along to his sons. Tucker remarks:

> He manages his time well. He, like all productive people, is in a constant state of agitation about how lazy he is. My father is one of the least lazy people that I have ever met. But he is convinced that he is lazy, and he is always fighting an ongoing battle with himself about how little he is accomplishing.

Dick is always looking for the next adventure, the next opportunity, and because of this, he has been able to accomplish much in life. Dick's been a wire service reporter and newspaper rewrite man, a night-shift crime reporter, a television and radio correspondent, a leg-man for columnist Louella Parsons in Beverly Hills, a television anchorman and a host on multiple TV and radio shows, a documentary filmmaker (he wrote and produced three TV films—two for ABC, one for NBC), a magazine writer for *Time* and *Look*, an organized crime expert, and a beat cop in Ocean City, Maryland, about which he has written extensively.

As Dick's skills progressed, so did his responsibilities. Not many people can attest to doing even half of the things Dick had done at this point, but

Dick prepares for his radio show.

because of his ardent desire to learn and because of the manners that kept him in high regard with whomever he met, Dick was just getting started. He ran the Voice of America for the last six years of the Cold War, the same for Radio Marti to Cuba. He was assistant director of the U.S. Information Agency, and spokesman for the agency. All of these appointments were by President Reagan. He was appointed, by the first President George Bush, as the U.S. ambassador to the Seychelles Islands, a beautiful archipelago in the Indian Ocean, far off the east coast of Africa, famous as a haven for spies and international rogues and site of a large U.S. spying operation. (CBS's *Sixty Minutes* did a segment on it called "Islands of Spies.") He returned to the United States to be president and CEO of the Corporation for Public Broadcasting, the parent to PBS and NPR. Later, he was president and CEO of a King World company, the most financially successful TV syndicator in America, with *Oprah*, *Wheel of Fortune*, and *Jeopardy* among their cash cows.

For the past six years he has been Vice Chairman of the well-known counterterrorism think tank, the Foundation for the Defense of Democracies, with offices in Washington and Brussels. The FDD was begun by Malcolm Forbes, Jr., former U.N. ambassador Jeanne Kirkpatrick, former CIA director Jim Woolsey, and foreign correspondent Cliff May, in the aftermath of the attacks of 9/11. For many years Dick has also been Chairman of InterMedia Research, of Washington, D.C., and London. InterMedia does sophisticated polling and opinion studies in difficult-to-access parts of the world such as China, Tibet, North Korea, Burma, Laos, Cambodia, and many parts of Africa.

Dick does effective and important work. He writes a weekly newspaper column on national security. He hosts the international radio show *Dan-*

ger Zone, which runs on Sirius/XM satellite radio in the United States and Canada twice a week and runs on British Sky Radio and the World Radio Network in Europe, Asia, and Africa. He broadcasts from the Christian Science Monitor studios in downtown Washington and the World Radio Network studios in London.

Dick has certainly made a difference. He's been at the center of many of the major engagements and important political and cultural developments of the latter half of the twentieth century. Why? Because, as Tucker says, Dick will not pass up an interesting and newly challenging opportunity. As Dick himself tells, he did indeed go with Tucker to Afghanistan. On his trip, Dick's wish for an interesting experience was more than granted. He describes the exciting flight:

> My son and I boarded a Pakistani International Airlines plane in Islamabad on the evening of October 21, 2001, to fly to Dubai. We had spent the week in Rawalpindi, Islamabad, and in Peshawar, up by the border, trying and failing to get into Afghanistan. Tucker was attempting to interview the one-eyed Mullah Omar, leader of the Taliban, for CNN, where he was a correspondent at the time. That was the plan. I have a close English friend, Lord Michael Cecil, who was a major owner of the phone company in Afghanistan. He had been helpful with some logistics (including Mullah Omar's cell number), but it didn't work out.
>
> It was an interesting but uneventful week, other than one day when we drove from Islamabad to Peshawar on the old Grand Trunk Road. We were near the entrance to the Northwest Frontier when we had a flat tire, a blowout. This is an incredibly dirty, dusty road jammed with thousands of people trudging, lorries packed with animals, crates, and vegetables, thousands more people squatting along the roadside. After the blowout, the driver took the wheel off, thinking he could get a repair nearby. Tucker and I got out of the beat-up Fiat to help him. Within a minute, Tucker and I were surrounded by a dozen hostile Pashtun men. They began shouting "CIA, CIA" at us. They were working themselves into a spit-fit. (We kept shouting back, "No, no, we are Canadians!") One of them was waving a rusty hunting knife, stabbing the air with it. We threw the tire into the backseat and careened away on three wheels.
>
> In a couple more days we headed out of the country, flying from Islamabad back to Peshawar, where the plane stopped to pick up some more passengers, and then on to Dubai, in the Persian Gulf. The U.S. bombing runs in Afghanistan were really heavy, preventing us from flying over

Afghanistan on the way to Dubai—too dangerous. So we flew around the country. Twenty minutes from Dubai, high over the water, there was a terrific explosion. I thought we'd hit another plane. We made it to Dubai airport shaking violently and flying, it seemed, somewhat sideways. We came in for a crash landing and skidded into the desert. Tucker and I jumped into the inflated slides. We went down those rubber tubes like greased lightning—something I've always wanted to do.

Many people spend a lifetime trying to avoid such moments. Dick doesn't look for these dangerous events, but he doesn't turn away from them either, and seizes them as they appear. He lives life. He pursues his interests. He ran for mayor of San Diego many years ago. He was a top vote-getter in a primary crowded with candidates, but later lost to the incumbent Mayor after a tight and nasty runoff. It was a grueling run, but even losing was worthwhile for what Dick gleaned from the experience.

Dick's myriad adventures have not only provided him with a rich array of experiences, but they've also put him in a position of power to help others. Once, three years before the end of the Cold War, Dick visited Soviet Moscow as part of his work with Voice of America. There, he and his wife Patricia met, late at night, in a grim Moscow flat with a twelve-year-old Russian girl named Vera, a VOA fan who listened surreptitiously to the jammed broadcasts with her parents. Vera had curly red hair and bright blue eyes, spoke perfect English, played classical piano, and loved the idea of democracy. Most of all, she said, she loved the cartoon character Garfield, who she had once seen in a British newspaper. Why?

"Because he's my hero," said Vera. "He's tough. He doesn't put up with a lot of foolishness from others. He is free. He is American."

When Vera hugged Dick and Patricia goodbye, she said, "I will be coming to America some day; I will see you again." The poignancy of this moment was underscored by the Carlsons' knowledge that Vera's father was a Soviet physicist who had applied to emigrate with his family, and had been vehemently refused by the Communist authorities.

Dick was struck by Vera's charm and intelligence. When he arrived back in Washington, he wrote Jim Davis, the creator of Garfield. Dick explained about Vera's affection for the cartoon cat, and asked for a drawing for her. Davis sent one signed to "My friend Vera," which Carlson put into the diplomatic pouch at the State Department and had delivered to Vera through an embassy officer in Moscow.

A few weeks later, at a Washington dinner party, Dick told the story of

Vera and Garfield to a Reagan administration speechwriter. "Why don't you ask the President to help her get out?" Dick said.

At that time, President Reagan was preparing for his historic trip to the Soviet Union to meet with President Gorbachev. The message got to President Reagan. A deal was secretly struck with the Soviets. One month after President Reagan returned from Moscow, Vera and her mother and father stepped out of a U.S. government limousine in front of the Voice of America offices on Independence Avenue in Washington. Dick and Patricia Carlson were waiting on the front steps. Vera bounded up and hugged both of them. The first thing she said?

"I told you I would see you again—in America!"

Vera Zieman and her parents settled in Massachusetts. Vera graduated from Tufts University and is now a respected scientist and an accomplished musician. She was recently married, and has a baby and enjoys a good life in America. Dick Carlson made this possible because he cared about her, loved his country, and wanted a young girl with big dreams to realize her desire for American freedom.

Despite all these adventures, the most important thing about Dick's life is the relationship he has forged with his two sons, Tucker and Buckley. They are grown and independent and have families of their own—five children, between them. Today Dick's role has shifted from a caretaker-father to his sons' best friend. But once, and for many years, fatherhood was his most important job. Tucker recalls how his father tried to pass along to himself and his brother the many life lessons he had learned, at the most ordinary moments:

> His main strategy for dealing with adversity is not complaining about it. He made a decision early on that he'd rather die than whine in public. All through our childhood, that was the central lesson: never complain. He coupled that with humor—he is the funniest person that I have ever met. He believes in humor. It's more than just that he is funny. He is committed to seeing life through that lens.
>
> [As kids,] growing up in La Jolla, California, which is a warm, almost tropical climate, we would almost always get bugs in our breakfast cereal, and we would complain about it. And my father would always dismiss our complaints as the whining of affluent, spoiled kids. He is very tough. And one morning we were all sitting at the table—my brother, Dad, and I, all three of us living together—my brother poured his Captain Crunch in the bowl and said, "Yuk! There are bugs in here!" And my father said,

"That's not true! There are no bugs in there!" And we all look down and there are these insects floating in the milk. My father said, "The fact that a few bugs bother you is just pathetic." He took the bowl and ate the whole thing just to prove the point!

Tucker recalls how very seriously Dick took his duty towards his sons. Not a day went by that Dick did not write his sons a letter:

My father wrote me when I went to boarding school at fourteen—and I never lived at home again—a letter every single day all four years while at boarding school. Every day. When I was a little kid, for years, my father made brown-bag lunches for my brother and me. Our school didn't have a lunch truck or cafeteria, and every single day he put a note in our lunches, a different one for each of us. And every day it was a quote, a joke, or a riddle. And I saved every single note, and I saved every single letter. I have massive boxes of them in my basement. I know how hard that is now that I have my own children. I know how hard that is.

I'm forty years old, and my father writes me every week. Not e-mails, but letters. The other thing he did was to introduce ideas to us as children, and I mean little children. I read *Animal Farm* in second grade; it was one of the first books I ever read. And he explained that this was an allegory. This is Trotsky. This is Stalin. But he sent me, every day, articles and books and magazines. I had subscriptions to every single magazine known to intelligent man by the time I was sixteen.

Dick knows that when all is said and done, his relationship with his sons and with his wife Patricia will be what matters most in his life:

When you're gone, pushing up the petunias, they won't remember you long at the law firm or at IBM or in the newsroom or at the hedge fund or machine shop; and after a short while they won't remember that you were ever there at all. That's the way it is in life, and always has been, and you are a fool if you don't face it. Billions of completely forgotten folks have come before us, and memory of them has vanished. What you did as an occupation will mean nothing, gone in the snap of two fingers.

But what you did or are doing with your sons and daughters will mean everything, both to them and to you. It will pay you dividends unending for the rest of your puny life. And the memory of what you do, what you say, what you think, will survive long after your death; it will live through your children and their children, maybe for generations to come. I didn't really know this when I was young, but I figured it out later, and it is true.

Many would be envious of all of Dick's experiences. Others, having had such adventures, would rest now on their laurels. Not Dick Carlson. He's sixty-nine years old and still working full time. He has no intention of retiring. When the time comes to cross the final river, he plans to help row the boat. That is the life of Ambassador Richard Carlson—so far.

Paul F. Eckstein, Esquire

"To be a person of truth, be swayed neither by approval nor disapproval. Work not needing approval from anyone, then you'll be free to be who you really are."

—*Rabbi Nockmen of Breslaff*

Paul's lifelong commitment in Phoenix to law, as an undertaking of service and trust, is a story that almost did not happen. Paul promised himself three things when entering law school: (1) he would never practice law; (2) he would never move back to Phoenix; and (3) he would not marry until he turned thirty-five. In 1965, providence changed all that, and smitten by the law and by a girl named Flo, he revised all three of his promises.

In the summer of 1964, the growing momentum behind the Civil Rights movement presented Paul with the opportunity to go to Mississippi and participate as an aspiring lawyer in the social changes of the 1960s. It was a chance to fulfill his youthful idealism and "make a difference." But Paul was pulled in another direction. Jack Brown, founding partner of the

Brown and Bain law firm in Phoenix offered Paul what then seemed like an honorable but pedestrian summer clerkship and he accepted.

By the summer of 1965, Paul had married Flo, moved to Phoenix, and committed himself to the law under Jack's tutelage. An irreplaceable mentor and friend, Jack Brown molded Paul's professional character. Jack's impact on Paul was plainly visible in Paul's moving eulogy of Jack:

> With Jack's passing ten days ago, his family, his friends, his law firm, and indeed the entire community suffered an enormous loss. We can no longer see his warm smile, hear his reassuring voice, feel his strong presence, or benefit from his wise counsel, unparalleled intellect, and unending generosity. His good and stout heart has ceased to beat, but his legacy has just begun—and what a legacy it will be.

As he had done for other young associates, Jack took Paul under his wing and gave him a great deal of responsibility from his earliest days in the firm. Jack's principles and work ethic rubbed off profoundly on all the young lawyers who worked with him. "Never cite a case that holds against the position you are seeking," went the first rule of Jack Brown, "even if there is favorable language in the case." Jack also told his young associates to "Never brag about what you have done or what you are going to do." Indeed, Paul recalls:

> Long before the Nike ad, those who learned from Jack know to "Just do it." To illustrate this rule, on my first day of work in 1965, Jack cited a passage from *Death of a Salesman*, where Willie Loman has talked with Bernard, who is a contemporary of Willie's luckless sons, Biff and Happy. Willie learns in this conversation that Bernard is going to Washington on business, but he does not learn why. Later, Bernard's father visits Willie and tells him that Bernard is going to Washington to argue a case before the Supreme Court of the United States. Hearing this, Willie exclaims, "The Supreme Court! And he didn't even mention it!" Bernard's father responds, "He don't have to—he's going to do it." Jack did not tell us about his successes. He simply brought home the results. The casebooks and boardrooms are filled with Jack's victories.

Finally, Jack told all his associates to "Think big, but master the details." Paul saw how to put this into practice, within just a few short days: Jack knew a client's business and industry better than its principals. He could

Paul and his wife Flo enjoy an evening together.

explain the most intricate of details in everyday language. Thus, because of preparation and attention, neither Bill Gates nor Nobel Prize–winning economist George Stigler gave Jack any difficulty in his cross-examination.

Paul believes that when you're responsible for making an argument, there is no substitute for total understanding, knowledge, and control of the situation. It's hard, and that's why practicing lawyers don't really make good businesspeople or good politicians—because they're not good delegators, and as lawyers *shouldn't be* too good at delegating. Litigators should be masters of the law and the facts and have control. Others develop evidence for the law, put things together, but litigators sign off on all the evidence and details. Paul learned from Jack that being a lawyer, whether on the transactional or litigation side requires detail-oriented organization.

Hard work. Truthfulness. Loyalty. Soon, as a lawyer, Paul acquired an outstanding reputation of his own. His practice in Phoenix at first encompassed everything: litigation, real estate transactions, and tax work. By 1968, Paul was doing litigation virtually full time, and for the next fifteen years spent a high percentage of his time on lawsuits involving technology issues. Paul's practice reflected a combination of autonomy, complexity, and a close connection between effort and reward. As Paul's skills and experience increased, so did his reputation for outstanding work and the complexity of the legal issues that he tackled.

But for Paul, the law represents a much deeper passion than merely serving his clients' needs. Paul sees the role of the lawyer as central to the virtue of our Republic. As Alexis de Tocqueville wrote:

> In America there are no nobles or literary men, and the people are apt to mistrust the wealthy; lawyers consequently form the highest political class and the most cultivated circle of society. As the lawyers constitute the only enlightened class which the people do not mistrust, they are naturally called upon to occupy most of the public stations.

"A modern-day de Tocqueville undoubtedly would liken [lawyers] more to used-car dealers," writes Paul. Why?

> Who knows whether our fall from grace has all taken place in the last half of this century, but if one is to believe the high priests of our era—the public opinion pollsters—our fall from grace is complete. As we have come to rely more and more on technology as a substitute for clear thinking, as our services are beyond the reach of all but the most wealthy and stubborn in our society, as statutes and regulations have become so complex that lawyers must hire lawyers who must hire other lawyers to ferret out their true meaning, and as we have abandoned our present historical calling... we must surely wonder what we can do to recapture the respect and station we long ago enjoyed.

Paul did more than wonder about restoring the practice of law to an honorable station; he made it his life's work. In 1988, Paul was called upon to render an important, but unfortunately necessary, public service as co-prosecutor in the impeachment of Arizona governor Evan Mecham. The Mecham impeachment was really a trial that should not have taken place. Mecham's Republican Party controlled the state legislature, and his deficiencies made perfect fodder for the minority Democrats.

But almost immediately after taking office, upon winning just a plurality of the vote in 1986, Mecham began drawing the ire of his political opponents and his party alike. By 1988, he faced the triple threat of a recall election, felony charges, and impeachment. Paul was originally brought in to evaluate the case against Mecham, prior to formal impeachment charges being brought. So thorough was his work that both parties sought Paul's counsel as a co-prosecutor before the state Senate. Paul successfully convicted Mecham on two of three impeachment charges brought before the Arizona Senate.

With regret, Paul recalls that at multiple times Mecham had the opportunity and counsel to avoid becoming the eighth governor in U.S. history removed from public office. "Impeachment is a process that rends the political fabric of society," Paul wrote. Nevertheless, for doing his duty well, Paul bolstered his already strong reputation among fellow lawyers in the Arizona bar.

Such a moment cannot be anything but difficult for any political society. Paul follows well the advice of Edmund Burke in his 1775 "Speech on Conciliation with America":

> All government, indeed, every human benefit and enjoyment, every virtue and every prudent act is founded on compromise and barter. We balance inconveniences, we give and take, we remit some rights that we may enjoy others. We choose to be happy citizens rather than subtle disputants.

As Paul sees it, lawyers must dedicate themselves completely to their profession, to bring about just compromises. In doing this, they also ensure their own happiness. As Malcolm Gladwell remarks in *Outliers*, "Working hard is really what successful people do." Paul believes that the lawyer today has all the tools to be successful, but all the incentive to cut corners and be satisfied with complacency. He describes the challenge and satisfaction of working hard in law today:

> We live in an era in which we have the technological tools to do legal research, write briefs, and prepare documents at near–mach three speed. Lawyers on the other side of matters who send e-mails expect instant responses, clients expect immediate turnaround, and courts expect rapid and accurate replies. In this environment, lawyers are tempted to believe that they know more than they do and are prepared to do more than they can. It takes time and repetition to be successful and considerably more time to be at the top of the profession, no matter how fast we do the things we do. If this sounds like drudgery, it is not. Just as it is fun and satisfying to be able to write elegant computer code or great music, it is fun and satisfying to be able to make cogent appellate arguments, conduct hard-hitting cross examinations, and negotiate solutions to intractable problems.

Paul's advice echoes the words of his mentor Jack Brown. Former Supreme Court Justice Robert Jackson once remarked that the law is "like a religion" and "more than a means of support, it [is] a mission." Paul lives the law as a noble calling, an honorable vocation to excellence. Its practice brings fulfillment to lawyers through their selfless dedication to the public good. Paul writes:

> The ultimate key to happiness in the practice of law is to understand that however frustrating the task and relentless the pressure, when you are called to the bar, you are called to an undertaking of service and trust. If you view the practice as a means to acquire goods in an acquisitive society, you will be inordinately unhappy. If you view the practice as a challenge to solve seemingly insolvable problems and to employ the law as an instrument for positive social change, you will be able to find fulfillment and happiness. If you take seriously your obligations of public and private service, the next de Tocqueville will be able to say that your generation of lawyers is like those who helped found and nurture this Republic—an enlightened class in which the people once again can place their trust.

One period that was difficult in Paul's noble calling to law, however, was when he was called upon to testify about conversations he'd had with Bruce Babbitt about an application by three Indian tribes to take land in trust for an off-reservation gaming casino. Babbitt was the United States Secretary of the Interior during Bill Clinton's administration. Paul knew he was going to put Babbitt in a bad light. He didn't sleep very well. In this difficult time, Paul stalwartly responded with the truth. He told exactly what happened. It wasn't easy. While it fractured a friendship (although not a close friendship), and caused a lot of people in his community to view Paul differently, he understood that doing what is right often has a price.

Paul and his wife Flo copy the good example of their parents as they put family first, faithfully live their Jewish faith, and selflessly serve their community.

In 1981, the Ecksteins purchased the *Phoenix Jewish News*, to provide news to the Jewish community of the greater Phoenix area. Over many years, Paul has been a founder, board member, and chair of the Arizona Center for Law in the Public Interest, a non-profit law firm dedicated to ensuring government accountability and protecting the legal rights of Arizonans. Paul has also served as a member of the board of the Phoenix Children's Hospital for twenty-three years—and as its chair for two of those years.

At Christmas, Paul may be found playing Santa Claus for a group called Chicanos por la Causa (Chicanos for the Cause). The group puts on a massive charity event to distribute five to fifteen thousand gifts to the very poor children from the inner city. Paul, a Jewish Santa Claus, sees this as an opportunity to be charitable before our common God.

Paul's most treasured community work, though, has been his membership on the board of trustees of Pomona College, a service that he has provided since 1983. In addition to chairing a number of standing committees of the Board, Paul has twice served as chair of Presidential search committees. Paul also enjoyed teaching a course at his alma mater in the fall of 1997, entitled "The Fiction of American Politics." The course explained the relationship between literature and an understanding of U.S. history. He also served as state chair for the regional selection committee on Rhodes Scholars.

Paul dabbled formally in politics by serving as the campaign manager for his senior partner, Jack Brown, in Brown's run for Congress in 1972. Brown ran a good race in a difficult year for a Democrat, no thanks to Paul's maiden efforts at national politics. Paul likes to joke that his law partners delegated him to manage Brown's campaign because they knew he would do so incompetently and Brown would, therefore, return to running the firm he had founded. Paul did not disappoint his partners.

Temporarily losing his sanity twenty years later, he likes to joke, Paul considered running for the United States Senate against John McCain in 1992, but pleas from his family and some soul searching caused him to regain his sanity and avoid (as he believes) seriously embarrassing himself.

Paul believes that six simple rules can guide any lawyer in his work, in the honorable practice of law. Paul's principles do not simply guide success in law, they also guide success in political life:

1. Practice civility with your opponent before, during, and after battle; a lack of civility and cordiality diminishes the joy of any practice.
2. Do what you do well, and take care with each word you write and each thought you put forth.
3. Seek out and master new areas of practice, however foreign and intimidating they may at first appear.
4. Make the time to read great novels, listen to fine music, and keep a watchful eye for new architecture so that above all, you develop a deep appreciation of America's history and governmental institutions.
5. Be prepared to resign your position or fire your client when asked to participate in or bless unjustifiable conduct.
6. Give constant attention to the quality of your work.

Admiral Thomas C. Lynch (Ret.)

"Always work as hard as you can, pray as hard as you can, and leave the rest up to God."

—*Marie Lynch*

Tom Lynch is a man of uncompromising ethics and limitless optimism. He was born in April of 1942, the second son of Rodney and Marie Lynch, in Lima, Ohio. Tom has two brothers and one sister. Tom's extended family, including his maternal grandparents and his father's four married sisters, all lived within a block of him. Tom's paternal grandfather lived with his family. His childhood was lively and raucous, and revolved around school, church, and neighborhood activities, which meant many Irish and German interfamily rivalries, arguments, and feuds. Kids went outside at first light and remained there playing sports, games, and whatever their imaginations would permit.

Tom's father was a large man, a stern disciplinarian, and—like his father before him—the Superintendent of the West Ohio Gas Company. It was not uncommon for him to receive a call in the middle of the night alerting him to a gas problem anywhere within a fifty-mile radius, and he would have to dispatch a crew to solve the problem. At age eleven, Tom inherited his older brother's 224-customer paper route. Tom did not have a vote in this. He hated delivering papers—and the weekly collections even more so, because many customers would dodge him, or not answer the door, to avoid his twenty-five-cents-per-week delivery charge. Then after a number of weeks, these customers would declare that they owed less than Tom's records indicated. Tom was learning human behavior, discipline, and the value of twenty-five cents. His persistence in performing his first job, whether he liked it or not paid off; after a year of saving, Tom became the envy of the neighborhood with his new Schwinn suspension bicycle with chrome fenders!

Although Tom's parents did not have a college education themselves— or maybe *because* they did not—they drummed into each of their children the vital necessity of obtaining a college degree. Tom was blessed to have priests and nuns as mentors, in his parochial elementary and high school, who re-echoed the values of his parents. Education, respect for authority, and love of God were the pillars of his formative years. And if a nun felt that her disciplinary measures, which included corporal punishment, were not getting through, the punishment at home would be even worse, no questions asked.

Tom was a good student and athlete, and by his senior year weighed around two hundred pounds, which attracted several schools to recruit him for football. The nuns urged Tom toward Notre Dame, but the school offered him a meager academic (not an athletic) scholarship—and there was little money at home. Then Coach Rick Forzano of the Naval Academy entered Tom's life. Tom went to Annapolis upon graduation in 1960 because he needed a free education; he wanted an opportunity to play major college football, and as a local sports writer quoted him at the time, "I hope someday to be in a position to do something for my country." On the fourth of July, 1960, he left Lima, Ohio, and headed by train to Washington, D.C. From there, Tom took a bus to Annapolis, and after a six-block walk, with great trepidation, he entered the U.S. Naval Academy. The next day he was inducted, with 1,200 others, into the class of 1964.

Life at a service academy is like no other. At the time, the Academy was homogeneous: all male, mostly white, and mostly athletically and academically strong. Each was a superstar in some aspect of life. Tom felt overwhelmed, but he fell back on his mother's dictum: "Always work as hard as you can, pray as hard as you can, and leave the rest up to God."

The mission of the Academy is to develop leaders for the Navy and the nation. Plebe (freshman) year at the academy is designed to teach each student that before being placed in a leadership position, the student must first learn to accept orders and discipline, with a degree of humility. Tom hated it at the time and thought about leaving the Academy many times, but it worked, and over his time there, Tom developed strong bonds with his classmates and teammates that have shaped his life and remain important today.

Tom had the opportunity to play major college football on the same team with Heisman Trophy–winner Roger Staubach. Tom captained the 1963 Navy team, which had a 9–1 regular season record, beating Notre Dame, Michigan, Pittsburgh, and of course Army, among others. The team lost to Texas in the 1964 Cotton Bowl for the National Championship. The 1963 Navy team has recently become the subject of Michael Connelly's enjoyable work *The President's Team*. Among all the stars, Connelly's book recognizes Tom as the heart and soul of the team:

> Assistant Coach Steve Belichick [father of Patriots coach Bill Belichick] said Lynch was the most charismatic leader he had ever coached in his decades in football. Lynch came to the Naval Academy from Lima, Ohio, where he was captain of the football team, a basketball forward, and shot-putter for Lima Central Catholic High School. At the conclusion of his career, he was awarded the Thunderbird Trophy for his "leadership, adherence to discipline, and team spirit." The inborn leadership skills that bloomed at Lima Central Catholic were further strengthened at the Naval Academy. Lynch eventually served as Superintendent of the Naval Academy and reached the rank of Admiral.
>
> A bond connected the 1963 Navy football team, and Tom Lynch was the custodian. Lynch pushed his teammates from day one to be the best they could be. The 6-foot, 1-inch, 210-pound Captain—who was a two-time heavyweight boxing champion at the Academy—was able to command the attention of his teammates without needing to ask for it. Players were inspired by his words and his actions.

Tom's gift of dealing with adversity appeared with his leadership of the team during the nation's difficult days and weeks following the assassination of President Kennedy:

> After JFK's assassination, Captain Tom Lynch led a contingent of players, including Skip Orr and Roger Staubach, to the Chapel; others went back

to their rooms to listen to the radio or gathered in their company room, where the lone television was located.

The moment had particular import because usually the President himself tosses the coin at the annual Army–Navy game:

> From the moment Tom Lynch and Dick Nowak had been named Captains of their respective teams, they had looked forward to the traditional coin toss with the Commander-in-Chief. But now they stood at midfield reminded again of the void the nation felt. What was intended to be a lifetime memory turned out to be a sad remembrance (for the Army and Navy teams). Lynch won the toss for Navy.

A week after the Navy victory, an envelope showed up in the mailbox of Navy Captain Tom Lynch. When he opened it he found a silver dollar. Accompanying the coin was a letter from the Secretary of the Army, Cyrus Vance that read:

9 December 1963

Dear Midshipman Lynch,

I am forwarding the coin which the late president would have used and would have presented to you had he made the toss of the coin at the Army-Navy football game this year. Please accept this memento of a memorable football game.

With best wishes,
Sincerely, Cyrus R. Vance
Secretary of the Army

Admiral Lynch would treasure the coin, and the victory, for the rest of his life. In that game, Tom displayed the charisma of a great leader: Following the suspenseful game against Army to close out the 1963 regular-season schedule, Lynch spoke of the spirit that had consumed the team throughout the year:

All season, we had a kind of motto that the way to really accomplish something worthwhile was to fight your way through tough spots. So when we found ourselves down there with defeat staring us in the face, I think all of us subconsciously thought about this spirit that we have believed all along. It's kind of what we had in the back of our minds, and it helped us throw ourselves in there and hold Army.

As if football were not enough, Tom spent his off-season boxing, to stay in shape. He won the heavyweight boxing title both years that he participated. Winning these titles probably served him well in his role on base as Company Commander.

In June 1964, Tom graduated with distinction and selected the surface warfare community for his follow-on naval service. Although obligated to serve for four years, he was unsure about making Navy a career. That September, Tom married his high-school sweetheart, Kathy Quinn, at the Naval Academy Chapel and recently buried her at the same Chapel. At last count, they have three children and ten grandchildren. Tom didn't fully understand the magnitude of the decision to marry at age twenty-two; it seemed to be the natural thing to do. Kathy has supported Tom throughout his thirty-one-year Navy career, which meant guiding the helm of the family through nineteen moves, little money, lengthy deployments, and some hardship—but through it all she never wavered.

Upon graduation, and following a six-month-stint coaching the plebe footballers, Tom reported to his first ship in December 1964: the World War II destroyer the *U.S.S Stribling*, whereupon he began a six-and-a-half-month deployment. Over the next ten years, a series of intermittent deployments followed. This included a tour aboard the *USS Dickson* as Chief Engineer, and another WWII destroyer that was highlighted when—despite being the oldest ship in the battle group—it completed a six-month deployment to the North Atlantic and Mediterranean with fewer engineering casualties and equipment failures than any other. Tom took pride in this and considered it a reflection of the pride and hard work of his engineers.

In December 1968, believing he most likely would be sent for duty in Vietnam, Tom was informed that he was being sent to the Naval Academy to work for the Dean of Admissions. By then, Tom had his second daughter, Alison. He was still unsure about choosing a naval career, but he accepted the orders nevertheless. What he learned subsequently was that the antiwar hysteria sweeping the country and the Academy made the leaders of the Academy fearful that they might not have enough first-rate applicants to fill the next year's incoming class. Tom, along with three others, arrived in Annapolis over the Christmas holidays and immediately divided the country in quarters, donned their dress blue uniforms, and proceeded to cross the country telling the young men of America that the Navy needed the best and brightest at Annapolis. Within the first year, they generated over 7,000 applicants for the 1,200 spots, and the Academy has not had a recruitment problem since.

Tom was introduced to the Naval Academy's Superintendent, Vice-Admiral James Calvert, who was responsible for Tom's career decision to stay in the Navy. In 1970, Tom's third child, and first son, was born. In 1971, Tom received a Master's Degree from George Washington University, which he attended in the evenings.

In January 1972, Tom began a six-month school in Norfolk, Virginia, to prepare him for joint-military operations. It was a period of study, thought, and reflection, with no sea duty and the opportunity to meet and learn from officers of the other services and from NATO allies. Over the next eighteen months, Tom was moved from Norfolk to Newport, Rhode Island, and then to Charleston, South Carolina. He was appointed Executive Officer of a brand-new Knox Class Frigate, the *USS Jesse L. Brown*. The ship was named after Jesse Brown, the first black naval aviator. To be a part of a ship's commissioning crew is a great experience—and a responsibility as well. Each ship develops its own persona among the fleet, so it is important that the initial crew sets a high standard and establishes a reputation for professionalism, competence, and a can-do spirit. While Tom was busy motivating his men to achieve such a reputation, he remembers how disappointed he was when he was commanded to leave the ship in the middle of another Mediterranean deployment. However, he realized that he was now prepared to have his own command someday: the dream of every military officer.

By April 1975, Tom was back in Virginia, this time for his first tour at the Pentagon. Duty in the Pentagon is all "half-days," 7 AM to 7 PM, which is no joke for those stationed there. During the next two years, Tom experienced decision-making at the highest levels. He was screened to command a destroyer and selected for the rank of Commander. He received orders to command the *USS Truett*, a frigate home-ported in Norfolk, Virginia. Tom's tour aboard the *Truett* was a defining moment. The Navy in this post-Vietnam period was experiencing a 20,000 petty-officer shortfall because of the dearth of ships. The consequent load on the fleet resulted in seven- or even eleven-month deployments with short turnarounds, followed by another deployment. Drug and alcohol abuse and racial tensions were rampant, not unlike the civilian culture at the time. Many Navy families qualified for food stamps because the pay was far less than what was available in the private sector.

Amid this difficult environment, Tom embraced and promoted the philosophy of "Ship, Shipmate, and then Self." Before every thought, word, or deed, a sailor must first ask himself what effect this may have on the ship, then on his shipmates, and then on himself. Tom held a formal recognition program for all the *Truett* "superstars" who always abided by this philosophy.

Although it required Tom to spend the next thirty of thirty-six months at sea, his three years in command of the *Truett* were the most rewarding of his life. The *Truett* was tops in battle efficiency, awarded the Arleigh Burke trophy for most improved ship in the fleet and the Golden Anchor for highest re-enlistment rate in the fleet. It completed a seven and a half–month deployment to the Mediterranean and to the Red Sea, including sophisticated surveillance of the Soviet carrier *Kiev*, and a three-month operation in the Gulf of Aden with no liberty. The most searing events were the deaths of six *Truett* sailors during those three years. It is unusual to lose a sailor in peacetime, but the loss of six—four to freakish accidents ashore, and two to separate suicides on board—certainly raised questions within the chain of command.

In August 1980, Tom reported to the Pentagon as administrative aide to the Secretary of the Navy. Within a short period, Ronald Reagan was elected President and John Lehman was appointed Secretary of the Navy. Tom was selected Captain and detailed to Senate Liaison in the Russell Senate Office Building. This was the last job held by Captain John McCain before he retired and returned to Arizona. Tom quickly learned the power of politics, as well as the dedication of many devoted men and women who worked long, stressful hours to keep their senator apprised of the issues. Tom's job was to make sure Congressional staff and their bosses understood the Navy's needs, as stipulated in the Defense budget.

In 1985, Tom left for command of a tactical operation destroyer squadron in Norfolk, Virginia. He led a group of ships around South America to operate with the Navies of all the United States' South American allies. Shortly before Christmas of 1986, Tom was informed that he had been selected for flag rank—the Naval term equivalent to a general in the Army General—and would be returning to Washington, D.C., as the Navy's Chief of Legislative Affairs, working directly for the Secretary of the Navy. Tom's job was to get the next carrier funded as a major part

Admiral Lynch (ret.) served as
Superintendent of the U. S. Naval Academy
from 1991–1994.

of the six-hundred-ship goal, and to get the F-18 and Tomahawk missiles funded and integrated into the fleet.

In 1989, Tom was assigned as Commander, Cruiser Destroyer Group 12, in Mayport, Florida. Tom soon embarked aboard the carrier *Eisenhower*, and when he deployed in March 1990, they became the Eisenhower Battle Group. He conducted a major live missile exercise in the Gulf of Sidra. He responded to the Iraqi invasion of Kuwait in August of that year by being the first U.S. presence in the Red Sea prepared to strike if called upon (Operation Desert Shield). The Eisenhower Battle Group returned home with over 21,000 flight hours recorded, no major mishaps, and a proud record of achievement for the country during a tenuous period.

In June 1991, Tom achieved his dream job: Superintendent of the U.S. Naval Academy. Unlike any previous assignment, his lovely wife Kathy was an integral and very visible professional partner and asset throughout this period because the job required planning, supervising, and hosting innumerable Midshipmen events, entertaining Congressional visitors, recruiting and caring for guest speakers, receiving visiting dignitaries, and overall management of the staff who cared for the Superintendent's residence at

Annapolis. Although Tom's three years of service as superintendent were marred by several Midshipmen deaths and a cheating scandal that rocked the Academy, he reflects that he would gladly return and do it all over again. The opportunity to help develop and train the future leadership of the Navy and the country is a privilege few are given.

In 1994, Tom was told that his next assignment would be a fleet command. Instead, following another Pentagon assignment, Chief Naval Officer Mike Boorda called Tom to his office to inform him that he was to be promoted to three stars but there would be no fleet command. Tom had other offers to consider, so with that news, he decided to reconsider them and change careers. He retired on November 1, 1995, and on that very same day, began a new civilian career in venture capital with Safeguard Scientifics, located in a suburb of Philadelphia.

Tom remained at Safeguard Scientifics until June of 2000. During that time, he participated in bringing more than a dozen companies public, worked an eighteen-month stint in Dallas as President and COO of CompuCom Systems, a billion-dollar NASDAQ company, and served as a board member for a host of small technology companies within the Safeguard portfolio. Tom next joined his close friend and former teammate Roger Staubach to assist the Staubach Company in establishing a federal real estate practice in Washington, D.C.

Today, Tom serves on numerous boards of public and private corporations and foundations. Presently, he is a partner in the Musser Group, a mainline Philadelphia venture capital firm, and makes his home in Villanova, Pennsylvania.

Ambassador Charles T. Manatt (Ret.)

"Born not for ourselves, but for the whole world."
—Chuck Manatt's High School Motto

Ambassador Charles Manatt is the founder and senior partner of the law firm Manatt, Phelps and Phillips, LLP, and former Chairman of the Democratic National Committee.

Born in Chicago in 1936 but raised in Audubon, Iowa, this son of a farmer and schoolteacher first tasted politics at age fifteen. The event was on April 14, 1952, in the nearby town of Carroll, Iowa. Chuck paid three dollars to attend a teenage-targeted Democratic Party fundraiser to support Adlai Stevenson's presidential campaign. Chuck graduated Iowa State College in 1958, along with Kathy, his wife of over fifty years whom he had known since the fifth grade. He served with the U.S. Army in the Quartermaster Corps and JAG. Shortly after graduating with his law degree in 1962 from George Washington University, where he was on the Board of Editors for the *George Washington Law Review*, he, his wife Kathy, and their baby daughter Michelle moved to Los Angeles, where Charles and Kathy's two sons, Tim and Dan, were born soon after. In 1965, Manatt founded his own law firm, capitalizing on his experience in banking and finance. Today, that law firm has offices in major cities across the country, and Manatt remains a principal partner.

Understanding Chuck begins with his family. The Manatt family believes they are descended from Huguenots who migrated from France through Belgium and Scotland to Northern Ireland in the seventeenth and eighteenth centuries. This family knowledge stems from Robert Manatt, Jr., who was born in County Down in 1792. He, with much of the rest of the family, came through Philadelphia in 1817, and eventually settled in Holmes County, Ohio. With the Homestead Act in full swing, he hitched up the horses to covered wagons and moved his family to Poweshiek County, Iowa, in 1847. It is believed that the Manatt family was the second family of European decent to settle there—just a year after Iowa joined the Union in 1846.

The Manatts thrived in Iowa. As a young man growing up there, Chuck was greatly influenced by formative experiences as a member of 4H, the Boy Scouts, and the Future Famers of America. The creed of the Future Farmers of America: "Learning to earn, earning to live, living to serve," continues to be Chuck's mantra guiding his career and public service.

Chuck has developed his professional career in five major areas: law, banking, politics, farming, and democracy building. It begins with law. His interest in pursuing a legal degree came, in part, from watching the leaders of the Iowa Young Democrats, all of whom seemed to be lawyers. Chuck enrolled in law school at Iowa and then transferred to the George Washington University School of Law in 1959. He served as the school's representative to the George Washington Student Body Council and as an associate editor of the *Law Review*. There he met one of his eventual law partners and lifelong friends, Tom Phelps, also an Iowa State grad.

After he completed law school, Chuck and Kathy traveled to Los Angeles, where he learned about banking. His training at O'Melveny was especially good. There he learned about the savings and loan chartering and bank approval processes, as the firm was just beginning to represent one of the first new banks chartered after World War II.

By the fall of 1964, Chuck and Kathy had firmly planted their roots in Los Angeles. They bought their first home, in Van Nuys; they learned that their son Tim was going to join the world; and Chuck opened his first law office above the Pantages Theater in Hollywood. The practice developed on the chartering and representation of new banks and savings and loans. San Luis Obispo Savings & Loan, Saddleback National in Tustin, and Palm Springs National Bank, and Valley National Bank in Salinas were among his first clients. In addition to the financial institutions work, Chuck started working on representing developers of some shopping centers, both in the San Fernando Valley and in Palm Springs.

The next winter, Chuck had extended discussions with friend and fellow Iowa State and George Washington law graduate, Tom Phelps. They came to an agreement, and Tom joined Chuck in a law practice in April 1965. Alan Rothenberg, also from O'Melveny, joined in 1966 as a litigation partner. In subsequent years, although the practice has had the ups and downs of most law firms, it has grown to four hundred professionals, with law offices in eight cities. In 2001, Chuck and his partners established Manatt/Jones Global Strategies, which is an international consulting firm headed by Ambassador James Jones and focused on client representation regarding incoming and outgoing investment in the United States. The consulting firm has offices in Washington, D.C., Mexico City, and Sao Paolo, Brazil.

Chuck's involvement in the banking industry resulted from his work in law. His very first client at O'Melveny & Myers turned out to be the FDIC application for American City Bank. Since O'Melveny had not handled a bank application in many years, they thought a young freshly minted lawyer might be the right one to do it. Eventually, that application, and that of the San Luis Obispo Savings and Loan, led to a flurry of activity in the bank chartering area. Among the benefits of this work, the young counsel was able to learn a great deal from the Directors of these banks, who were generally twenty to thirty years older than he was at the time.

The independent banking trend took off after many of the new savings and loans had been chartered, post-War. After completing about forty bank applications for clients, Chuck had the idea to start a bank directly. Tom Phelps, Alan Rothenberg, and he were founders of First Los Angeles, in Century City. Chuck was the Chairman of the bank and the largest stockholder.

This role gave Chuck recognition in the greater Los Angeles community, which he would not have received there as a lawyer. He was involved with the California Bankers Association (CBA), elected president of the organization in 1979. The banking work led in turn to numerous overseas activities.

Yet, despite his involvement in law, banking, and politics, Chuck never forgot his roots in Iowa and farming. His interest in farming developed especially when he was in 4H and FFA in high school. When city kids or town boys were running their paper routes, dirt farmers' sons were caring for their hogs or cattle as part of their 4H or FFA projects. The hogs Chuck raised were of the Hereford breed, which no one else in the county raised. This meant that Chuck would always have the Grand Champion Hereford Hog of Audubon County and then go on to show at the Iowa State Fair. Chuck's FFA instructor, Jim Hamilton, drilled into his head the importance of knowing how to fill out and read a financial statement and how to plan a project that would have a positive cash flow. When he finished his high school years, Chuck had four steers, twelve Hereford hogs, and about $3000 in the bank.

Manatt graduated from Iowa State, studying agricultural business, rural sociology, and agronomy. Over the next few years, while working in law and banking, Chuck began purchasing Iowa farmland. Today he has twenty quarters, composed of 2,400 acres of cropland and 800 acres of pasture. His agricultural portfolio spans six different farmers in Cass and Audubon Counties in Iowa. In addition to the corn and soybean operations, they run 600 stockers on the pasture, which are fed out during the wintertime at a feed lot before going to market.

The recent capstone to Chuck's agricultural activities was the building of the Taylor Hill Lodge on Highway 71, north of Audubon. He had the lodge built by Tom Testroet, who is an amazing carpenter as well as the son of one Chuck's high school classmates. The joy of the lodge is that it serves as Chuck's family home when they are in Iowa and, otherwise, is available for the community's use. Donna Bauer manages the lodge, and Ted Bauer manages the overall farming operation. Happily, these managers have worked with the Manatts since the time when Chuck's father was running the farm operations.

Perhaps the area where Chuck is most well known, though, is his involvement in politics. As mentioned earlier, his first political event was a Democratic Party fundraiser to support Adlai Stevenson's Presidential campaign. Richard Rausch was the promoter of the fundraiser. Little did Chuck know how thoroughly this event would hook him for the future. Chuck immediately made himself useful to the Democratic Party, serving in roles such as President of the Iowa State Young Democrats, National College Chairman of the Young Democrats, Executive Director of the Young Democratic Clubs of America, and Legal Counsel for the California Federation of Young Democrats.

In Los Angeles, Chuck started out as the treasurer of the 26th District

California Democratic Club. That was, in part, a grassroots movement started in the 1950s, which was championed by future U.S. Senator Alan Cranston. In 1964, Chuck was the Chairman of the Young Citizens for Johnson/Humphrey, in southern California, under the patronage of Earl Warren, Jr., and the new young Senator Birch Bayh. Throughout the '60s, Chuck was especially active in supporting Congressman Jim Corman and Assemblyman Bob Moretti, who later became the California Speaker. This eventually led to his working with Nelson Rising, Fred Port, John McAllister, Burt Pines, Gray Davis, and others in the Tunney for Senate campaign in 1970.

Following up on the Tunney campaign, political operatives raised the idea of Chuck running for State Chairman. The previous summer, Chuck had lost in a twelve-way race for LA County Committee from the San Fernando Valley Assembly District. Chuck dug in and visited fifty-two of California's fifty-eight counties in his quest to be successful this time.

The actual election is a story in itself. During his California Chairmanship, Chuck generally had good luck in electing Democrats to office. After his first try at reappointment didn't succeed, the state did it a second time, and that, along with the Watergate scandal, ushered in more new legislators. The exciting times of being a Party Chairman included trying to build from the ground up a political organization that would be supportive of office nominees and progressive policies around which most Democrats could rally. This marked the first time Chuck had to rebuild Democratic operations, following the era of Ronald Reagan.

The concluding year of Chuck's State Party Chairmanship reflected a national victory for Governor Carter and, unfortunately, a loss for Senator Tunney. As Larry O'Brien's book of memoirs reflects, "There are no final victories in the party business." Following his California experience, Chuck was elected Chairman of the Western Conference of the Democrats, and in 1978 he was tapped by DNC Chairman John White to be the National Finance Chairman of the Party. Both of these new assignments gave Chuck the chance to travel much of the country and work quite closely with party officials and some office leaders in rebuilding party activities. Unfortunately, the 1980 election results were reflective of the Reagan magic and limited the progressive policies that had been attempted in the Carter era. Chuck decided to run for Democratic National Committee (DNC) Chairman to again concentrate on "the rebuilding after the Reagan phenomenon" that he had experienced in his service to California.

The DNC Chairmanship brought both great joy and great frustration during Chuck's term. He was able to modernize the party, computerize the national headquarters, establish the Harriman Media Center, and build the first-ever National Party Headquarters. In 1982, Democrats had good gains in the House and in Governorships.

Chuck's presumed replacement as National Party Chairman by Burt Lance was one of the biggest fiascos Chuck would experience. As literally hundreds of Chuck's friends were coming to San Francisco for the weekend of the Democratic Convention, they were buffeted with the news that the Mondale campaign wanted Lance as the National Chairman. (While in the Carter administration, Lance had been accused of mismanagement and corruption as Chairman of the Board of Calhoun National Bank of Calhoun, Georgia, leading to his resignation as director of the Office of Management and Budget in1977. Lance was acquitted of all charges in 1981.)

Fortunately, the *Wall Street Journal* ran an article in favor of Manatt for Party Chair, and Chuck prevailed.

During the 1980s and 1990s, Chuck's work continued, as a National Committeeman from California and as a Co-Chairman of the Clinton/Gore ticket in 1992. Happily, that election campaign was successful, and the Democrats came into their own with a progressive President.

But politics did not remain domestic for Chuck. He has also made a lifelong commitment to spreading democracy around the world. Chuck's first involvement with the international democracy movement came with a NATO Young Political Leaders conference in 1961. They met in D.C. that year, and in 1962, they met in Aurhus, Denmark. From that activity evolved a group called the U.S. Youth League and its Washington affiliate, the American Council of Young Political Leaders. There was much activity across borders, with and into Communist countries, which went under the guise of study tours or learning missions. Chuck's first trip abroad for the Young Political Leaders was in 1974, when he enjoyed an extensive trip to Japan. He continued to pursue other similar activities, including visiting with the Peace Corps in Colombia and going on a study mission to Germany with the Republican leadership of the California legislature.

Chuck's more serious involvement in promoting a democratic form of government around the world started in 1978, when Bill Brock, as the Republican Chairman, and Chuck, as the Democratic National Finance Chairman, got together to form the American Political Foundation. The Foundation conducted a variety of activities, and with Larry Silverberger's help, President Reagan gave a speech in the House of Commons on June 9, 1983, encouraging Americans to form the National Endowment

Chuck and Kathy Manatt display their souvenir flag from Chuck's appointment as the U.S. Ambassador to the Dominican Republic in 1999.

for Democracy. It was Chuck's pleasure to serve as Vice Chairman of that group, and he was founding Chairman of the National Democratic Institute, the Endowment's Democratic affiliate. In 1999, then-President Clinton appointed Manatt Ambassador to the Dominican Republic, where Chuck emphasized election administration reform, commercial development, and greater cooperation between the Dominican Republic and the United States' criminal justice systems.

Chuck has been honored numerous times for his professional abilities, including being named in *The Best Lawyers in America* and being awarded two honorary Doctor of Laws degrees.

In addition to his prodigious professional and political activities, Chuck has dedicated himself to numerous causes and organizations. Currently, Chuck is the Chairman emeritus of the George Washington University Board of Trustees, having served as its Chairman from 2001 to 2007 and as a member of the Board since 1980. Since Chuck's joining the Board, the university has seen rapid expansion and growth, including the construction of a state-of-the-art facility for its medical school and other key programs.

Chuck is also a member of the Board of Trustees of Grinnell College, in Iowa. His commitment to his home state and to higher education was demonstrated most recently in 2002, when he established the Manatt-Phelps

Lecture in Political Science at Iowa State University. Since giving its inaugural lecture, Chuck has brought such luminaries to Iowa State as then-Senator Biden, Senator Hagel, FedEx founder Fred Smith, and international political dignitaries from Mexico and Sweden.

Chuck is also the Director of the National Museum of American History, a branch of the Smithsonian dedicated to inspiring a broader understanding of America and its many peoples. He is Director of the National Capital Boy Scouts of America. He is committed to social justice and works to improve the lives of the poor as a trustee of the Wesley Foundation, the Red Cloud Indian School in Pine Ridge, South Dakota, and the Meridian Center International, a leading nonpartisan, not-for-profit organization dedicated to strengthening international understanding. In 2009, Chuck became the President and a Director of the Council of American Ambassadors, a nonprofit, nonpartisan association of over two hundred former and incumbent non-career U.S. ambassadors. Chuck serves as a Director of the Center for the Study of the Presidency. He is also an advisory member to the Paladin Capital Fund.

Above all else, Chuck believes in the goodness of people and in helping those in need, when possible, to do the best they can for themselves, their families, and their communities. Throughout his life, Chuck's career reflects a commitment to helping those who are less fortunate. Helping others motivates many of his life's activities. Chuck truly believes that people are not born merely to improve conditions for themselves, but to improve the governments and the lives of the whole world by giving generously of their resources and talent. This Iowa farmer truly has lived by the Future Farmers' creed. He has learned to earn, earned to live, and lived to serve.

The Honorable Richard J. Santorum

"I pattern myself after Wilberforce in many respects, because I see the struggle for the recognition of the rights of the unborn as a similar civil rights struggle."

—*Rick Santorum*

Rick Santorum, former Senator from Pennsylvania, is a lawyer, a public intellectual, and the father of eight children.

Born in Virginia but raised in Pennsylvania, Rick started his political career working in the State Senate in Harrisburg in 1981. Rick ran a surprisingly successful campaign for the U.S. House of Representatives in a suburban Pittsburgh district in 1990, the same year he married Karen Garver. After four years in the House, Santorum was elected to the first of two consecutive terms representing Pennsylvania in the U.S. Senate. Rick was an active leader in his party, eventually rising to the third-ranking member of the Republican leadership. His signature legislative achievements included spearheading both the passage of the landmark 1996 welfare reform as well as legislation outlawing partial birth abortion.

Today, Rick continues to pursue his passion to strengthen families and improve American culture. As the president of a Virginia-based DVR set-top-box manufacturer, he leads a company whose software gives parents the power to edit scenes out of television content that they find objectionable. This technology will shift the power to shape our children's character back from Hollywood to the parents, where it belongs. He also heads Program to Protect America's Future, an institute that educates citizens about the threat of terrorism to America at the Ethics and Public Policy Center. He remains engaged in the public square as a public speaker, writer of a semi-weekly column for the *Philadelphia Inquirer*, Fox News commentator, and recently as a radio host on the Friday edition of Bill Bennett's *Morning in America* program.

Rick describes his brand of conservative political philosophy as a "stewardship of patrimony." Born on May 10, 1958, in Winchester, Virginia, Rick inherited from an early age his parents' tenacious work ethic and strong core values. "Rooster" was his childhood nickname, on account of a tuft of hair on the crown of his head, but it stuck because it fit his outspoken personality. Rick grew up attending Catholic schools in Butler, a steel town north of Pittsburgh, made up of well-defined ethnic neighborhoods. As a son of an Italian immigrant, the old-world Catholic traditions of both his family and his community formed an integral part of his identity from an early age:

> I went to Catholic school; most of my neighbors turned out to be Catholic, and just my whole being, whether it was a fish fry on Friday, the things you just sort of did as a young person when you lived in that era, you did along with the Church, which you didn't necessarily see as religious, but as part of the community, as part of that era, of what Catholics did.

In 1980, Rick graduated with a bachelor's degree in political science from Penn State University. During his undergraduate years, Rick got his first taste of politics. As an indicator of things to come, in his freshman year Rick took charge, becoming President of Students for Senate Candidate John Heinz. Shortly after the election, he started the College Republican Club and became its chair. He continued his education, receiving an MBA from the University of Pittsburgh in 1981 and his JD from the Dickinson School of Law in 1986. Concurrently, Rick became more involved in

Rick and his wife Karen enjoy the campaign trail.

Pennsylvania politics, working as an assistant to State Senator Doyle Corman and as Director of the Pennsylvania State Senate Transportation Committee and the Pennsylvania State Local Government Committee. In 1986, Rick also began practicing law in Pittsburgh at Kirkpatrick and Lockhart, where, among his other clients, he represented the World Wrestling Federation.

1990 was the pivotal year in Santorum's life. First, he married Karen Garver, a law student, former nurse, and the tenth of twelve children of an Irish Catholic family:

> Meeting my wife was as important a moment as any. It wasn't necessarily her, but it was we. We happened to be the right people for each other to begin this new journey. Neither of us on our own was on this journey, and we would not have gone on this journey but for each other. We both came in respects broken as we started our relationship and understood that as we grew in our relationship, the seeds planted would grow. She grew up in a Catholic ghetto, one of twelve kids; she went through the same thing

I went through: a little rebellion, a little living the '70s in college and afterward. Once we got off the secular treadmill that the world likes to have us all on and realized that we loved each other, wanted to marry, and wanted to have a family, well, family all of the sudden snapped us back to our families, and what we would want for us and for our family now that we've gotten off the pop culture siren song. That's where we were both of one mind, and integral to that was faith. We had to find the faith that we really weren't practicing. It was a wonderful journey that still continues.

Together he and Karen are raising eight children and are approaching their twentieth year of marriage. Karen is the author of two books: *Everyday Graces: A Child's Book of Manners* and *Letters to Gabriel*. The latter book details the Santorums' experience with their son Gabriel, who lived only a few hours due to a congenital birth defect. Rick and Karen discovered their son's condition literally a week after Rick began shepherding the bill to ban partial-birth abortion through the Senate. The discovery of Gabriel's condition was very hard on Rick, but he pressed on during a dire situation:

> A week later, we had that sonogram. The doctor kept looking at this one dark area and finally said, "Your baby has a fatal birth defect and is going to die." (He had obviously flunked bedside manners in medical school.) That wasn't the news we wanted or expected, but I must tell you that our reaction, after the shock and grief, was not to avoid the pain, the cost of the struggle; it was not to get rid of the "problem," and it was not to put the baby out of his misery like something that was less than human. Karen and I couldn't rationalize how we could treat this little human life at twenty weeks' gestation in the womb any different than one twenty weeks old after birth. At either age, he is helpless, unaware, and thoroughly dependent on us, his parents, to protect him, care for him, and love him unconditionally. So instead of giving our child a death sentence, we gave him a name: Gabriel Michael, after the two great angels.

To understand Rick is ultimately to understand how central family life is to his life. Around his wrist, Rick wears a wristband with the acronym FAMILY, which stands for, "Forget about me, I love you." It is a reminder of the centrality of family in his life, which defines Rick and provides him with strength:

For my wife Karen and me, marriage is a sacred vocation. We give ourselves to each other, mind, body, and soul. Nothing in this world is more
important to me than the happiness and well being of my wife and children. It is my most important job. All of my strength comes from my love
for them and God's love for me.

In 1990, at age thirty-two, Rick ran for the U.S. House of Representatives in the heavily Democratic 18th District. Few thought Rick stood any
chance against a popular seven-time incumbent; indeed, the Republican
National Committee refused to donate one cent to his campaign. Nevertheless, Rick surprised everyone, even himself, with his victory in 1990. It was
a near-impossible win:

> I ran against a seven-term incumbent who had always been easily re-
> elected. I did a poll six months before the election, and 6 percent of the
> people in my district had heard of me. I spent less than $250,000 and
> was outspent three-to-one in a Democratic district. But with the help of
> a great campaign manager, Mark Rodgers, and many devoted and hard-
> working volunteers—including my chief volunteer, my bride, Karen—we
> did the impossible. The year was 1990. It was a bad year for Republicans,
> both in Pennsylvania and nationally, and a rather unremarkable year in
> American history, but it was a big one for me. I was married to Karen in
> June; in August we found out we were to be parents; and in November I
> was elected a Congressman.

This impressive upset was soon followed by his equally unexpected reelection in 1992, when his district lines had been redrawn to produce a two-
to-one Democrat-to-Republican ratio. Why did he have these surprising
victories? Rick came to Congress with a clear vision of America. Rick prizes
the freedom of Americans above all else, and he believes that our freedom
can be secured by the promotion of virtue. In his book *It Takes a Family*,
Rick explains:

> As Americans, we enjoy historically unparalleled personal freedoms guar-
> anteed in our Constitution, and we take great pride in understanding our
> country, correctly, as "the land of the free." In our judgments of other na-
> tions, we make respect for liberty and human rights our priority. But too
> often, the freedom we boast of in America is not the freedom envisioned

by the likes of Washington, Adams, Madison, and Jefferson. It is different today, in tone and substance.

The freedom enshrined constitutionally by our founding fathers was a freedom that both gained its vitality from, and was limited by, the social bonds between fellow citizens. America's founders understood [that] the securing of freedom was the ultimate aim of politics; but they also saw the promotion of virtue as the ultimate aim and the indispensible support of freedom. As Samuel Adams wrote, "we may look up to Armies for our Defense, but Virtue is our best Security. It is not possible that any State should long remain free, where Virtue is not supremely honored.

The safeguard of freedom is virtue. Rick looks to John Adams' view on virtue. In 1776, Adams wrote:

Statesmen, my dear Sir, may speculate for liberty, but it is Religion and Morality alone, which can establish the Principles upon which Freedom can securely stand. The only foundation of a free Constitution is pure Virtue, and if this cannot be inspired into our People in a greater Measure than they have it now, they may change their Rulers and the forms of Government, but they will not obtain a lasting liberty.

Later, in 1798, Adams said this, as President:

We have no government armed with power capable of contending with human passions unbridled by morality and religion. Avarice, ambition, revenge, or gallantry, would break the strongest cords of our Constitution as a whale goes through a net. Our Constitution was made only for a moral and religious people. It is wholly inadequate to the government of any other.

The man called Rooster by his high school friends soon garnered another reputation in Congress: reformer. He joined a group of Representatives known as the "Gang of Seven." Together, they uncovered longstanding corruption in the House, including embezzlement investigations involving the House's bank and its post office. These schemes lead to several members' conviction for stealing taxpayer money and gave impetus the to "Republican Revolution" and takeover of Congress in 1994.

In 1994, Rick again bucked conventional wisdom and unseated Pennsylvania's incumbent Senator Harris Wofford. Just thirty-six years old, Rick continued quickly advancing as a leader on the Senate side of Capitol Hill. He spearheaded the landmark bipartisan reform of welfare. This reform was successfully recognized as having "ended welfare as we know it" according to President Clinton, who signed the bill in 1996. In his typical less-talk-more-action fashion, Rick then hired nine people off welfare to work in his Senate offices in D.C. and Pennsylvania.

Santorum also worked tirelessly to ban partial-birth abortion. He led the legislative fight to pass laws in 1996 and 1998, only to face a presidential veto. Following a subsequent Supreme Court decision striking down a similar state law, Rick passed a new version of the ban in 2003, which was signed into law by President Bush. In 2007, the Supreme Court constitutionally upheld the law. But perhaps the most moving impact was the effect of Rick's persuasive arguing from the floor of the Senate, even amid his several defeats. After his defeat in overriding the President's veto, Rick received this email from a young college student:

> Recently while my girlfriend and I were flipping through the channels, we came across C-SPAN, and were fortunate enough to hear your speech regarding the evils of partial-birth abortion. We saw the picture of the little boy with the headphones on, who was lucky enough to have parents who loved him and brought him into this world, instead of ending his life. Both of us were moved to tears by your speech. And my girlfriend confessed to me that she had scheduled an appointment for an abortion the following week. She never told me about her pregnancy because she knew that I would object to any decision to kill our child. But after watching your emotional speech, she looked at me as tears rolled down her cheeks, and told me that she couldn't go through with it.
>
> We're not ready to be parents ... but I am grateful that our child will live. It is a true tragedy that the partial-birth abortion ban failed to override Clinton's veto. But please take some comfort in knowing that at least one life was saved because of your speech. You have saved the life of our child.

Rick's leadership skills were apparent throughout his Senate career. He became the youngest member of the Republican leadership in over thirty years. He assumed leadership of the Senate Republican Conference in 2006. In addition to chairing the GOP Task Force on Welfare Reform, Rick served on various senate committees: Agriculture, Banking, Rules, and Aging, as well as stints on both the Armed Services and Finance Committees.

Additionally, Santorum founded and lead the Congressional Working Group on Religious Freedom.

Despite serving only two terms in the Senate, Rick succeeded in passing a broad range of key legislation: the Welfare Reform Bill, the American Community Renewal Act, the ban on partial-birth abortion, the Born-Alive Infants Protection Act, the Combating Autism Act, the Farmland Preservation Act, the Abandoned Mine Lands Reform Act, the Multi-Employer Pension Reform Act, the Global Aids Authorization Act, Health Savings Accounts, the Syria Accountability Act, and the Iran Freedom Support Act. Santorum additionally focused his efforts on religious freedom, promoting democracy and religious liberty worldwide, lowering the tax burdens on working families, combating the HIV/AIDS epidemic, and strengthening and enhancing national security. In 2005, while still in office, Rick published *It Takes a Family: Conservatism and the Common Good.*

Toward the end of his second term, the Senator was an outspoken defendant of the War on Terrorism, in particular supporting the wars in Iraq and Afghanistan. Running primarily on this platform in 2006, he was defeated in his bid for a third term by his challenger, Bob Casey. Rick describes his defeat as engendering "nothing but gratitude" in him toward the people of Pennsylvania for the opportunity to serve them. "God's got something else planned for me." Indeed, taking things from God's perspective is the cornerstone of Rick's approach to life:

> I try to look at success as Thomas More would: through the eyes of God, as opposed to through the eyes of man. If you look at success through the eyes of God, then it is very easy to figure out the virtues that lead you to success. If you look at success through the eyes of man, you are caught with the reality, particularly today, of how fallen man really is.

Phrased another way, Rick's comfort is that of a duty done well. He comes to serve, not to be served. Rick feels that these words paraphrase those of the great American thinker, Orestes Brownson, who in 1843 said,

> Ask not what your age wants, but what it needs; not what it will reward, but what, without which, it cannot be saved; and then go and do; and find your reward in consciousness of having done your duty, and above all in the reflection that you have been accounted to suffer somewhat for mankind.

One of those plans was to have the opportunity to spend more time with his wife and growing family. Another gift from God was the blessing of the birth of a special baby in 2008 who needs special attention that Rick now has time to give. Santorum remains dedicated, whether through his family or his work advancing the common good through his conservative political philosophy. At present, he is contemplating a run at the 2012 Republican presidential nomination. But if not as President, Rick hopes to find new ways to leave a better country for his children and for all Americans, echoing the words of John Adams in 1780:

> I must study politics and war that my sons may have liberty to study mathematics and philosophy. My sons ought to study mathematics and philosophy, geography, natural history and naval architecture, navigation, commerce and agriculture, in order to giver their children a right to study painting, poetry, music, architecture, statuary, tapestry, and porcelain.

Rick Santorum lives by one mantra: *Non nobis Domine, non nobis, sed nomini tuo da gloriam.* "Not to us, O Lord, not to us, but to your name, be glory."

Ten Characters with Character

Their Conversations

If politics does not build character, it certainly provides the opportunity to display it. The personal interviews that follow allow the reader to meet ten principled political players and get a glimpse of their good character in action. The questions asked and answered will help the reader understand how these people deliberated in crisis to maintain their moral compass.

The interviews cover three main areas of questioning: about the character's personal life, about values, and about life in politics and the workplace. Each person faced the same thirty questions, ten in each section. Each answered independent of the others. The answers are arranged alphabetically by last name. Not everyone answered every question. The answers are also not even in length. As happens in many conversations, an initial question spurs tangential thoughts. In several cases, some of the richest material emerges from these digressions, so the response has been kept intact for the reader's enjoyment.

The conversations often reveal similarities. For example, many of the interviewees emphasize the important role family played in forming their sense of right and wrong, and their work ethic. All of them speak of defining moments, points in their lives where they made choices that enabled future success. And each is quick to point out examples of role models they knew and admired in their own lives. Good character seemingly begets more good character.

There are notable differences as well. Partisan politics plays into several answers. But even when this occurs, the interviewees remain civil. They rise above pettiness. Many of them are even willing to call out those in their own parties who don't display principle. Conversely, many are also willing to find the good and praise it, even when it blossoms on the other side of the political aisle. For example, Democratic Senator Ben Cardin explains that knowing what he knows today, he would vote to confirm the conservative Justice Scalia to the Supreme Court, because of his high regard for Scalia's integrity and good character.

There are alternative ways to enjoy the interviews that follow. While this requires much flipping back and forth, one may focus on a single interviewee and read all of his or her responses in sequence, question by question. The benefit of this approach is that it provides a complete picture of the person. One sees how important mentors promote good character during formative years, how values become internalized, and finally, how good traits, once acquired, resurface during one's professional life.

Conversely, the reader may prefer to focus upon a single question of interest and compare the different responses across the collection of characters. This approach serves to stimulate self-reflection, encouraging one to answer the questions along with the interviewees. Either way, the conversations that follow should be insightful.

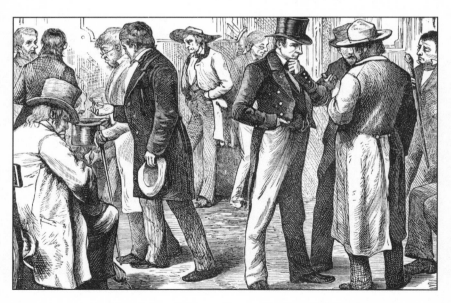

Vintage engraving, 1877, of conversations at the White House among men who await the President. Restoration credit: Steven Wynne Photography.

Personal Questions

Among the people you know, whom do you most admire?

What do you most respect in a person?

Was religion important in your home? Does religion continue to play a role in your life?

Can you identify something like a "defining moment" in your life?

What worldview guides your thoughts and actions?

How do your natural tendencies or habits relate to your character?

Can you identify the most important decision in your life?

When have you had to make principled compromises?

Have you ever violated your principles? What was the outcome?

Do you have any regrets about any past decisions?

Among the people you know, whom do you most admire?

Black, Charlie: Certainly in a political context, I would say John McCain, because of his totally unselfish service to his country, the courage he has shown in doing what's right, and as we said in the campaign, he is always putting the country's interests ahead of his own interests. It's beyond integrity. It's being willing to sacrifice your personal interest. There are other people I admire as much, but probably not in politics.

Bulger, William: Recently for a gentleman who was my majority leader, one Walter Boverini, I was asked to deliver a short eulogy at his funeral Mass up in Lynn. I was reminded as I looked at his life how he, as such a young man, born in the year 1924 and by the end of World War II in 1945 had flown thirty-five missions, the limit of the number of missions one could fly in the B-17 "flying fortresses" across Europe, and engaged in the huge effort to bring Germany to its knees. And he flew those thirty-five missions. Since he was only twenty-one when the war ended, he surely must have been between ages nineteen and twenty for the larger number of those missions. Yet, he was a very easygoing and modest person, who didn't know his own virtue, the soul of integrity. I just knew him as a very reliable, straightforward man, and I liked the virtues that he stood for, though I don't think I ever heard him seek to preach. But he did preach by his example.

Dr. Johnson said, "Example is always more efficacious than precept." That's my observation also. Those are the kinds of people I do admire. They are not very conspicuous, nor are they very appreciated during their time. These are the type of people who don't need any kind of appreciation. They do what they think is right. They do what they think they are called to do.

Cardin, Ben: For my generation it was John F. Kennedy. I was in high school when John Kennedy was president of the United States. We really took what he had to say seriously. It was not unlike the current situation with President Obama. Kennedy called upon my generation to get involved and make a difference.

In public life, my parents I admired greatly. They really taught me the value of family and of public service. [My father] was in public office before he was married. So it was a combination of in public life of John Kennedy and a governor named Theodore McKeldin, who was a Republican governor who opened up opportunities beyond just the traditional people who had gotten involved in politics. He appointed a lot of different people and believed in diversity.

Bliley, Tom: My father. He graduated from college at age nineteen, valedictorian of his class, with a 3.6 in Chemical Engineering. He went on to run the family business, and eventually (but reluctantly) decided to support my efforts in public service.

Carlson, Richard: My two sons, Tucker and Buckley, come immediately to mind. They were wonderful kids, and they have grown into men of character, strength, and courage. They have great intellectual curiosity and incredible good humor. They have kept their kind and humble hearts from childhood—not always such an easy thing to do. Accomplishments and accolades and a lot of attention sometimes wipe that away, but it didn't in their case. Both are exemplary fathers and fine husbands. Their wives, by the way, are like daughters to me. The two families live about a minute from each other in Northwest Washington and about five minutes from Patricia and me. Very nice for us.

Another man I admire is my close friend Bill Cowan, a retired U.S. Marine colonel. I have been hosting the *Danger Zone* radio show for more than five years every week, usually with Bill as co-host. Bill is also a Fox News military and terrorism analyst. I have come to know him really well. He's an accomplished person, unconventional in his thinking, catholic in his interests. He was a longtime Special Forces operator within the U.S. government, which is unusual for a Marine officer, and has been involved in some hair-raising events, which he will never tell you about. He was a member of the highly secret unit at the Pentagon called the ISA.... He personally is brave, resourceful, and a loyal friend. Loyalty is a trait in every person I admire. In Bill's case, he is smart and has a wonderful sense of humor, too. He is one fine, cheery, friendly guy. *Semper fidelis* is his watchword: always faithful.

P.X. Kelly is another man I admire. I guess it is no coincidence that he is also an ex-Marine. In fact, P.X. was commandant of the Marine Corp. I sometimes go bird-shooting with him. The Ruger shotguns that my boys and I all sometimes shoot came from P.X. He's a remarkable person who comes from a remarkable family. This is what I like about him: P.X. Kelly, who is getting up in age yet is still very active and still [stands] ramrod straight, grew up in Boston. He came from a modest background. I'm a little uncertain about the details, but his father died when he was a boy about twelve or thirteen. Yet, his sister and his brother and he all ended up being very accomplished Americans. I'm sure a lot of that is attributable to their mother.

P.X. told me a story that I love. He wanted to go to college, but he didn't have the money and didn't get a scholarship to Villanova, which was what he wanted. He decided to enlist in the Marine Corps. He and a friend went downtown and signed up at a recruiting office. This was around 1946. Then they went down to Cape Cod for some partying for the weekend, their last days of freedom before the misery of boot camp at Parris Island, South Carolina.

P.X.'s sister called him on Sunday before he was due to report in to the Marine Corps. She said, "There is a letter here from Villanova University. It says you have a scholarship." P.X. had already signed up for the Marines. Ah, he was too late! So he went down on Monday anyway and saw the same Marine Captain who had inducted him, and he explained what had happened.

The captain said, "You have a contract with the Marine Corps. This institution is built on honor, among other things, and you have agreed to join, you have given your word."

And P.X. said, "You're right, I understand."

And the Marine captain then said, "I'll make a deal with you, son. If you will agree to join the Marine Corp as an officer when you graduate from Villanova, I'll make your signature on this paper disappear. I'll take your personal word of honor that you will do this."

P.X. gave his word, and he kept it. Four years later he graduated from Villanova under the NROTC program, became a Marine officer, and rose through thirty-seven years in the Corps—Silver Star winner, Bronze Star winner, Master Parachutist, leader of Force Recon, to become leader of the entire Corps.

When he became commandant in 1983, he thought, as he had often done over the years, about the Marine captain who had helped him begin the career that he loved. Without his kindness, P.X. would not have succeeded as he had done. He asked some assistants to find the captain, last seen at the Boston area recruiting office in 1946. They soon did. He was still alive, had retired as a colonel, and was now an old man living in New Hampshire.

P.X. called him on the phone. He said something like, "Colonel, this is General P.X. Kelley, Commandant of the Marine Corps. You probably don't remember me, but I remember you," and told the surprised colonel the story from more than three decades before. P.X. said, "I want you to come down and be my guest in Washington. Come to the parade next Friday night at Marine Barracks at 8th and I Streets. I'll send a plane for you." And the old colonel did. That story was typical of P.X. Kelly.

Eckstein, Paul: It's probably not uncommon for people to start with their parents, and I will start with mine. Following that must come John Ahern and Jack Brown.

My father was born in Hungary when it was part of the Austro-Hungarian Empire, in 1908. He came to the United States in 1926, and he was seventeen at the time. He attended the University of Pittsburgh, where his family had settled, and graduated from the University of Pittsburgh in 1931. It was in the midst of the depression. He was interested in going to medical school. He applied to the University of Pittsburgh, but he was not admitted. At the time there were strict quotas called *numerus clausus*— no more than around ten percent of the students admitted to the medical school [could be] Jewish. He had to find some place to go if he was going to be a doctor. I don't think it embittered him particularly, but I will tell you a little sidelight on that.

He applied to and was admitted to the Goethe Medical School in Germany, in Frankfurt. While the Nazis were a minor party on the rise, they had not yet come to power. He was admitted and started medical school in the fall of 1931. Exactly on January 30, 1933, Hitler came to power and it became evident to him that virtually everyone in the medical school, students and faculty, were Nazis. Here he was in Germany, studying medicine in a language that was not his native language, as he had studied in the United States in English at the University of Pittsburgh. Because he was an American citizen at the time, he was able to continue medical school there, where he met my mother, married, came to the United States and started a new life.

My mother came from a wealthy Frankfurt Jewish family who [were] pretty much wiped out in the Weimer inflation in the 1920s—and [those who weren't] dissipated during that decade [were] taken by the Nazis in the 1930s. [My parents] both started from nothing, if you consider my mother coming to the United States with nothing, and had the most admirable success and made the absolute most of their lives, enjoyed life, worked hard, raised a family—and it all starts with him.

[Paul greatly admires not only his parents, but John Ahern as well.]

I admire John Ahern for a lot of things. John was a person who lost both his legs on Utah beach on D-Day. He lost them trying to save some paratroopers who were in the middle of a minefield; he tried to rescue them. They warned him not to come; he came anyway. Lost his legs. He was awarded the Distinguished Service Cross for that. Many of us thought he should have been awarded the Congressional Medal of Honor, and we tried to get him that. In some ways, that was just a small part of why I admired him. He died several years ago. I admired him because he was in pain every day of his life. He was in the hospital for several years. After his legs were amputated, he went to law school, became a lawyer, a candidate for office. He ran a number of races and only won once. He was a man who was never defeated. He was really undefeated.

[And Paul wouldn't be Paul if he were not honoring the memory of his mentor, Jack Brown.]

There are many things about my mentor, Jack Brown, that I admired. Because I was closer to him, I could see his faults, but he had more moral courage than anyone I've seen. It was displayed primarily in the spring of 1981, in a trial he was leading and I was assisting on, in which the judge had turned on our case, in the sense that he didn't like our case, and was really making life miserable for our side of the case. Every day Jack would take a fair amount of abuse from the judge, work at night, come back, and keep our spirits high. I admire Jack and revered him for many, many things, but never more than for what he did at that period of time.

Well, we won. The case was a bifurcated trial, meaning we tried liability to the jury first and the jury returned a victory for us. We were supposed to try the damage part of the case two weeks later, but the judge postponed that and entered a judgment notwithstanding the verdict, in which he took away the jury verdict. We then appealed to the Ninth Circuit, and Jack argued the case in the Ninth Circuit, which reversed the decision of the trial judge to grant the JNOV. The other side then filed a petition for the writ of certiorari to the Supreme Court, which was denied. Then the case went back for a trial on damages and settled on $52 million, at a time when that was a lot of money. It is not chicken feed now, but in 1982 or 1983, when we settled, it was a considerable sum of money.

You had to be there every day to see how stalwart Jack was. It wasn't put on; it was sincere, and there were a lot of depressed people on our team. Both sides had enormous teams. We may have had twenty lawyers on our case. The other side had close to a hundred lawyers. We rented a couple of floors in a building in San Francisco and had anywhere from seventy to one hundred employees: file clerks, secretaries, computer people, and artists. Every day after court Jack would hold court in one of the open areas of our building to keep spirits high. I don't know if I could have done it, but I sure learned how to be a leader at that time.

Lynch, Tom: Without doubt, Roger Staubach and Senator John McCain. Roger Staubach is a tremendous athlete and has been recognized as such. He was awarded the coveted Heisman Trophy his junior year at the Naval Academy, symbolizing the best college football player. Following his four-year active duty commitment as a naval officer, which included thirteen months in Vietnam, Roger joined the Dallas Cowboys and went on to become All Pro, and has since been inducted into both the College and Professional Football Halls of Fame. Roger Staubach also is the most genuine person I have ever known. Despite his fame, he has remained grounded and strives to maintain balance in his life. He remains a devout Catholic who does not preach his faith but demonstrates it by his words and actions. A successful businessman, father, husband of forty-four years to Marianne, he is blessed with a loving family and fourteen grandchildren. Roger has worked hard and achieved a great deal, but because of his quick wit and sense of humor he never makes you feel uncomfortable around him, no matter who you may be. He has maintained his life's priorities of faith, family, and friends.

I respect John McCain because as a politician and a naval officer he has endured a great deal for his country, especially his years as a POW in North Vietnam. John is a feisty guy who is willing to stand up for the little guy and will take a position and not back down if he believes it to be for the good of the country. He was the first to talk about a cause greater than himself, and there is no doubt in my mind that his campaign for the presidency was not about himself but for the country, and that's why I supported him then and will do so in the future. He has been assailed for his positions, taken the heat and all the flack that goes with it, yet he continues on. He is incorruptible and can always be counted upon to do what is right for the country.

Manatt, Charles: My brother, who is four years older and five grades ahead of me. He also taught me about the birds and the bees and about lots of things in life. Without him I would have had to ask other people who were not as objective a source as my brother was.

Santorum, Richard: *[Rick Santorum began his answer to the question with a disclaimer, saying that not only was it a tough question to answer, but in a way almost impossible.]*

In the political world, it's tough. I'd say there are qualities I admire about a lot of different folks. In terms of the number of individuals that I raise to the level of total admiration, it's an empty well. Let's talk about George W. Bush. There are qualities about George W. Bush that I certainly admire. But at the same time I can't say that I admire George W. Bush, because there are also a lot of qualities where he falls woefully short.

When I came into office, I admired and tried to pattern myself after Dan Coats from Indiana. I got to know Dan well. He had the heart of a servant. Dan is not a Catholic, but he is my "Protestant Catholic." I looked at the way he looked at the world, and I saw someone who cared about the poor, who understood that part of the Gospel, and who understood though the concept of subsidiary. A few evangelicals—and Dan was one of them—he was a great role model to me in dealing with those issues. I served with him on the Armed Services Committee, and he helped me understand a lot of those issues well and develop my worldview. Certainly if there was anyone out there early in my career that I saw as "This is the kind of guy and Senator I aspire to be," then it is Dan.

What do you most respect in a person?

Bliley, Tom: Truth. Plain and simple.

Black, Charlie: What I respect most in a person is integrity—it is a threshold requirement for someone to get a lot of respect from me. But also, unselfishness, the ability to follow the Golden Rule, the most important of Christ's teachings: "Do unto others as you would have them do unto you." Which means to do that—no one can do it perfectly—you have to sacrifice and put someone else's interests ahead of yours.

Bulger, William: One time, President-elect John Fitzgerald Kennedy outlined these qualities for history. I had been elected to the House of Representatives in 1960. In the month of January, we were sworn in, and then we had a joint session, where President-elect Kennedy came and spoke to us. He was, of course, well known to us. He was a heroic figure for anyone running for public office at that time. Almost everyone saw in him a huge inspiration. I still recall, at the time, qualities that he said that in the judgment of history we had truly been men of these characteristics. He cited courage, integrity, judgment, and dedication. Then he just said a few words about each of those.

Courage—you just had to have the courage of conviction. He wasn't speaking of physical courage, but the courage to stand up for your point of view, because without courage, you can't really assert your other good characteristics.

Integrity—being absolutely honest so that you are always mindful of your integrity. You allow nothing to challenge, to impair it, a total honesty.

Judgment—it's interesting that he had judgment there, as I believe it was the third one he had cited—that's a very important one. That's where we are frequently at fault, because people who are in public life have more responsibility to find out what everyone's thinking. You can't ignore what everyone is thinking, even if you disagree with him or her. You have a right to consider it as you are making a decision. But I think the best words spoken on the subject of judgment were from Edmund Burke in the eighteenth century: "Your representative owes you not just his industry only, but his judgment; and he betrays, rather than serving you, if he sacrifices it to your opinion." Edmund Burke is exactly right.

Finally, dedication—you must place this entire public obligation before yourself each day and pursue it with vigor and never deviate from your purpose.

John Fitzgerald Kennedy's admonitions to us were sound, and I've always been grateful to have been present for that particular speech.

Cardin, Ben: People who prepare to be themselves, who aren't really trying to impress people—people who are genuine. People who try to listen well; that's important, instead of speaking all the time. I admire people who can really engage and get the best out of other people.

Carlson, Richard: Personal integrity—which for me includes courage, kindness to others, and a sense of humor. These three traits together are a wonderful combination. There were a number of people in my life, with those attributes, who had an effect on me.

One of the first of them, a man who I really looked up to in my early years, was Louis Lurie of San Francisco. I was a twenty-two-year-old UPI reporter when I met Mr. Lurie through a friend's father. Mr. Lurie was a backer of Broadway plays. Mr. Lurie also owned the legitimate theaters in San Francisco, and his son would later own the San Francisco Giants.

Mr. Lurie gave me a great deal of his personal time. He was a successful man from another and very different time, a man of deep wisdom and broad experience, willing to help a much younger fellow, me, who had limited amounts of each. Uncle Lou was the richest man in San Francisco, and one of the most popular, when I met him in 1962. He still wore wing collars made of celluloid. He sported a boater hat in the summer and a homburg in the winter. He carried a gold-headed cane. He had an impish sense of humor and a straightforward honesty.

What I admire about old-fashioned people like Mr. Lurie is their endurance. They hang in there; they keep doing the same thing over and over again because they like it, it agrees with them, and they form a tradition out of it. Mr. Lurie ate in the same ramshackle restaurant every day, six days a week, for about sixty years—a great joint called Jack's, in the old downtown financial district. Jack's Restaurant was even older than Mr. Lurie—it had been serving since 1864, and it too died not long after he did.

A couple of the people whom I met at lunch with Uncle Lou affected my life. Another person I greatly admired was Uncle Lou's best friend. Jake Ehrlich was then one of America's most famous criminal lawyers. This was the golden age of courtroom attorneys, when their flamboyant antics were lionized by newspapermen—Louie Nizer, Greg Bautzer, Jerry Geisler, Mel Belli, etc. The TV show *Perry Mason* was based on Jake.

Jake was born around 1900. He ran away from his home in Maryland at age fifteen after the ninth grade, joined the U.S. Army's horse cavalry, fought in Mexico, and later hooked a freight-train ride to San Francisco. He boxed for money (and forty years later still carried himself like a professional boxer) worked on the docks, and found a way to get into law school. He passed the California Bar in 1920.

Jake went on to write nine books. (*A Reasonable Doubt* and *Ehrlich's Blackstone* come to mind.) Like many successful men I have known, Jake had primarily educated himself through voluminous reading.

Jake was sartorially splendid, with starched white shirts, a collection of hundreds of gold cuff links, and a snowy handkerchief always perched in his breast pocket. "Never Plead Guilty" was monogrammed in blue on one cuff of each of Jake's starched white shirts.

I was covering a lot of crime stories at the time. Soon, Jake invited me to "read law" in his Montgomery Street office. At that time a person was allowed to take the bar exam in California without attending law school and without an undergraduate degree if he had the recommendation of a member of the bar and put in sufficient hours studying with him. Jake Ehrlich represented an endless stream of society women and actresses accused of murdering their husbands or lovers. He held a winning murder-case defense record that exists to this day. Out of sixty-three clients accused of first-degree murder, Jake got fifty-nine of them acquitted and four of them convicted on a reduced charge of manslaughter.

I was sitting at Jake Ehrlich's desk, listening to him, when I noticed a thin yellow line painted on the dark wood desktop. It ran all the way across, from side to side. I asked what it was. He said. "I tell new clients I expect cash on the line for my services. There's the line; you can put the cash right there." I used to use that with new clients—once in a while I still do.

I watched Jake in courtroom action many times. He could quote dozens, maybe hundreds, of passages from the Bible. He had written a book called *Ehrlich's Holy Bible and the Law*, and in the drama of opening and closing courtroom remarks, he would offer religious homilies that fit the case, citing their specific biblical origins. Once in every trial he would mention to the jurors that "Ehrlich" is the German word for "honest," and he invariably said that though he surely was an imperfect man, he had always striven for total honesty in a courtroom—not the only lie he would tell in a day.

Eckstein, Paul: A number of things... I'd say truthfulness, hard work, loyalty—but truthfulness is *the* most important thing in my world.

Lynch, Tom: Trustworthiness. If you have a person you can trust, then that tells you that you have an honest person and a person of character, who won't let you down. Trustworthiness is the most important quality.

Santorum, Richard: There are so many characteristics that I would say are essential. There is faithfulness to God and to his call for you in your life. It is important that someone understands that they are part of something bigger than the here and now. America is a country blessed by divine providence, and we have a role to play, through God, to serve him and serve this country, which he has so blessed. You approach the public life with the idea that you are a little piece of a big puzzle and that you are there to serve something greater than self, greater than this country—but that this country is part of God's plan—and by serving America faithfully, America can stay with its core principles and with its purpose and stand under the protection of God in doing so. One of the great concerns I have is that we have strayed from under his hand and suffer consequences as a result.

Was religion important in your home? Does religion continue to play a role in your life?

Bingaman, Anne: Truthfully, no. Nobody in my family, on either side, was ever religious. My father's father, from Croatia, was Catholic. He came to Jerome and married a Swiss woman who was Lutheran. They had my father baptized both as a Catholic and a Lutheran. But my grandmother left when my father was five years old. My grandfather divorced her, and he was then excommunicated from the Catholic Church. So that was pretty much it for him on religion.

My grandmother never remarried; it was completely over religion. She was an evangelical. Maybe there was a lot of that at that time; I don't know. She stayed that way her whole life. She later changed her name to Marie Liberty. She was a registered nurse who made a living taking care of elderly people, but she was totally flipped out on religion.

She went to California first when my dad was about five. Much later, when my father was in his twenties, she disappeared; nobody knew where she was for over twenty-five years. My father stayed close to his grandparents, her parents. And when her mother died, my great-grandmother—I was eleven when she died; I knew her well—my father hired an investigator to try to find his mother to tell her that her mother had died. And the investigator finally said, "We think she is not alive; we can't find any trace of her." Well, in fact, they couldn't find her because she had changed her name. Who knew she was now calling herself Marie Liberty? But when I was twenty, at Christmas one year, home from college, the doorbell rang, and I opened the door, and here was this little old woman, hair up in a bun. And she said in a Germanic accent, "Are you Anna Lena?" Her original name was Lena also. And I said, "Yes" and she said, "I'm your grandmother."

After my Croatian grandfather was excommunicated, my mother used to tell me that he would say, "All religions are no damn good, but if you've got to be a religion, the only thing to be is a Catholic." But because he had been excommunicated and raised my father by himself, my father was raised without religion. My mother's family, for a reason I don't know, was just not religious. My mother's mother had been widowed when she was forty-one, with six children, all of whom she raised.

Bliley, Tom: Absolutely. It has guided my entire life, in and outside of public service. My father's brother was prior of the Benedictine Abbey in Belmont, North Carolina. One of my sisters was a Benedictine nun in Virginia, and another was a Sister of Charity in Emmitsburg.

Black, Charlie: Yes. I grew up going to Sunday school and church every week, and it was important to my parents. I went through a stage in my twenties and thirties, where it was always important to me, but I wasn't practicing my religion the way I should. Since I was in my late thirties or so, I am back to having it play a daily role in my life.

Bulger, William: Again, Dr. Johnson says, "Men do not need to be informed, so much as reminded." Very early on we're informed about the right and wrong of various things. But then the big lesson comes, and that comes from example. I can think of one person who lived—as we would say back in the old Haverhausen Project—"in my hallway," and her name was Catherine Prior. She lived on the second floor. Mrs. Prior had five children. They were a great, great family. She was a widow; her husband had died when the children were very young. Mrs. Prior had the full responsibility for those children. Invariably she had to be struggling, just terribly hard, to feed them and to keep up with the rent, which was modest but, of course, very heavy for her. In the meanwhile she was a fervent Catholic woman. She had been born in Ireland, in the county of Galway. She was kind to everyone. I don't recall one word of formal preaching from Mrs. Prior, but I do remember thinking how deep her religious spirit and fervor must be.

She was living her belief: she was dedicated to her children, kind to her neighbors, a very responsible human being.

For the rest of my life, whenever I would be somewhere where someone was saying someone had "a touch of class," wearing those words out, I would be saying to myself, they were talking about apparel or superficial features of their manner, but for class that was deep, meaningful, profound, I would think of Catherine Prior. She, to my view, was class, which made it rough for everyone else, who could not measure up to her, but that's what I used to think of as class.

Cardin, Ben: Yes. I grew up in an Orthodox Jewish family. My neighborhood was 98 percent Jewish. My religion was part of my life. It was a very important factor. It was an important factor through my young years. When I decided to go to college, I made sure there was support for my Jewish traditions. So it was a very important factor. Religion and the ethics of Judaism are a very important part of my life. [...] You're always learning.

Carlson, Richard: I went to church every Sunday for the first dozen years of my life. My father was a deacon in the Congregational Church of Norwood, Massachusetts. My mother was an Episcopalian. I was a regular at Sunday school. I won a prize for memorizing the books of the Bible when I was eight. After my father died, I dropped away from church and religion. I believed in God, but going to church was something I had accepted without personal interest. My mother didn't go to church much after my father died. I become more interested in religion later in life. I had my first son baptized as a Christian more out of social obligation than anything else, I'm a little embarrassed to admit. My wife's uncle was an Episcopalian bishop, and he did the honors at Grace Cathedral in San Francisco. There was a cocktail party afterward, at my wife's grandmother's house. This was typical of life in San Francisco society at the time. Baptisms like that didn't have that much to do with religion. I was divorced a few years later. I failed to have my second son baptized as an infant, something about which I've felt guilty over the years. My excuse was that my marriage was not doing well and I was distracted. Buckley was baptized years later in Washington, D.C., when he was eighteen. It was his choice, and that made it more meaningful. Patricia, who I married when the kids were small, has a strong Christian faith and played an influential role in Buck's decision. She was their mother for all practical purposes, and when they were each age eighteen they asked her to adopt them legally, and she did.

My children are both Christian men of firm and positive faith. So am I, but getting to that place for me was a much slower deal. "I once was lost, but now am found. Was blind, but now I see." That refrain fits Dick Carlson. I do regret that I didn't spend much effort with my boys helping them with faith. I took them to church infrequently. I didn't talk against it, but I didn't talk in favor of it. It's water under the bridge now, but it worked out all right in the end. They've both said, "Hey, no problem, we didn't feel like we lost anything."

My faith is now a great part of my life. It's not a foxhole situation for me, either. I am a faithful Christian; I strive to do good things and not do bad things. I feel the same way about it in times of calm and in times of crisis. I have to say that when the going gets rough, faith is awfully nice to have. I was very seriously shot at, multiple times, in a car in Albania. I thought it was over for me, but I was calmed by my belief in God.

Eckstein, Paul: Religion was important in our home. My father had a classical Jewish education in Hungary. He knew more than any of the rabbis at the synagogue that we belong to in Phoenix. My brother and I didn't have the kind of religious education my dad had; I wish we had. We had more of a classical Jewish religious education. A lot of what I have learned, I've learned later, either taught myself or perhaps learned by going to synagogue. My son Tim really became a religious Jew in the sense of understanding the liturgy, being able to read Hebrew relatively fluently, knowledge of the prayers, to the point that he led High Holiday services in his home this Rosh Hashanah and Yom Kippur.

My mother came from a German Jewish Reform family, where it was said her grandmother's way of observing Passover was, instead of having ham and cheese in a sandwich, to have ham and cheese on matzo. My father was clearly a religious person. He abandoned the Orthodoxy in which he had been raised, but clearly understood and made some effort to impart lessons to us. We went to religious school, we had our bar mitzvah, confirmation, and we were married in religious ceremonies.

Religion plays a very important role. I try, but I am not always successful in trying to observe the Sabbath day and not do work on it. Flo and I light the candles every Friday night. The serenity and peace that comes from having a break from the heavy work of the week and sitting down and saying the prayers and reflecting on the week, I find very comforting. I like to, as much as I can, at least eighty percent of the time—I'm pretty good about staying home on Saturday, on the Shabbat, and reading the Torah. I do try to read a portion, called in Hebrew a *parsha*, of the Torah each day in English, and when I see something that interests me, I dig deeper. I wouldn't say that is praying. It's more learning, observing, trying to understand the world. I've probably read the Torah twenty times. And every time I read it, I see something different.

Lynch, Tom: I grew up in a Catholic family in the Midwest, around northwest Ohio. My father and my mother were practicing Catholics. My grandfather was a thirty-second-degree Mason. He and my grandmother were married in a Catholic church. He says it was to keep her happy by walking down the aisle with him. Being Catholic, I attended parochial school, so we had the nuns and priests as teachers and mentors. We had daily Mass. We prayed the Rosary at home. We always turned to the saints, to the Blessed Virgin, in prayer for any special need.

In my own family, I've tried to emulate that with my own children. As it turns out, all three of my children are long married to Catholic spouses and all practice their faith. And we continue to do so as well, because I believe we're all here on earth for but a short period. During our time here, we need to have purpose in our lives, which I get through my Catholic faith.

Santorum, Richard: *[Rick didn't immediately answer the question, but first talked about his time in a Catholic ghetto growing up and being entirely immersed among people of the same faith.]*

I was an altar boy, I lectured, and religion was certainly a part of my life. I look at how religion was a part of my life, and I see how I am raising my kids, and religion is much more a part of their life: they're more prayerful, much more knowledgeable about the faith. To me faith was just in the air, and it wasn't something that you read. I didn't read the Bible. I didn't study. You had religion courses that were, by and large, rote that was drummed into your head, Catechism and such.

I take this all as seeds that were planted, but they were planted with a sledgehammer, which doesn't mean they're going to grow very quickly, because they are compacted down so hard. I look as my progression as someone who was surrounded by Catholic culture and Catholic presence and drifted away in my college years and mixed up that ground a little bit. So when the right rain came along, the change in career and meeting my wife, the seed was ready to grow again.

Can you identify something like a "defining moment" in your life?

Bingaman, Anne: Well there are really two. Marrying Jeff changed my whole life. I don't know what I would have done if I had married someone else, but I know I wouldn't be doing this, and I wouldn't have gone to New Mexico. For everyone, who you choose to marry is a crucial decision, no less so for me. Second, I got tenure teaching law school and decided I wasn't going to do it forever, and once I decided that, I figured, "Why am I doing this any more time at all? I'm wasting time. I ought to figure out what I really want to do." So I quit.

Yes. I didn't care about tenure. I did have tenure. But what was it really to me? I worked hard at teaching; I was a good teacher. And so I was trying to figure out what to do next. And my father kept saying to me, "Honey, why don't you start your own law firm?"

And I'd say, "But, Papa, I don't have any clients."

"Just try it! Try it for a year! I'll pay your rent. Just try it," he said.

Well, he called me every day. I talked to him every single day, from the time I was twenty-eight or twenty-nine to the day he died; we talked every single day, and he wasn't in great health, and we both enjoyed and looked forward to our talks. His dream for me to have my own firm was a defining moment.

When he died, he was sixty-four. But when I quit teaching, law firms in Santa Fe wouldn't hire a woman. I had worked for state government and didn't want to do that again. My old firm in Albuquerque offered me a job, but I had to commute two and a half hours a day. So, finally I listened to my father and started my own law firm. I had sent out these announcements. I had a half-time secretary that I shared with the lawyer next door.

And then this law firm in Santa Fe, which had this billion-dollar case, called me and said, "Hey Anne, I've got your announcement. I bet you're not too busy. Come on over; we'll give you some work on the case." So I said, "Okay," and the next morning I go over there to meet with the lawyer who had recently quit the New Mexico Supreme Court to come back to this firm to help try the case.

And he says, "We hear you're smart. Go to the library and start with *AmJur.*" So I walked out of there, and eight months later a very courageous state court trial judge granted our motion for default judgment under Rule 37 for refusing to produce documents and answer interrogatories submitted to the uranium cartel.

United Nuclear vs. General Atomic. Brown and Bain knew all about it. They were, in effect, on the other side, with Cravath representing Shell. It had changed my life. It gave me the self-image that I was a person who wasn't writing for a firm, but I was the founder and head of my own firm.

It totally changed my self-image. It changed my own view of myself. I saw myself as heading a law firm, being in charge. Women in those days had a very different self-image than this. When I got out of law school, I didn't have an image that I was going to start a law firm. It just never crossed my mind. It wasn't that I dismissed it. It just didn't occur to me. Anyway, marrying Jeff, moving to New Mexico, and starting my own law firm were the really key things from which everything else flowed.

Bliley, Tom: October 1955, when my wife, Mary Virginia, agreed to marry me. Nothing before or since has meant anything without her guiding presence. I am blessed.

Black, Charlie: Two things. When I was hired in 1975 to work for Ronald Reagan's first campaign, John Sears hired me, and that set in motion the entire career path that I have been on. As well, that period gave me a lot of self-confidence that I could perform and be successful in national politics and public affairs on a national level. The other defining moment would be when I married my wife, Judy Black, which changed my personal life and also strengthened my faith and my participation in my church and in my religion. Certainly that was the greatest defining moment in my personal life. From a professional standpoint, it was certainly being hired by John Sears to work for Ronald Reagan and proving that, in fact, I belonged in national politics at a high level.

Well, I was just a regional field guy for five or six states in the campaign.

And through that, I was promoted in the campaign to bigger and better things and also gained a good relationship with the Reagans and had their confidence. Sears really had two other people whom he relied on the most in the campaign, and I became one of them.

Bulger, William: I had been sitting between two individuals, Joe Clark and Walter Clifford, one of whom went to Boston College High School and the other to Boston Latin School. And they were talking about school. We were at the Sunday school class at Saint Monica's. And the conversation went on, and I was completely out of it because I knew nothing about it, because where I was going to school, no one was doing homework, let alone talking about it. So at some place in that moment, I decided that I wanted to go to BC High.

The preparation at the Hart school just would not allow me to walk into BC High in the second year. So, on my own, I went over to Boston College High School, and I approached the fellow who was the treasurer there. I didn't know him, but I came to know him later. And I said to him, "If I went back one year, do you think they would let me into BC High?"

I thought I was going to have to go in front of some tribunal to get this decided, but he said, "Yes, they would!" He appears in my little political memoir, the gentleman himself, who was always happy he had been singled out for the reference. He, of course, read the book later in his life.

So I went over to BC High. I began as a freshman, even though I had finished my freshman year at the Thomas B. Hart school, and I did nicely at BC High. The tuition was $150 a year. $37.50 a quarter. And I had help. I worked at John's Meat Market. And I also had some help from my sister Jean, who was very generous to me and made it possible for me to go and pay the $150 a year.

Cardin, Ben: I've had a lot of defining moments. I had two tough political decisions to make. The first was giving up being Speaker of the House, which was a wonderful job. There was no pressure on me to leave, but I moved on and ran for Congress. It was a very tough decision, because I knew it meant not only giving up the safety of my legislative seat and the power of Speaker, but I would also likely lose my ability to be a lawyer, which I loved greatly, by being in Congress.

The second tough decision was giving up my seat in Congress after being there for twenty years with a lot of seniority, and running for the United States Senate. Both decisions were the right decision, but they were difficult in my professional judgment. Professionally, they were the two most defining moments in life.

Carlson, Richard: Asking Patricia Caroline Swanson of La Jolla, California, to marry me. This beautiful and charming woman said, "Yes." She has been a wonderful mate and friend for the thirty-three years we have been together, and I am grateful for the large part she has played in my life. I am a better man because of her.

Another defining moment was surviving a plane crash, mostly because my son Tucker was with me. It is every man's desire to die before his children. Cashing in at the same moment is not many fathers' Plan B. Anticipating its possibility lends itself to deep thought. It was about 2 A.M., and Tucker and I were sitting in first class, second row, across the aisle from each other, on a Pakistani International Airline flight to Dubai from Pakistan. One minute we were reading quietly, the next we were holding hands in a firm belief that the plane was going down.

It had been a smooth flight. We were about sixty miles from Dubai, over the Persian Gulf, when there was a terrific explosion. The plane started shaking. This was an Airbus 300, with one huge engine on each wing. I thought a bomb had gone off in the cargo hold below or that we had hit another plane. It turned out that the starboard engine had blown up and was hanging off the wing. This significantly affected the smoothness of our forward motion. The pilots were clearly struggling to control the plane. We were like a piece of paper in a wind tunnel.

The lead steward scrunched down in his jump seat in front of us. He pulled on his shoulder harness, dropped his face into his bushy beard and began to shout "Allah Akbar." I could hear people behind us crying. Nearby, four Arab men in white robes lit cigarettes and began to chain-smoke. Tucker and I held hands as we came in. We said the Lord's Prayer aloud. The Airbus hit the runway and slid sideways. The starboard engine went under the fuselage and up under the cockpit, and the right wing struck the pavement. The shriek of metal on asphalt was deafening and seemed endless. I still hear it occasionally. Because I had been in the news business for so long, all the plane crash stories I'd read popped into my head. I pictured us plowing into the terminal or hitting a fuel truck. We actually went between some buildings, out into the desert sideways and missed everything but the sand dunes we stopped on.

The plane began to fill with smoke. Flames were rising on the starboard side blocking those exits. The steward yelled into his microphone, "Stay in your seats, wait for the captain." We hadn't heard one word from the captain, or any other crewmember, since the explosion. There seemed no point in hearing from them now.

Tucker shouted an obscenity at the steward. The man reminded Tucker of the guards at the New York Trade Towers who told people, on their way down the stairs, to go back to their offices and wait for official word to evacuate. (We learned later that the captain and his cohorts had already escaped from the cockpit and abandoned ship.) We ran to the port exit. With a CIA officer from Islamabad, Tucker worked the locks and threw open the door. It wasn't armed. No chute. It looked like a forty-foot drop to the ground, as the plane was tilted on the damaged right wing.

Tucker pulled two toggles on the deck, and the chute inflated and shot out. Good deal. A small woman in a burqa ran up behind us and pushed her way to the open door. Perfect timing, Tucker yelled, "Jump!" and she did. We watched her slide right down that chute. Then the CIA man jumped, then Tucker, then me.

The lights and sirens of fire engines were almost upon us. We ran up a sand hill as firemen began to hose the plane. Tucker wheeled around and gave me a high-five. He said, referring to his brother asleep in Washington, "It's going to kill Buckley he's not here."

About 270 people were on that plane, more than sixty were injured. Tucker and I were not among them. We survived for a reason…

Eckstein, Paul: The Mississippi decision. To not go to Mississippi. To go back to Phoenix, to see the practice of law and whether I liked it. I went to law school at age twenty-one knowing three things for sure: I was not going to return to Phoenix; I was not going to practice law; I was not going to get married until I was thirty-five. By age twenty-four, I was married, practicing law in Phoenix. At age sixty-eight, I'm married to the same woman; I've lived in Phoenix all my life; and I've practiced with the same law firm. Looking back, it seems obvious. Looking back it seems clearly this was the right thing to do. It wasn't so obvious to me when I was twenty-one years old. The most important thing that I did in my life was to decide to take a job at Brown and Bain in the summer of 1964.

Lynch, Tom: The moment was August 19, 1977, when I assumed command of the *USS Truett*. Really, it was the three years that I was in command that were the defining period in my life, because never before outside of my own family had I felt any all-consuming responsibility. When I took command of that ship, from that moment forward every thought, word, and deed was how would it affect the ship, and the men on the ship, and not "What's in it for me?" or "How would it affect me?" I've told many youngsters, it's almost like being a saint: a saint focuses on God in every thought, word, and deed—what effect does this have on God? I truly believe that to be an effective, strong leader, you have to put yourself last. We used a slogan aboard the *Truett*: "Ship, shipmates, self." If you first think about "What I am doing, saying, or thinking, and what effect does it have on my ship, on my shipmates—and only then what does it do for me?"

That was a very arduous period and a very tough period in the Navy. For my crew and me, we were gone for thirty of thirty-six months which included a seven-and-a-half-month deployment and an out-of-homeport overhaul in Boston. I commanded the ship for three years, from August 1977 to August 1980. The crew was mostly young healthy males, and it is very unusual to have a death on board, outside of hostilities. But we had six deaths while I was in command. Two of which were suicides on board. I had a lot of people asking questions. Each death was tragic and a unique circumstance. Plus, we had all the things that happened on that ship. I knew every man on board that ship, about 280.

The *Truett* command tour allowed me to mature as a person and as a leader; it was a wonderful experience. During the deployment to the Mediterranean and the Red Seas, we had an unusually high tempo of operations and spent our Christmas and New Year celebrations in a repair depot outside of Athens, Greece. I prided myself that I knew every crewmember as an individual sailor, and I also knew most of the families. I was cognizant of the stress each was experiencing. The crew performed admirably, and we were recognized for our performance when we returned to the States. And we shared many happy and sad remembrances of the deployment... Nearly running aground in the Djibouti harbor, learning of family deaths, catching a shark off the fantail, reacting to word that President Sadat of Egypt had been assassinated.

It was a lot of unique experiences and happenstance that shaped my life. But it all gets back to selflessness, because that really is the essence of a great leader. You have to be a selfless person if you want to be an effective leader or even a great father to your children and husband to your spouse. Whatever you do, selflessness is so important.

Manatt, Charles: *[On getting into politics.]* I started so early. I started at fifteen. My first event was a fundraiser in Carroll [Iowa], when Harry Truman was in the last year of his Presidency. And the interest and concern we had at that point related especially to Civil Rights and fair and equal opportunities for a variety of Americans. And being in western Iowa at the time, there weren't many minorities, but it was just a fair shake for everyone for whom we were campaigning.

Santorum, Richard: Meeting my wife was as important a moment as any. We happened to be the right people for each other to begin a new journey.... It is a wonderful journey that still continues.

What worldview guides your thoughts and actions?

Bingaman, Anne: I have thought it consciously for a long time. I am not religious, as I've said, but I am a huge believer in the Golden Rule: do unto others, as you would have them do unto you. I try very hard and very consciously to help people, and particularly to help them when things are bad. I feel better about myself doing it. It is a way to remind myself of my blessings, the need for the Grace of God, and to try to place myself in the shoes of people to whom life has not been as kind as it has to me.

Black, Charlie: The most important part of the worldview is faith, and those of us who are Christian try to aspire to follow the principles of Jesus Christ in everything we do. But also being involved in politics and government, I believe that the United States is the greatest country on Earth. And the key to that, as de Tocqueville identified when the Republic was new, is citizen participation and service to community, state, and country. I have been able to spend a majority of my adult life in politics and make a living doing it. And I have spent many, many hours in politics and helping others in volunteer work. There is an obligation for American citizens to do that to keep the country great.

Either a calling, or I was just really lucky to end up in the right place at the right time on a number of occasions. My first paying job out of school was working for Jesse Helms in a campaign he wasn't supposed to win—but he did win, and I came to Washington, D.C., with him. And he was a friend of Ronald Reagan, and I got to know the Reagan people, and that launched me onto the national political path. I've always felt like that part of it was luck to be at the right place at the right time, but once I had the opportunity, I felt called to help good people run the country.

Bliley, Tom: I'm a son (well, maybe a great-great-grandson) of the heart of the Confederacy, but I could not be more proud of the progress, liberties, and freedoms that our country enjoys today. America is the greatest country in the world. I celebrate it every day.

Bulger, William: I see the active role of political life as a very important role. I don't know that everyone is ready for it. It can call for huge sacrifice. Very often exceedingly good people are disparaged, and they watch precious reputation savaged. Our system of jurisprudence is wrong in America. A person who steals your money faces severe criminal and civil penalties for doing so. But to steal your reputation—that can be done with impunity! We don't have the legal protections we should have. I have spoken and debated on the libel law in America. There should be a libel law that allows people to bring to court traducers, people who tell untruths that do damage to a person. There should be a forum where that can be brought. I don't mean that you ought to be able to become rich by suing these traducers, but you should be able to sue in court and at least get some sort of vindicatory relief that says the person is lying and it has been deemed an untruth, and that says that they should have to pay some sort of nominal cost for having caused some damage. There should be, and there isn't. And as a result, just about anything can be said, and as I said, I've debated on the subject, and I hold a minority view that there should be some forum where we can bring people and take them to task for bringing falsehoods. And we don't have it.

And while we don't have it, people who run for office have to be able to stand up to the most terrible of abuse from the worst elements of the press. The fact of the matter is that most parts of the press don't engage in these sorts of things, as most people don't commit murder. Still, we have laws against murder. Most people don't rob people, but we have laws that say you shall not or you'll pay a penalty. And similarly, it is not very many in the media who engage in this sort of thing, but they are a criminal element in the press, and they should be brought to task. As the law is presently constituted, especially in the case of the *New York Times vs. Sullivan*, it is very, very tough for a public person to hold someone accountable for bad conduct as a journalist.

Cardin, Ben: I spend a lot of time with parliamentarians in other countries. I really do find there is a lot in common. The crazy system we have here, where an individual can make such a difference, is so admired around the world. So I think what really binds us internationally is the desire of a person to make a difference, and this is really admired internationally. A person can make a difference, whether as a senator or as an activist in the community, or as an author.

Carlson, Richard: My worldview is simple in theory but not at all simple in social practice: It is to be allowed to live my life as I wish, and to let others live theirs as they wish, as free from interference as is humanly possible. It is difficult for cultures to achieve this—if the majority of people want it in the first place—as we have seen in spades over the centuries. Man's natural inclination is to control others when he can; to impose his will on them, to censor them, to inhibit them, to make them do what he wants them to do. This is why people who care about personal freedom should watch big government with a jaundiced eye. Government is the greatest example of the kind of arbitrary exercise of power I am talking about. Some aspects of this are just low-end, but wildly annoying. I am speaking of "Nannyism." This is a specialty of the Nancy Pelosi/Hillary Clinton wing of the Democratic Party, making citizens do what the government wants them to do in their everyday affairs, even against their individual wishes, because it is "good for them." Jeez, I hate that. Get away, I'll decide for myself what is good for me, thank you very much. It is amazing to me how many totalitarian hearts thump heavily under do-gooder breasts.

[Dick then gave an example of what he means by "Nannyism": a perplexingly parental law on a beach in Hyannisport. He was forbidden from using his snorkel; the beach had outlawed them because, according to local authorities, they "wouldn't be able to tell if he was snorkeling or maybe dead and just floating." Dick explains.]

I favor Jeffersonian liberalism—respect for individual liberties and human rights, the rule of law, limited government, as I said, and a free market. These are the things that bring political freedom and the greatest economic opportunities for the greatest number of people. I am opposed to the idea that an increasingly complex culture needs more government. It does not. Just the opposite is true. Central planning may work somewhat in a very small, homogenous society, but increasingly less so as societal complexities increase. To paraphrase Thomas Jefferson, "A government big enough to give man everything he wants today is big enough to take it all away tomorrow—and worse." The collectivists in the former Soviet Union, in China—in Romania, Bulgaria, Poland, East Germany, you name it, from North Korea to Cuba to Cambodia to Burma, have killed or made truly miserable hundreds of millions of people more than have ever died in all wars in all of the world's history. Yet, with that as a blood-drenched lesson, Western leftists, academics, and some intellectuals are still praying at the Church of Marx and Lenin. More government is wasteful and counter-productive and in the long run, very, very dangerous.

Eckstein, Paul: In much of what I do and what I try to persuade my clients to do and in the political realm, there are so many things that are fought over that don't matter, in that it's important to understand that it is important "to be happy citizens rather than subtle disputants." You don't have to win every argument. That's something I believe in.

I have a number of quotes I try to live by. A number of years ago a friend of mine gave me the Stephen Mitchell translation of the *Tao de Ching*. The Ninth *Tao De Ching*, comes close to what I believe in. Then I found years later that Rabbi Nockmen of Breslaff says something very similar. So here's what the ninth *Tao de Ching* says: "Fill your bowl to the brim and it will spill, keep sharpening your knife and it will blunt, chase after money and security and your heart will never unclench. Care about other people's approval and you'll be your prisoner. Do your work and step back. The only path to serenity."

I have found that when things are falling apart, I get more comfort out of taking a breath than just digging into work. Do your work and step back and you'll get serenity. Now here's advice from Rabbi Nockmen of Breslaff: "To be a person of truth, be swayed neither by approval nor disapproval. Work not needing approval from anyone; then you'll be free to be who you really are."

I'll also quote Edmund Burke on credos. This didn't apply to every situation, but it is something I try to look for so my principles don't get compromised. This Edmund Burke from a speech "On Moving the Resolutions for the Conciliation with the Colonies," given on March 22, 1775. Here's what he said as he's trying to persuade the crown on compromise. It clearly does not apply, however, to compromise on important principles:

> All government, indeed every human benefit and enjoyment, every virtue
> and every prudent act is founded on compromise and barter. We balance

inconveniences, we give and take, we remit some rights that we may enjoy others. We choose rather to be happy citizens than subtle disputants.

I've had a blessed life. I don't know if you've heard this, my view of the world, that it is very common in my readings of the lives of great men and women, who have achieved a lot, particularly in politics, that they had some tragedy that occurred in their life early on. Lincoln. Roosevelt. Kennedy. Bush (the elder). Clinton, who loses his father before he is born. Barack Obama. John McCain. It is startling. A death or near-death experience causes a person who has the skills and temperament to go into politics to realize that life is short, and if she or he is going to accomplish what they think they've got to do, then they've got to get on with it.

One of the tragedies of my life is that I never had a tragedy, I think. I don't view it as a tragedy. I had a very good and happy childhood. I had four grandparents at my birth. One died when I was two or three. The metaphor I've used is that I've been floating down the river for a long time. I've withstood some rapids, but by and large, it's been good.

Anyone writing or thinking of character and integrity in politics would be well advised to read some of the works we read, including *All the King's Men*, which is by far the best American political novel; *The Last Hurrah*, which is okay; Ward Just's books *Jack Gance* and *The Congressman Who Loved Flaubert*, a collection of short stories. *A Man for All Seasons* is another exemplar of a book that ought to be read as part of trying to understand how things work or ought to work or can work in the political world. If you're only going to read three, then it is *Jack Gance, The Last Hurrah,* and *All the King's Men.*

Lynch, Tom: Early on my worldview was peace through strength. Many times I considered whether or not I should continue my naval career, but I believed we would someday have a confrontation with the Soviet Union and the only way to prevent it would be our military strength. I believed then, and still do today, that a strong military will maintain the peace by deterring war. The end of the Cold War made it all meaningful. A military life is not the easiest, and caused me to question it many times; however, I always asked myself, "If not me, who?" Hopefully, I could make a positive impact, so I continued my career, and I'm thankful that I did.

Today, my worldview has not changed, although I worry that we have become complacent. We have the highest standard of living of any country and are blessed with so many freedoms that it's easy to take it all for granted. However, when you understand that many people have an extreme hatred for the United States because of what we have, and what they do not have; and so that anger and hatred can easily turn into a motivation for attacking us. You realize that we must keep our guard up and be prepared. So I believe we will always need to maintain a strong military as a deterrent—and thankfully, our young people today are stepping up to meet the current challenge.

Manatt, Charles: My worldview would be more open, allowing people to do their own things commensurate to the customs or standards of the day's civilized society. It might be perfectly all right fifty years ago for us neighborhood boys to go around the neighborhood and tip over all the neighboring farmers' outhouses on Halloween. And everyone set them up the next day, and life went on. But today there aren't any outhouses. To extend that logic today, letting all the air out of someone's tires, or doing physical damage to a house would be out-of-bounds, based on the current custom.

A worldview starts, at least in my case, from a very early period, in terms of what is positive and constructive behavior and what is not. One of things I am proudest of—and I still have no memory of how it came about—is our high school class motto. It was, "Born not for ourselves, but for the whole world." And our 1954 graduation occurred in the deep recesses of the Cold War and Vietnam, and a whole lot of things opened our eyes to possibilities. So my worldview has evolved over a very long period of time.

When I grew up, as a kid in Iowa, speed limits were [given only as] "reasonable and proper." Reasonable and proper—that was a relative law. So on a dark, dreary night, when it's wet and you've got cows out, reasonable and proper might be fifty miles per hour. But on a dry moonlit night with no cows out, reasonable and proper might be eighty-five miles per hour. That's a relative law. We don't come across too many relative laws today.

A lot of situation ethics right today is being rebranded as proper business and corporate governance. And if you understand that situation ethics is common sense—98 percent of the fees paid for wonderful lawyers to tell perfectly intelligent members of the Board of Directors what their governance procedures should be, would be unnecessary. Situation ethics is common sense and character and should be well-defined by what you think. … A gentleman may be very pressured about something to be done for his child, so much so that he then, after the fact, puts wonderful gifts in a satchel and has it delivered with no card and no identification on the doorstep of the professor who did the good things for the child. A bank cashier with seven kids is probably making $85,000; he's got seven children, and he's got lots of demands. New bicycles appear on his front doorstep, one for each of his seven children. A bank customer gave them. This customer will come into the bank a week later and for a big loan. On and on and on. The examples never cease. That is something that makes it very tough. It is so very tempting. I am not sure that Senator Stevens's problems in Alaska aren't somewhere in the nexus of what we're talking about here.

One of my most troubling times, and one of the things I'm proudest of, was once when [some] rascals were doing the wrong thing—I was a very young legal counsel of the bank, twenty-eight or twenty-nine years old—and I told the bank Directors [what was going on]. And they lined up the votes ahead of time, and I got fired. So I drove home that night—a bit shaken, because I had two kids at the time—and six months later he was arrested, six months later he was sent up the river. I think I did the right thing, but it was very troubling.

Santorum, Richard: The Catholic Church. The teachings of the Magisterium. I've been very up-front about the fact that the teachings of the Catholic Church have a very profound impact on my faith—not [just] because the Pope says it, [but] because it is true. I believe in applying both faith and reason to the moral dilemmas that we face in our lives. And if the faith is true and the reasoning is true, you'll arrive at the same conclusions. Obviously, from different directions, but the same conclusion will be there. The church teaches that. The church teaches the importance of reason and using the gifts that God has given you to discover truth. God reveals himself through his creation, and we are part of his creation and the order of the world. It is perfectly ordered because God created it. I have no doubt that through philosophy as well as theology and faith we can arrive at what is best for the United States and mankind.

I look back, and I am blessed with over two thousand years of great thinkers who have thought through these problems in different contexts and different circumstances, so it is a matter of finding that right lever that gets you to the solution that you need.

How do your natural tendencies or habits relate to your character?

Bingaman, Anne: Oh, I've always worked very, very hard. Like a lot of people. I'm certainly not the only one. I don't kid myself on that a bit. I always believed I had a duty to whatever I was doing to give it my all and to do the best that I could—usually [for] the client or the team of people with whom I was working. Doing your very, very best is actually hard. You have to keep yourself on a short leash. You have to focus every hour of every day on what you ought to be doing, not what you might want to be doing. I'm not saying I'm unique in this. Millions, billions of people work hard every day.

Oh, my whole family, my parents, aunts and uncles, my grandmother, all of them worked hard. My mother, father, aunts, uncles, and grandmother all had their own businesses, and they all worked basically all for this. No one told us to work hard. You just watched them. You saw it. You understood.

I'm a worrier. I worry a lot about anything that could go wrong. I've always kept a stack of Xerox paper with a pen near my bed, so if I wake up in the middle of the night, I can make notes so I won't forget something I need to do. Sometimes I'd have fifteen sheets of paper with ideas for a case or whatever on the nightstand in the morning. It was the only way I could go back to sleep. I was rarely, you know, surprised by something in a case because I usually thought of ten things that could go wrong but didn't. [. . .]

Well, basically, what it really comes down to is that you've got to care, really care, and if you do, you'll focus on it, think about it, work at it, stay ahead of the curve. As long as you care, it'll eventually be okay. One way or another you'll make it.

And usually you've thought of it. If you're really focused on what you're doing and you care about the right outcome, you're thinking about it all the time. I mean cases, big case litigation, anything really, you can, once and a while, get blindsided. Things come up that you could not have reasonably foreseen, or even a far-out chance of random things. But by and large that is not true. If you are really focused on it and working hard, you can usually anticipate most of what might hurt you and prepare for it and, therefore, keep from being hurt. And that, of course, is the whole point of anticipating it, to take actions to head it off and to protect the client, the case, the enterprise, whatever it is.

Black, Charlie: Discipline and work ethic… In my family, work ethic was emphasized as well as practiced [along with] the discipline that goes with that. Basic integrity, honesty, being a truth-teller—those things I was taught in my family. And obviously it was all reinforced by my faith and by the people I have worked with over the years. And some people who work hard and show personal discipline don't have high enough integrity. That's a third part of it. Because of my upbringing and the opportunities I've had to do big jobs in politics. I've got a good work ethic, and the discipline that goes with it, personal habits like you don't get to stay up late at night, drinking with your friends every time they go out.

Bliley, Tom: Growing up, we were a can-do, no-mistakes household. That ethic served me well. My time in the Navy reinforced that. In fact, the time in the Navy later served as a metaphor for my Chairmanship on the House Commerce Committee: you can turn the aircraft carrier, but sometimes it may take a while.

There's on old conservative saying, "not to be the first to adopt the new—nor the last to throw away the old." I think that sums up my approach to things.

Bulger, William: People are really at the best when they are struggling. I know no one escapes adversity totally. It's part of our lives. Facing up to it, handling it, is good. My friend Juvenal said, "Luxury destroys more efficiently than war." Along the way I've seen people who are friends who might have been in public life with me, whose way seems a lot easier because they have a lot of this world's goods. But time after time, I saw how their situations worsen, became so bad, because the person was affluent.

Cardin, Ben: Character is very important. It really does define you as to what is going to be important in your life. You set your own priorities. Each person sets his or her own priorities. And running through that is ethics. I teach ethics at Hopkins. So I've taught a couple courses in graduate programs in ethics. To me character and ethics are so very important. I got involved in the Naval Academy's ethics program, which I think is top flight, a really great program they have here in Annapolis. Your character and what you believe in, and your willingness to understand that, all are important. You have to have a moral compass; it is part of who you will become. The end does not justify the means. You have to have a sense of morality. It's part of me, and I think about it frequently.

Carlson, Richard: Of course, geography is destiny in the broadest sense. In my case, my background was sufficiently different that it surely has affected my character, for better or worse. I choose to believe it was for the better. But I am uncertain of all the specifics. I generally shy away from too much introspection. I have seen many people look inward so often they get hooked on the minutiae of themselves, fascinated by them, and they get on the fast track to boorishness. They become unable to bring their gaze back outside of their own psyche and id and the weirdness of the past. They wallow in real or imagined remembrances of unfairness or injustice they believe they have experienced. They identify with things so much that they join groups of similarly burdened folks—these are frequently women, so they can talk even more about themselves. They usually refer to themselves as "victims" of some kind, or "survivors" of something—cancer, incest, molestation, crack-smoking, "sex addiction" … Man, the list is endless. This is the Oprah Winfrey way: let's talk it to death. This is the Phil Donahue way. This isn't the Dick Carlson way.

Eckstein, Paul: Well, sometimes there is a disconnect. I like to think I'm disciplined, but while I was very disciplined in my work habits, as I've gotten older I'm less disciplined. I mentioned three things: truthfulness, hard work, and loyalty. The only time of the year I am not truthful is at Christmas. *[Paul dresses as Santa Claus for the poor children in Phoenix.]* And these little kids, most of whom are Mexican American, come up to me, and they ask me to bring a Barbie doll, a Game Boy, or a bicycle, and they give me notes, and they ask me to come by. I tell them I'll come by, and they'll have a good Christmas. And I know most of these kids, whatever they are going to get—and at the beginning it was a Frisbee, a stocking, and some Cracker Jacks; the gifts have gotten better over time—but, still, it's not true. They're not going to get what they asked for, and I am facilitating this. And it bothers me.

For many years I was the Chair of the state Rhodes Scholarship Nominating Committee, and then I was the Chair of the Regional Selection Committee. The process for the Rhodes scholarship is that people apply to the committee made up of Rhodes scholars—except for the chair, who cannot be a Rhodes Scholar, at least in the days when I did it. So I was selected as Chair and wasn't a Rhodes Scholar. They'd get together, collect the resumes, and interview the students, and the practice is for the students to hang around while the committee discusses who will go to region; or at region, who will get the Rhodes scholarships. Everyone sticks around. The Chairman of the Committee says Mr. X and Ms. Y will be awarded the scholarships. Then it is customary to say something comforting to those who applied. Here's the point. Every time I would say, "You are unbelievably talented. If you hadn't already accomplished much in your life, you wouldn't be here. There are thousands-plus people who put in their applications and didn't get interviews. There are hundreds of people who got interviews at the state level, but only two were passed onto the region. I know you feel that the world has fallen out from under you and you are a failure. You are a grand success, you will be a success, and you are on top of the world, so keep doing what you are doing."

To a person, I know they didn't believe it. The students, who had been turned down or rejected for the first time in their lives, thought that I was lying to them. And the little kiddies who were at the Chicanos program thought I was telling them the truth, and I always want to write something about that—the contrast and juxtaposition of those two moments, and they happen within three or four days of each other each year.

Lynch, Tom: The most basic is taking responsibility and being held accountable for your actions. With responsibility comes accountability, which leads to maturity. We see this at an early age in the Boy Scouts, newspaper and delivery persons who display a little more maturity than their peers because they must be responsible, demonstrate discipline, and are held accountable. I began as a newsboy at age eleven and learned quickly that if you fling a paper and break a window, you repair it. The paper is to be delivered on time. You're denied ballgames with your buddies in the afternoons, and you're up very early on Sundays. You're engaged in an endeavor where you are seeing discipline for the first time. You and only you are accountable for the results. Your character is being formed.

Parents can instill this in their children at an early age. I hope my wife and I have done so with our children. I think it is very important. As human beings we all need discipline. The younger you are, the more you need it— yet the more you rebel against it. Regardless of your age or circumstance, we all need discipline in our lives.

Manatt, Charles: Part of the building of the character—and this may not be fair to expect a city boy to necessarily understand this—but 4H and FFA and Boy Scouts had an enduring and continuing effect on building my character. Happily, two weeks from now I'm doing a court of honor for four boys who are becoming Eagle Scouts in our hometown of Audubon, Iowa. It's kindness, it's trustworthiness, and it's reliability, and we'll remember the other six to eight precepts of the Boy Scouts. They certainly ran true in my time and certainly throughout my life, as things have developed. Yes. Fifty-six merit badges and Eagle Scout. I've got a son-in-law and a son who are Eagle Scouts, to add to the discussion.

The FFA creed, on the other hand, is "Learning to earn, earning to live, living to serve." And it's obviously simplistic, with twelve or sixteen words, but when you think about it—to use your modern term "matrix" and, in my earlier time, "framework"—that's a lot of what I've tried to do in life.

Some people go off the track for a variety of reasons. One gentleman I know, who just passed away in L.A., who had been a leading lawyer in L.A., about ten years older than I would have been—all of the sudden he got divorced, got estranged from his kids, and got into the sauce real heavily. And then, happily in his case, he got two thirds of the way back: he got off of the sauce and he re-established relationships with his kids, but his marriage was gone at that point. But ever since then, he seemed like a totally different type of personality—positive, decent. I don't know if it was the sauce or what all the demons were working within him. And he bordered on being a bad, bad man. Then all these bad things happened to him. And two to three years later, he was much better.

A lot of it is circumstance, as far as how they are dealt their deck of cards. You can see it perhaps a bit more clearly when you have a high school class of seventy-three—and happily we've still got sixty-four of our seventy-three classmates still with us. And happily Kathy and I [were in] the same class, so we go back to the reunions, as we will next summer. And a third of the class has done quite well, a third has done okay, and some are missing in action. They never had the chance health-wise or motivation-wise to fully develop the lives they might have had.

I think really it is those three or four characterizations: age, geography, ethnicity, culture. The South, I was there in the service—a co-ed going to Ol' Miss or SMU is going to have a different set of experiences on the face of things than one going to the University of Washington or the University of Idaho. Different things are going on. Different weather patterns. In a big city versus a small college town.

Santorum, Richard: If you look at me, the institution that built my character more than anything was my family. I wasn't a Boy Scout, never went to a military academy. I've been un-institutionalized. It was the rigors of an Italian father who drove into me from the very beginning [with] very high expectations. He was an immigrant who loves America. He didn't wear it on his sleeve and didn't talk about it a lot. But he did talk about the great opportunities America has given him, the great opportunities for service and giving back. He talked about how you earn everything. Hard work. Work, work, work. I heard the word every day, usually in the sequence of work, work, and work. Every day. Work hard, serve others, and give back to this country, and you'll be okay. And that was it.

It was never a question of *if* I was going to college. He really didn't care what college I was going to go to. I didn't know what college I was going to go to. I applied haphazardly to a few schools, late in the application process. I'm going through this process with my daughter right now, and it is a huge ordeal. My dad didn't care what college I went to, so long as I went to college. Go wherever as long as you work hard: community college, wherever. You'll get a good education if you work hard, and you'll be fine. We weren't into the prestige game or anything like that. We ended up going to a school because my mom's family went there, and so I went to college.

Work hard, do your best, and things work out. I don't know if there is any institutional thing. It's just the basics.

Can you identify the most important decision in your life?

Bingaman, Anne: Yes. Starting the law firm. Very much so. But it was because of the self-image and not the work itself—although the work and the people were fantastic. It was the happiest work experience of my life. It was out of this world. It was so much fun. Well, if you see yourself that way, and if you pull it off, and if it goes well, then it changes how you see yourself, and then you [can] do other things.

I've had [this] great luxury. I had my own firm to work for myself almost my entire life, so I didn't have to compromise. I was with Brown and Bain only one year. And then at Powell-Goldstein, for nine years, I had my own practice. And I joined them because I had my own practice; I didn't want to work for anyone else, with some senior partner telling me go take depositions or write a draft for a brief he would go on and sign. I wanted to develop my own practice, be on the line for it, and I wanted it to be mine. And it was, and it was fine. So I didn't have to compromise anything, in the sense of my principles. And then in the government and in the business world, even at LCI, I've started my own companies. I've been in the top position, and I had the ultimate responsibility for the organization or enterprise, so the buck stopped with me, as Harry Truman liked to say.

I am an entrepreneur. And my father was, and my grandmother on my mother's side, and my grandfather, all my aunts and uncles. And my father used to tell my brother and me when we were just kids in high school, "Don't work for anyone else; work for yourself. It's the only thing. Don't work for anyone else." He really pounded that into us, and then he gave me the chance, in the sense that basically he pushed me into starting my own firm. And, really, this compromise stuff comes when you don't have complete freedom of action, which is what I mean when I say it is a luxury. It is. And I virtually always have had it. I think the compromise comes when you are subject to a lot of other external forces. Politicians are subject to constituencies. Votes are tough. People in corporations are [subject to external pressures], if you're not the CEO. If you are in a big corporation and your boss wants you to do something, and it affects your promotion... I think that kind of thing comes up when you are in a position to be acted upon by a lot of outside influences, and your own freedom of action is constrained by that. That's how I think of it.

[On being an entrepreneur.]

It's a luxury. In our society, it's not that common. Small-business people have it, but back in the city, in these big firms, you're on the line for income, you're on the line for revenue; you have to take cases you don't want to take. And corporate life is rife with that. I've seen it, although I've never personally experienced it.

Black, Charlie: For any Christian, the most important decision in your life is to follow Christ. From a professional standpoint, an everyday standpoint, probably the decision to drop out of law school and go work in campaigns [was the most important decision in my life]. I did finish law school at night, because I promised my mother I would. It would have been a safer choice to turn down that first job in politics and finish law school, and I might well [have become] an ordinary, garden-variety, run-of-the-mill lawyer.

Bliley, Tom: That's easy. Other than marrying Mary Virginia, it was in 1968, the day I announced for City Council in Richmond, Virginia.

Bulger, William: Staying the course as a member of the Senate. I still remember being encouraged by Senator Boverini. He used to say, "Where are you going to get to do something more significant than this? Your actions are brought to bear on this important matter or that one."

I realize that, as President of the Senate, I was in a pivotal situation. So frequently, people used to ask me, "Wouldn't you like to be the Mayor of the City of Boston?" Well, the Mayor of the City of Boston was always having to come up to my office! And even the Governor, a hugely conspicuous position, yes, but governors can't function very well without Speakers, without legislative bodies, for we are co-equal branches of the government.

This sounds as though we are speaking of it as a self-important matter, but no, it was this: it was for us to realize that we have a position that is so unlike others, and we're held accountable, and we know, ourselves, how we behave. Why not do it and do it well? It is not important that everyone else in the world knows that. It is enough that you know it yourself! When I have spoken to people who are thinking of public life, I say, "Expect no gratitude for it. Do it and do your best. And if you know it, and no one else knows it, even though they would dispute it—'All you did was engage in selfish behavior, in self-important behavior'—the fact is, if you know otherwise and you are true to yourself in your effort to give your very best public service humanly possible, then you will have something that many people don't have."

We're earning a living, and we do something that is worthwhile. That is a good word to describe it: worthwhile. Something good in and of itself. Why not, since we are able to it, and we seem to be doing okay at it?

And it's not that everyone is cheering us on: "You seem to be doing a great job, and you should be very happy with yourself." No-o. It was quite different.

Carlson, Richard: It's probably not one clear-cut decision in my case. But reading as I have done, devouring information on dozens of subjects, played such an enormous role in my life. I was never particularly interested in school, but I always loved books. I did well in school. Then I got bored. When I was twelve, after the death of my father, I totally lost interest. By the end of the tenth grade, school and I were of only passing familiarity. I never was bored by reading, however. Never. I was energized by it, Thank God, because I had become very independent.

This was good, and it was bad. I was getting too old too quickly, without the maturity of judgment to always handle it well. I was swimming in tricky, if not dangerous waters. Three things saved me from criminal delinquency: reading books, having good manners, and no availability of drugs like marijuana or cocaine as a temptation. If you're going to be a juvenile delinquent, which I was, it pays to have excellent manners. For one thing, it makes life easier in dealings with the parents of girls in whom you are interested. Their critical judgment is often softened, even mollified, by a boy with good manners—though in their heart of hearts they always know, or should know, not to trust any teenage boy with their family's little flower. By the time I was sixteen, I had pretty much stopped going to school, had hooked up with a remarkably varied field of women and girls, and was a regular at a couple of Providence, Rhode Island, gin joints. (Ever notice there is no such thing as a vodka joint? Gin was my choice of booze when I was a drinker.) No drugs, as I said, because they weren't available. But plenty of liquor. I thank God I was never hooked. I hardly drink at all now.

The strongest factor in my not becoming a full-blown juvenile delinquent, and ending up behind bars, was that I read so much. Because of that, through the characters created by the great J.P. Marquand (*The Late George Apley*) and Erskine Caldwell (*Tobacco Road*) and John O'Hara (*Appointment in Samara*) and Bud Schulberg (*What Makes Sammy Run*) and Nelson Algren (*The Man with the Golden Arm*) and Robert Penn Warren (*All the King's Men*) and Graham Greene (*The Quiet American*) and Nathaniel West (*Day of the Locust*) and the thinking of Eric Hoffer (*The True Believer*) and the incredible history volumes of Will and Ariel Durant (*The Story of Philosophy* was one of my first), I became completely enamored with life outside of my own limited world, and that fired me up to succeed in my personal and professional life, and to find interesting work.

Books helped keep my future life in some perspective. None of those books, or hundreds of others I read in the 1950s, would have been read by me or my confreres in my public high school classes, so what was the point of being there? (I'm sure there was one, but I didn't see it at the time.) I considered it a waste of good time, just ticket-punching to make the authorities in your life happy.

Eckstein, Paul: Clearly, [my most important decision was] going to what was then a very small firm, Brown and Bain, in the summer of 1964 as a summer clerk and then accepting a job as an associate the next summer. Nothing else compares.

I'm not comfortable talking about achievements, except that I've served as a mentor for a number of lawyers and, I hope, a role model. And if I've done anything that's meaningful, it's to try to pass what was passed on to me by Jack Brown and Randy Bain, primarily, to other young lawyers in my office.

As legal successes, the impeachment trial and the resulting conviction of Evan Mecham was a unique event in my life. I really don't consider it the most important thing I've done as a lawyer or the best thing I've done as a lawyer. The impeachment trial was difficult, in the sense there was a lot of public pressure. I always felt that we would always win, even though there was a certain political aspect to it, maybe because of it, because the

Republicans in the Senate really didn't want to have the governor, who was a Republican, around. The Republicans in the House impeached him and sent it to the Senate, and it was pretty evident they didn't want him. I guess the case could have been lost if the Democrats in the Senate had voted against conviction, not because they believed he didn't commit the acts he had been charged with, but because they wanted to keep him around as a political liability [to the Republicans].

Lynch, Tom: Obviously, the day I got married was an important decision. There is no greater decision you can make as a young person than the choice of a spouse, the companion with whom you're going to share your life.

There were "go" or "no-go" decision points where I questioned my commitment to a naval career. I was out of the Navy for a while. Very few people know about it. In 1974, with ten years as a commissioned officer, I was stationed aboard a ship in Charleston, South Carolina. We had had a tour of duty at the Naval Academy, followed by a six-month school in Norfolk, Virginia, and were then to be assigned to a ship there. However, Secretary of the Navy Chaffee reassigned the ship to Newport, Rhode Island, and after [my family and I] moved there, bought a home, and became settled, the Newport base was closed as an operating base, which necessitated another move, to Charleston. As I neared the completion of my tour, I was told that my next job would be in Washington, D.C. I pleaded to stay in Charleston, because the kids had refused to make friends because of all the moving. We needed family stability, and besides, duty in D.C. means horrendous hours and a very high cost of living, which we felt we could not afford. Out of the blue, a unique business opportunity presented itself in Atlanta. So I resigned my commission, stayed in the reserves, and we left for Atlanta, Georgia. After about six months there, we quickly realized that this was not for us. We missed the excitement, the adventure, and the camaraderie of the Navy life. One day, on a whim, I called the Navy to see if I had an option to return to the Navy and was told there was a freeze on accessions, but if I wanted to come back I had to do so immediately. I chose to do so, and that was certainly a major decision for me. At the time I was a Lieutenant Commander.

[…] When I chose to retire from the Navy, the decision to relocate to Philadelphia and enter the venture capital world was a major decision, but it turned out to be the right decision for us.

No matter what decisions you make in life, often I hear people say, "If only I had come back to college or high school, I would have done things differently." I don't believe that. You make the decisions based on the level of maturity, experience, knowledge, and emotional factors that are in play at that particular moment in time. Therefore, whatever decision you make, you make the best decision for yourself at that point in time. Twenty or thirty years later, it may turn out that it may not have been the best financial decision, or in hindsight there was a better path you could have taken, but I don't believe anyone should ever look back and say "would've, could've, should've" or "if, if, if." You made the best decision you were capable of making at that point in time, for yourself and your family. And looking back at some later point, another decision may or may not have been better, but it's only wasted energy on your part. It's always best to look forward, never back.

Manatt, Charles: That's very simple: [the most important decision in my life was] to start my own law practice, which then became starting my own partnership, which then became starting the law firm.

Santorum, Richard: Obviously, deciding to run for office was a huge decision. As far as the most consequential decision that changed my life while I was in office, it was the decision to walk to the floor of the United States Senate and begin debating the issue of abortion. I'd spent all four years in the House and never talked about abortion. I was a Republican in a Democratic district, and I just stayed away from those issues. I came to the Senate my first year, and it was "Keep your head down, I'm controversial enough" for all the other things I did. "People know that I am pro-life; people know that I am a conservative in a moderate and now liberal state. So you just best keep your head down." Then the partial-birth abortion issue came up, and I couldn't keep my head down. I went, in 1995, from making a two-sentence rebuttal to something Barbara Boxer said on the floor, to ten months later managing the bill on the floor for the override.

There were a lot of things going on in my life at that time. That decision to step up and lead the charge on the major abortion issue of the day changed me and people's perception of me. It changed me, well, because lots of things were going on in my life at the time, and lots of things happened as a result of me stepping up. I came to the Senate, a man on the move. Busy, busy, busy. ...Still sort of flailing away, in many respects, until we moved to Herndon and went to this little church in Great Falls called Saint Catherine of Siena, and ran into this priest named Father Jerome Fasano.

At the same time, I was encouraged by a couple of my colleagues to join the Bible study group on the Hill. And ran into a guy named Lloyd Ogilvie, who was the Chaplain of the Senate. And those two men had a huge impact on me: Fasano from the growth and development of my Catholic faith and Ogilvie for my growth in applying those tenets and teachings to the job at hand. Both were vitally important. I look back and I can't think of two better mentors to have, one Catholic, one Presbyterian-Evangelical, but both incredible men who helped shape me and my faith. Obviously, Lloyd didn't have a lot to do with Karen, so Fasano was the major player in helping us both come back to the Church. From his sermons on Sunday—I'd never heard stuff like this coming from a Catholic Church.

When have you had to make principled compromises?

Bingaman, Anne: Compromise is the essence of any enterprise larger than one person. Honestly, I saw that question, and I've certainly compromised to settle cases or work out a disagreement in business plenty of times. I don't remember compromising principles. I never did something that I felt ashamed of later—which, I take it, is the sense in which you are using that. Going against your fundamental values.

Black, Charlie: Without asking you for a definition for the term, having spent a lot of time in party politics, the basis of a two-party system is you support candidates for nomination, and if your candidate doesn't win, you support whoever does win. I have supported candidates on the Republican ticket who weren't my first choice or my second choice. And sometimes ones with whom I had personal disagreements on issues, and if they asked for my help, I would give it, which I guess would be in the nature of a principled compromise.

But also in doing client work for companies and trade associations, you are frequently trying to broker compromises. Whatever their public policy goal is, you might not be able to achieve all of it, so you deal with elected officials, government officials who decide that policy. Frequently, it is a compromise that they get. There are a lot of times I think the client deserves one hundred percent of what they are after, but rather than have them walk away empty-handed, I'll counsel them to get part of what they wanted.

Bliley, Tom: You bet. Did I mention that I was married? Seriously, I'm very proud of the number of bipartisan compromises that I managed as Chairman of the House Commerce Committee. For instance, I made principled compromises in working with Congressman Henry Waxman on the Safe Drinking Water Act; on food safety to get rid of the Delaney Clause, and in the Telecommunications Act of 1996 with Congressman John Dingell and Senator Fritz Hollings.

After the leaving the House, I have been involved in a number of key legislative initiatives, balancing policy and my clients' interests. Most recently, I was involved in the enactment of a bill sponsored by Chairman Waxman governing the regulation of tobacco. I'm also leading the charge on helping the autism community get some federal help in dealing with the many problems they face, which affect one in ninety-one kids today.

Bulger, William: First of all, "compromise" is not a bad word in my vocabulary. No legislator sees compromise as bad. He knows that to be effective is to have the ability to adjust your purpose. To be adjustable is to work with people who have different points of view. In the legislative body, people come from all different parts of geography and legislative view. And to function is to be able to give up and demand accordingly.

But to get to a specific area where I had to surrender on some fundamental principle, I don't know of [a case], right now, where I had to personally do it. It's the concern about that, always. It's a nice question and a wonderful academic question, and I'm sure we could conjure up an instance right now.

Cardin, Ben: Compromise is part of life: your willingness to listen, your willingness to compromise, and your willingness to be effective. If you are going to get things done, you have to be willing to compromise. But you should never compromise your principles. It's a fallacy to say that compromising is compromising what you believe in. It's not. It's being able to effectively carry out what you believe in by being willing to sit down and enter into compromises with other people. You do that throughout life. It's not just in the political sector where you'll be sitting down and figuring out how to do that. The manner in which you compromise really speaks to your effectiveness as an individual and your own personal character. If you never compromise, then you aren't really part of an organized society.

Lynch, Tom: I really can't. I don't know that I've ever had to compromise. I can remember as the Superintendent of the Naval Academy, the mantra to not lie, cheat, or steal is pretty clear-cut. But there were some extenuating circumstances at the time that, instead of dismissing a midshipman from the Naval Academy, instead of being pure black and white, no questions asked, I showed leniency based on the merits of the case, and maybe that's considered to be a compromise. As far as compromising core principles, I don't believe I've ever had to do that. If I had to live my life over, I wouldn't change a thing. So I don't know that there was ever a time where I have compromised my basic beliefs.

Santorum, Richard: The most famous principled compromise I made was supporting Arlen Specter for reelection in the United States Senate in 2004. I make the argument that was a principled compromise. A lot of my conservative brethren across the country, and certainly in Pennsylvania, didn't see it that way and punished me for it. To this day I believe it was the right thing to do. I look back and see the confirmation of Roberts and Alito, especially Alito, and say, but for Arlen Specter, that man may not have ever been confirmed. I can look at other things that may not have happened, but for [Specter]. I also believe in my heart of hearts, without question, that had Arlen lost that election, it would have had an impact within our caucus; we would have lost Pennsylvania—and look at it today: we would be at forty instead of forty-one.

There are all sorts of ramifications, and I believe that Arlen was certainly not someone who was right on many of the issues I care deeply about, but keeping a Republican majority and supporting the president on a whole set of issues was more important than one single race. That was the principled compromise that I made: winning and, as a leader of the Republican Party, supporting my colleague, a moderate, in an effort to hold our caucus together and get as many votes from the moderates as I was able to get, showing that I'd be willing to support a moderate was an important thing for me to do—and [allowed me] credibly to get votes from them. Secondly, it was very important for me to get the votes necessary for us to [do] the things [that needed] to get done.

Have you ever violated your principles?
What was the outcome?

Black, Charlie: Everybody, along the way, has times of weakness. You tell a lie and take the easy way out. You didn't sit down and premeditate it. You immediately regret it and sometimes regret it for [quite] a while. More frequently, someone else I was working with, or for, might have violated a principle, and whether I approved of that action or not, I supported what they did. That's the nature of politics, where you cannot just walk away from campaigns or candidates when something that's a small mistake happens, and it is not a huge mistake. Sometimes you do. I've walked away from candidates for huge violations of principle.

Bliley, Tom: Tough question. I winced a few times voting "aye" or "nay" on a House floor vote, but [I knew] that what I was voting for served the greater good. No regrets.

Bulger, William: The principles have been pretty much observed and adhered to. I hope that's the case. Even with Senator Boverini one day, there was a bill that would have allowed for sparklers [to be] legalized. Sparklers. They seem like innocent enough things. I said to Boverini, "Who wants this?" And he said, "Well, I'd like to see it done." And then he did something that was very unusual: he said he would like to do it for his constituent.

I would always jokingly say, "Let's see if we can handle these things on their merits," as if we could be totally impersonal. Now I know that's almost a human impossibility; we can't manage that.

He said, "Walt Dropo is representing them." We all knew the legendary Red Sox first baseman and Rookie of the Year, and he came from Lynn. Boverini pointed over his shoulder to the balcony, and there, sitting in the balcony, was none other than Walt Dropo. And we looked, and I gave him thumbs-up, and we put the bill through sight unseen!

Now that's something I'd be telling people: "Try not to do that, because we want to see if we can be like judges." The point is that we would frequently cite that as the Walt Dropo case: if we can do it for Walt Dropo. And I would frequently get on that and say, if a person was Rookie of the Year for the Red Sox, at least we owe them a sparkler bill.

Cardin, Ben: I think of a lot of issues where I might have done things differently, where at the time, it was the right thing to do. I remember the President of United States calling me on three separate occasions for a vote and voting against him—a guy whom I greatly admired. Then I think of times that one person coming up to me, talking to me about an issue, causing me to change my views, has impacted me. So I really do think there was a lot of pressure on me to vote for the war in Iraq in my district. And I thought it could affect my reelection. There are times that I've been influenced that I guess today I would have liked to do differently. I am not a purist by any stretch of the imagination. I do stand up for principle when I think it is critical to my beliefs, and it is the right thing to do. It's always a balancing, and in hindsight I certainly would have done things differently in my life on certain issues.

Carlson, Richard: I have probably violated enough of [my principles] sufficiently that I won't be able to enumerate them all. I would tell you if I could think of a good example, or at least an example I would want you and your readers to know about. Sorry, I can't. I can say that my principles have gotten stronger over the many years I have trod this good earth, and that means that they have gotten better. I was not as moral a person when I was younger. I was not overly burdened with the weight of too many scruples. I always had some, though, and I never deviated from them. I was never cruel or unkind to man or beast, not consciously, in my whole life. I did do a lot of other bad things. And the consequences were not as leavening as they probably should have been. I didn't strive to be as honest as I am now, or as truthful.

Maturity, Christian faith, and having children and a good wife changed me. You have close and longtime relationships with people who you don't want to disappoint, much less disappoint yourself.

Eckstein, Paul: In discipline, yes. I'm not very disciplined. Every year I tell the kids at Chicanos por la Causa that Santa Claus is going to come, so leave some cookies. Sissela Bok wrote a book a few years back, called *Lying*. I taught that book—that was one of the things I taught in my course on fiction and American politics, even though the book is not fiction. She posits, as Kant does, whether it is ever acceptable to lie. Ever. Kant comes pretty close to saying, if he doesn't actually say, that it is never acceptable. The situation posed is that the Nazis come to your door, they ask you if anyone is there, and if it is not acceptable to lie in that situation, it never is. In my mind, it is acceptable to lie to save a life. Is it then acceptable to lie to save people from serious injury or embarrassment?

I'm a big believer in compromising on small things that really don't matter, to get to the big things, so the small things don't tie you down. For politicians to succeed it's important to have people who are independent and who will tell you when you've crossed the line and when you've done wrong, and will really stand up to you. But in order to do that, you have to be independent. That's what I tell young lawyers who want to get involved in the political world: get a trade, become a competent lawyer if you want to go into politics, because if you get into a situation where a difficult decision has to be made and you have to give advice or point out something that is difficult for an officeholder to hear, you need to be in a position to do that. No one resigns on principle any more. People were critical of Colin Powell for not resigning on principle, and he was independent. He had a soldier's mentality, that you don't resign, that you soldier through.

Lincoln is getting all the credit for Obama's election, Doris Kearns' book *A Team of Rivals*. [Lincoln] had political rivals who had opposing point of views, but the important thing isn't to get rivals in there, but people who will see the world differently. Franklin Roosevelt did have people who gave him different advice. He often, it was said, would get people in his office, and they would debate. And it's important to have that kind of advocacy before you are an officeholder.

Manatt, Charles: I'm sure [I have violated my principles]. I have no memory of what circumstances they are. If anyone would say they have never violated their principles, it would not be your friend Manatt. I think virtually everyone has.

Santorum, Richard: Yes. Every day. It's called sin. And the outcome is always bad. There is always guilt. That is the one good thing that the nuns did a great job at. When I do sin, I know it, and I feel it. I know it is not worth it, and I still do. That's how it is. You keep trying to get better. You keep trying to get those things that you do. In the ordinary course, you try to work hard to exorcise those things out of you. It is a constant process. There is no question, with good formation, and it has taken a long time, and there is a lot more work to be done. With good formation you know what you're doing, you know why you're doing it, and you go in there with eyes wide open to the sins you commit. There are some things you look back and say, "Boy I wish I hadn't done that," but I didn't look at it that way. Most of the time, I'm just a stubborn sinner.

Do you have any regrets about any past decisions?

Bingaman, Anne: The only regret I have is that one time I let Jeff talk me into taking a job that I really didn't want to take, knew it wasn't right, but couldn't articulate it well. I learned a big lesson from that: you've got to make your own decision—end of story. You've got to listen to your own guts. And no matter how it looks from the outside, you've got to trust yourself. And in a lot of ways it was lucky that it happened when we were young. I learned early on that your life is your life and no one else's. You've got to do what is right for you. If you let other people make decisions for you, it's almost always a loss, so just don't do it.

Do I have regrets? I regret I have not taken the time to get to know some of the great people in this town—and there are some phenomenally decent, incredibly smart and talented people. And I know who they are. I know a bunch of them. And they'd say, sure, absolutely. Have I ever done it? No. I've never done it once in my life.

Black, Charlie: I have no [major] regrets. Small things. Occasionally I felt like I could have done a better job on something. It wasn't so much from making a bad decision as maybe not being perceptive enough or having good enough judgment. But I have had a lot of luck in most things I've worked on. And in most things I've contributed some value. No big decisions I really regret.

Bliley, Tom: No regrets. I'm at peace with the Almighty, my family, and the Republican Party. It doesn't get any better than that.

Bulger, William: Generally, I've been happy with my choices. I think I did ask a great deal of my family by remaining in the legislature for thirty-five years—ten years in the House of Representatives, twenty-five in the Senate, eighteen of which were as President. It's a very stormy position; the higher up on the mountain you go, the harder the winds blow. But it seemed to work all right. I was under all these heavy, heavy attacks. Each time I think I could be reelected back in my district, and then I could be re-elected as Senate president at the beginning of the new session, both seemed to give me some vindicatory relief: I had beat the critics!

I was not an easy person when dealing with the press. I do remember Tom Winship, editor of the *Boston Globe*, years ago, asking me if I'd come speak to the editorial board, and I said no. And he asked why. And I said, "You wouldn't like it if I came over to the Board of the Bank of Boston or John Hancock. And you're just a business for profit, Tom, you should not be able to summon me."

And he said, "I really resent it when you keep referring to me as a business for profit."

And I joked with him about it. He used to come in a big car from the town of Lincoln. [I said,] "Who do you think you are: Mother Teresa? Coming in here for your paycheck?"

He was a good person. I liked Tom Winship. I probably antagonized [the press] more than I should have, more than was necessary, so they probably saw me as quite arrogant, probably rightfully so. I, on the other hand, thought it was a way to assert my independence from them, which was a big factor in my life.

I will also say this: it had a big, strange kind of beneficial effect. I remained popular in the district. They knew the press was against me. And for whatever reason there was a healthy skepticism of the press in my constituency. They would say things that were very bad, especially the talk masters, and time after time, the people would reelect me. Even the senators themselves would like that idea that I didn't have that relationship with the press. It's ironic in a way, because if you were very popular with the press, it would mean that you were doing their bidding or you were a source for them in some way, that you might embarrass a person. I think [my poor relationship with the press] gave me an authenticity.

Carlson, Dick: I have no regrets that amount to anything—just piddling things. Everybody spills some milk; don't whine about it and don't think about it—that's my personal motto.

Eckstein, Paul: The most important decision I made was to go to Brown and Bain in the summer of 1964; I had been offered the clerkship that summer. Something else I could have done that summer, which I have always regretted I didn't do, was to join some of my classmates to go primarily to the South, to Mississippi, the so-called Freedom Summer in 1964, to be legal advisors to the Civil Rights movement in the South. That was the summer that Cheney and Shwamer and the other young men were killed. It required an incredible about of courage to be a white person seen with a black person in Mississippi in the summer of 1964.

I've regretted not going there, not knowing whether I was afraid to go, I didn't have the courage to go down there, or I was more interested in getting on with my career or establishing myself.

Now had I gone down to Mississippi with some of my classmates, number one, I might not be alive, and number two, I wouldn't be a lawyer at Brown and Bain and wouldn't have had the career I had. My career would have gone in a different direction. So clearly that decision to return to Phoenix, where I grew up, rather than go to Mississippi, was a key decision. While I haven't regretted my life, [what] my life became and has become, all of which is attributable to coming back to Phoenix that summer, I often wonder what would have happened had I taken the other course.

Lynch, Tom: First, I never look back. What is done is done, so I have no regrets. I had a thirty-two-year career in the Navy, and I can honestly say I enjoyed the Navy. I found the time in the Navy to be challenging, rewarding, demanding, and exciting. I was proud of my naval service and that I attained the rank of Rear Admiral; however, when I went to the private sector at Safeguard Scientifics, I never cared whether they called me Tom or Admiral or whatever; I didn't care. The military was behind me. I spent five enjoyable years at Safeguard Scientifics, and I'm now finished with that. That too is behind me. I look at what are we doing today and what do we need to work on together today. As I said, if I had to do it all over again, I would have done it exactly the same way.

Values-Related Questions

What does it mean to have character?

What will you do—or not do—to accomplish your goals?

Have you had to pay a heavy price for your integrity?

Good character is currently in short supply in politics today, where can it be found, and how can it be developed?

How can we reconcile the tension between principle and power politics in Washington?

Does how a person chooses to act under pressure reveal their character?

What traits do you think enable a person to avoid misbehavior?

Do you believe there are common traits that successful leaders display in political life?

What stories or anecdotes might you share that teach good character?

How might we move leaders to be touched by "the better angels of their nature"?

What does it mean to have character?

Bingaman, Anne: Well, as I said, I value honesty, with all that implies: it implies integrity, it implies personal honesty, and it implies keeping your word, and it implies honesty with yourself about yourself. I think it means trying to help other people.

Black, Charlie: Let's give it a broader definition than just the Christian view, because we all deal with people in politics and everyday life who don't share our faith but who do believe in character—the threshold quotient of integrity, people who are truth-tellers and do what they think is right. But I also think the true test of character is when you can put your own interests secondary to another person's interests or to the country's interests to do something that is for the overall good.

In day-to-day tactics and methods of doing things, you have to insist on integrity, and frankly, that's almost always the right approach for a client's success and a campaign's success. So when someone has a bad idea for being deceptive, shading the truth, or cutting a corner, it's not the right thing to do, and usually it doesn't work out for the accomplishment of the goal.

Bliley, Tom: A willingness to stand for what you believe in, even though it may not be popular. In my time on the Hill, I cast many votes that a majority of people in the Seventh District may not have agreed with—spending cuts, defense spending, abortion, just to name a few. But when you have the courage of your convictions, I think that people will judge you for your whole character.

Bulger, William: [Character] is a person behaving on sound principles. I knew the interview would be on character, but I have not thought much about it. There is a constant theme in my life, reading people like Demosthenes and Cicero. Samuel Johnson was a moralist in the eighteenth century, a friend of Edmund Burke and a friend of the writer of *The History of the Decline and Fall of the Roman Empire*, Edward Gibbon—people like that. And they're constantly on the whole question of moral behavior.

Character is the whole idea of giving a high premium to morality. Someone has written on that subject, noting the distinguishing characteristic: "However wise other creatures are, only man can make a moral decision." We're the ones who can make a moral decision. We decide what is the best way to get; we recognize if there is a right or wrong; we have to make a decision on it; it may not be there, but if it is, we'll see it, and we'll have to make the decision. If that is a distinguishing characteristic, then we're certainly more human by virtue of the fact that we take that as a very serious matter.

In my life I was fortunate, again, it was a constant theme. I go back to Father Carl Thayer; he urged us to remember the words of Juvenal: "*Summum crede nefas animam praeferre pudori, et propter vitam, vivendi perdere causas.*" "Consider it the greatest evil to prefer life to honor, and for the sake of life to lose all reason for living." Juvenal is saying if you put your life ahead of honor, and in order to save your life, you do something dishonorable, then you may have lost all your reasons for living.

Cardin, Ben: I strongly believe that to have character is to have ethics. When I was Speaker, I had a decision about the first bill I would get done. It was sort of a honeymoon phase, and I chose to reform our state ethics laws. I do think that character and ethics are important. When you are in public life, you can say it's an individual choice—any person can say that it is an individual choice and you don't have to have rules in a society because it is up to the individual to make those judgments. In reality we collectively make those judgments. So I think character and principles are very important. It is your moral compass. It's what gets you going every morning, what we are trying to achieve, and why we are here: to make our country, or our community, or our school a little bit better.

Carlson, Richard: [To me, to have character means] to possess the important defined values such as honesty and truthfulness, loyalty, straightforwardness—to be absent of hidden agendas in quotidian dealings with others.

It is not that I don't like complicated planning with multiple levels of truth, even professional deceptions, which can be okay, depending on what they're deployed for tactically. God knows I have been involved in some of them, but I have never used them with friends or trusting peers. I know something about propaganda and its uses, so I'm not adverse to second- and third-layer truths, but only if used professionally. There are too many genuinely duplicitous people in and around politics. You can hardly believe a word they say, regardless of how mundane the subject. They just lie and shade and twist as a matter of everyday intercourse.

Eckstein, Paul: I was reading Aristotle's *Rhetoric* this morning, which I don't do every morning, but reading your question reminded me to go back to Aristotle. Aristotle talks about the three components of rhetoric: *ethos*, *logos*, and *pathos*. In a way, you can call it credibility, reputation, what people think of you when they think of you: you can have a bad character, you can have a good character. So when people say, "What do you think of him?" "Oh, he's kind." That says something about his character. He's hardworking. He's charitable. It's what you do that causes a view that other people may hold. You may think that you are creating a view that really doesn't accord with what others around you think.

Lynch, Tom: Trustworthiness is so much to me. It's the old Robert E. Lee mantra:

> A man of character is a man who can look you in the eye, tell you a fact, and you know that is a truthful and honest answer to the best of his knowledge.

You can trust and believe him. A person of character is one who is totally trustworthy and genuine, a person who is selfless and has empathy for his fellow man.

Santorum, Richard: To seek the truth. And once arrived, to live it.

What will you do—or not do—to accomplish your goals?

Bliley, Tom: Faith and family never, ever hang in the balance for me. Plain and simple.

Bulger, William: Well, I hope that I always work very hard to accomplish my goals. I probably make some hard decisions. What is a worthwhile goal? Not all goals are equally important. I hope I'd always be willing to strive hard to accomplish a goal, but not at all and every cost. You know, I don't think it's always so tough. It's a time of great cynicism, but if you're closer to the political realm and understood it more, you'd probably see more things that would drive you to despair. But you also see so much that is noble and so much honest-to-goodness hard work done by good people that you would never again disparage the entire process and those involved in it. […] They see these humans for the way they are: imperfect, certainly, but with all sorts of great virtues. Once you've been exposed to that, you're actually more of an optimist.

I still recall the day one of the Massachusetts senators, a decent fellow, was having a nervous breakdown. It was very difficult to deal with him. He was disparaging members and accusing them of all sorts of terrible things; he was just out of his sane mind. I had to finally, after weeks of putting up with it, order him out of the Chamber. It was one of the worst things I ever had to do. As he was going, he said that it's the same as being thrown out of a brothel.

At that moment the Republican minority leader, John Parker, stood up and said, "Wait a second!" And Parker had a lot of years on [this man]. He said, "I have served in the Senate for so many decades. I have served with great men and great women who gave their all to do their job well." And he went on to praise the colleagues with whom he had worked. And he said, "I'm not going to stand here and let anyone disparage this institution and the people who have given so much to it, the way you just have done. I am pleased you are being expelled for doing something like that." So he made it clear that there was bipartisan support for my action.

I felt bad, as did Parker, for the whole episode. But the fact is the fellow had provoked Parker into saying something that deserved to be said. [Parker] had experience with all these people, and I am sure that at times he must have wrung his hands in despair at what they were doing, at what they weren't doing. We all go through that. To take it all *in toto* is to recognize there are lots of people doing lots of things, at great sacrifice, to bring about excellent results.

Cardin, Ben: The manner in which you get things done is equally important as the final result. You have got to be honest to yourself, and there are certain things you won't do. That has happened to me over the course of my life. When I was Speaker, I was in the most direct position to get things done. The Speaker has tremendous power, and how you use that power is critically important. I remember when one of my dear friends in the legislature was criticizing one of the governors of Maryland who abused power, who had power and didn't use it. I think that's just as important—how you don't use power—as how you do use power. Power is corrupting. You have to decide when you don't do something, just as when you have the power to do. That's a tough choice at times.

Carlson, Dick: I hesitate to respond to some of these questions, because of a lifelong fear of being caught trading in banality. To specifically answer the question, though, I would never lie to or deceive or manipulate an innocent party to any transaction, personal or professional, that I am engaged with, for gain—and I never have. But, you should know also that in the whole area of "goals and objectives," mine have been pretty thin. I didn't really have specific goals during much of my life, [either to] engage in interesting enterprise or to become a writer of some kind. I did develop a very specific goal of becoming a news reporter. That happened when I was twenty-one, close to fifty years ago—in part because of my close friendship, when I was a summer cop in Ocean City, Maryland, with a woman named

Catherine Mackin, a reporter for the Hearst Newspapers. Cassie encouraged me to go into the newspaper business, and it was because of her that I went to California and got a job at the *Los Angeles Times* as a copy boy. I became a reporter through desire, hard work, and very good luck. I didn't have to compromise anything to achieve it, other than to not talk too much, to keep my own counsel, and to listen and learn from others. I became a full-time general assignment reporter for United Press International six months into my twenty-second year.

Eckstein, Paul: I've never had goals in the sense of things I feel like I have to do. We've had discussions about this. Did I have the goal of having one million dollars by age thirty or age forty? Did I have a goal of having two houses? Did I have a goal of having sons?

My parents were very modest in their lifestyle. And it was in part because of my mother's experience coming from a family where she lost everything and my father's experience of coming from a family that didn't have anything. Some things you'll never forget. I remember my father saying, "I could have a Cadillac if I wanted to, but I'd rather spend my money on your education. We could live in a bigger house or a fancier neighborhood, but it is more important that we use our money for charitable causes." As a kid growing up, you don't realize how important a casual statement like that might be and how influential it might be. As a parent you don't realize it. My father may have said that to me only once. My father might have said it a hundred times. But I certainly observed the way they lived.

This was reinforced by some of my readings, particularly Thoreau. When Flo and I go to Boston, we try to go to Walden Pond; we try to read *Walden* once every five years. This may be the beginning of it. When I was about five or six years old, I wanted a holster set with two cap guns. My mother bought that for me for either Hanukah or my birthday. Within twenty minutes the holster set came apart because it was cheaply made. I didn't have what I wanted. Maybe I learned at that moment that material things really didn't matter. I didn't want for anything as a child. I went to great camps, I went to great schools, we lived a comfortable life, and we took great vacations. I didn't have a car until my junior year in college; I got my mother's hand-me-down car so my brother John and I could use it together. Things just didn't matter. Material things, toys, were never part of my life. Books are.

Lynch, Tom: What would you do to achieve your goals? I just go back to what I heard from my mother when I was a kid: "You work as hard as you can, you pray as hard as you can, and you leave the rest up to God." If you always do that, you'll always look yourself in the mirror and, if you didn't achieve your goal, you'll at least know you gave it all that you could to the best of your ability because you worked as hard as you could, you prayed as hard as you could, and you left the rest up to God. This philosophy of life solves a lot of problems for you in life; it has solved a lot of problems for me.

Maybe this better explains my response to your earlier question about when I've compromised my principles. Many people will compromise principles to achieve a goal, whether it is a financial goal, a personal goal, stature or something like that. But if they had the right attitude, just work, pray, and say, "Shit happens"—if it works out, it works out; if it doesn't work out, it doesn't work out. But you've done your best; don't worry about it.

Santorum, Richard: I'm going to take issue with the question. I've never been a goal guy.

[Rick possibly takes issue because in his world, he must change plans quickly, so setting a goal based on old facts may not serve him well. He gives an example.]

When I ran for the House of Representatives, a year before I ran, I'd say, "I'd never run for the House of Representatives. I have no interest in federal politics. I interned for a Congressman one time, and I hated it. And the issues were boring. I'm a state guy. My aspirations one day are to be a state senator, and maybe someday run for Governor." That was my political aspiration when I moved to Pittsburgh. When I moved to Pittsburgh, I picked the place to live because of the stability of the neighborhood in terms of home values, and because it provided the chance for election of a Republican to the State House. My Congressman was a Democrat. I thought I'd work as a lawyer and one day run for the State House.

I just got frustrated with looking at this Congressman. I had been around politics and worked for a state senator for five years and been around all stripes. The one thing I couldn't stand about any politician—it drives me crazy—are dishonest ones. I don't mean dishonest in terms of cheating or stealing. But he was not honest to the people he represented in terms of what he did and believed in. He would go to Washington and do one thing and then come back home and sound completely different.

I would go to his town halls and say, "You said this, and then you did this."

And he would say, "Well you don't understand; that was a vote about this…" And he'd just bloviate. It just drove me crazy. Yeah, he was liberal, but he wasn't the most liberal guy in the world. But he was dishonest, and so I decided to run.

I had no chance of winning. He had just gotten through the last two elections, where he had gotten 63 percent of the vote… I thought, "My base is 37 percent, and I only need 14 percent more to win." That's the way I approached it.

A year into campaigning—it's not making much headway—a State Representative took me to the top of Pittsburgh, the sixty-third floor of the USX Building, and told me of the seemingly insurmountable odds I faced. He laid out how difficult this district was and how rough this election year was going to be: mid-term, George H.W. Bush and Governor Casey were up for reelection, and he was going to win by a landslide. "You're trying to unseat a fourteen-year incumbent Congressman who is chair of the Subcommittee on Energy and Commerce and has all the money he would ever want," he told me. "But we can do this. We'll give you this money and you'll have this."

I said, "No. This is what I feel like I'm called to do."

And the guy said, "Look. Let me lay it out for you more clearly. It's 1990. You know what happens in '92: redistricting. So we're going to lose two Congressional seats. Even if you win, Casey will be the Governor; we'll probably still be in the majority of the House and the Senate. And we'll have to give up one Republican seat and one Democrat seat. So even if you win, you'll lose."

And I said, "That's really convincing. No thanks."

He said, "But you can't win."

And I said, "Yeah, but this is what I feel a strong call to do."

So, goals: if you had asked me three years ago what my goal was, I moved [to Pittsburgh] to run for the State House, and they handed it to me on a platter, and I said, "No, I'd rather take this." And guess what happened? In '92 they eliminated my seat, blew my district apart, and I still won.

Have you had to pay a heavy price for your integrity?

Bingaman, Anne: Only in the most ephemeral sense, but there is nothing to be done about it. I'm just horribly plainspoken and outspoken. My mother's family was from Oklahoma and West Texas, and believe me; those people talk straight, all of them. People out here [in Washington, D.C.] don't take it quite right; it's just not normal, and they just think you're kind of an oddball, but truthfully, what can I do about it? I didn't get here until I was thirty-nine. It was way too late to change my spots at that stage in life.

This is what I think you don't appreciate, maybe because you're from a big city and you have a different background… Jeff and I are really small-town people. Jerome was 4,500 people at its high point. What it is—small towns, my parents, and I am one generation from a small town; I was raised by small-town people, and Jeff grew up in a small town, and what's different is that everybody knows you. Everybody in the town knows everything about you. You get called out if you talk too big and look too smart. Kids will beat you up on the playground if you put on airs. And you're also very aware of other people. You know them. It's just very different from big cities, with layers and layers of people on top of you, around you, and you know a small, small percentage of them at best.

Black, Charlie: I don't think so. Again, occasionally you turn down clients and money, but I think there are a lot of clients and money that have come my way because of integrity and because of the track record that I've had. Some people would say that if I've ever paid a price, it is getting into campaign politics as opposed to the client business. Although sometimes in client business I've gotten into a controversial situation and have been personally attacked and not defended myself. I don't consider that paying a big price, because usually the right response is not to get into a tit-for-tat with people. And in a campaign and a client situation, you are not out defending yourself, and it is certainly not in the client's interest.

In a recent campaign here, where I worked for John McCain, I had newspaper stories and a lot of blog stories planted by liberals and Democrats that I was crooked and had conflict of interests and I should not be working for McCain. MoveOn.org had ads against me. I didn't counterattack, and if factual questions about these charges came in, I would answer them or have the campaign answer them, but I didn't retaliate and counterattack David Axelrod or the Obama campaign, or have a press conference and attack the leaders of MoveOn. Some people thought I should have.

To me, trying to stay above the fray is also good for your own integrity over the long run. And probably serves the interests of your clients and candidates better than making you the center of attention. But at the same time, I've had the housekeeper who has been helping us in our home for over twenty years show up with a mailing from MoveOn saying I was a crook. And at a restaurant I frequent for breakfast regularly in Alexandria, the waitress said, "Oh, I got a mailing about you!" And she was looking at me sideways with a look saying that it must be true that I am a crook. Sometimes you do wish you could correct the record for average people—not the people in politics, or in the press who probably *do* know better. It's better not to get into tit-for-tat contests.

Bliley, Tom: Well, politics can get rough. There were times when I felt bad for my family when I was under attack. But, fortunately, everyone realized that we were in it together.

Bulger, William: I feel bad for members of my family if they had to see unfair criticism or a drumbeat that was intended to drive me out of office. But I always say, "We'll come through it. We're going to be okay." If they don't like you and they're going to put you out, they don't say, "We do not like him. He will not cooperate with us. He will not speak to us properly; therefore we do not want him in office." No, they're going to say that you're a thug, a henchman. I've been described as the head of the mob and all of these things. It must be painful for those who love me and know better. But I always say, as long as we all know better, we have no control over what is said. We have to be brave; we have to take it. That's all there is to it.

Cardin, Ben: You always do. I go on talk shows all the time. I get bruised. Yes, you'll pay a price. But if you're honest with yourself, you have the right compass, and you are honest with your constituents, whether you're an elected official or not, they'll understand that. Clearly, I've cast certain votes and certain groups won't support me for a long time to come. But that's the price you pay.

Carlson, Richard: No, not at all, although sometimes there were momentary inconveniences because of honest positions I took. I stood up at the Voice of America on principle quite often. This is because the power of the international broadcasts at VOA—half a hundred languages, live twenty-four hours a day, were awesome and very appealing to other U.S. government officers engaged in national security and intelligence agency work. You can imagine. We had bureaus and reporters and transmitters and antennae fields around the world. We had tens of millions of faithful listeners, many of them tuned in at some personal danger to themselves—in the USSR, the Eastern Bloc, North Korea, etc. These were people who believed what we said. I had control of VOA and Radio Marti to Cuba, and in the last few years of my time, I controlled all government TV and film work as well. To use the VOA to spin some event in Albania or Cuba or China, or some other denied area of the world, had great appeal to some folks, quite understandably. There were always people in other parts of the U.S. government who would come up with bright ideas for some manipulation, and I would have to deny them. If I had ever done what they asked, it would have created an incredible slippery slope for VOA as an international broadcaster. The VOA had credibility with its fifty million-plus listeners every day because we didn't lie and we didn't spin and we didn't omit stories for geopolitical gain. Very important. The men who put pressure on me—and there were many of them over my almost six years there—invariably had good intentions, broadly defined. But I never gave in. We had a law to protect the VOA's integrity.

Let me add something to this, about honesty and integrity and the kind of sharks who patrol the political waters. This is also about paying an unintended price for unguarded candor.

Years after I had left government, I was under consideration by President George W. Bush as U.S. Commissioner of Customs. This was before Customs was folded into Homeland Security in the wake of 9/11. I had been a Reagan appointee and a George H.W. Bush appointee. The feedback coming to me was that the decision was going to be made in a few weeks. I was a finalist for the job. I then over-reached, and in so doing got shafted. I remembered a guy I had known when I was VOA director, a Reagan presidential appointee, as I had been. He had been head of the Drug Enforcement Administration, the DEA. I'd had lunch with him a few times; he was a former federal judge in Los Angeles who had gone back to private practice at a law firm there after the DEA. I already had a great list of influential supporters, but I thought I would add just one more. It was a fatal mistake.

The fellow's name was Rob Bonner. I figured his endorsement might help. He asked me a few more questions about it. Then he asked for copies of my support letters "for help in formulating one from me." I sent him copies of my entire package.

I never heard back from him. I called his secretary a half dozen times, but he was never in. I would ask about the endorsement letter, and his secretary would say, "Oh, yes. He mentioned it, but I don't think he has written it yet." Well, I guess not. Rob Bonner threw his hat in the ring to be Commissioner of Customs. He got the job.

But I guess this story is more about getting burned by another man's lack of integrity.

Eckstein, Paul: Did I pay a price for the Babbitt affair? I don't think so, but you never know what you don't get. I wasn't seeking any position. I never wanted to be a judge, so I didn't apply to be a judge. I never sought a political position. I explored the possibility of being a candidate for Senate in 1992. I'll give you an example of my lack of ambition. There was a time in my life when I did think it would be terrific to be a publisher of a newspaper or be president of a small college like Pomona. So Flo and I bought a small newspaper, and I got to sleep with the publisher of a newspaper, which is a whole lot better than being the publisher.

Lynch, Tom: There are a couple of things that stand out. When I was Superintendent of the Naval Academy, we experienced a cheating scandal, and I did everything that I knew to proceed as fairly, honestly, and openly as I could. Yet I personally took a lot of criticism because it was on my watch.

I remember another time. Ollie North had written a book, and it came to me whether or not we should allow him to sign autographs of that book in the Midshipmen store. The policy had been that a Naval Academy graduate who has published a book had the right to come to the store and sign autographs for the Midshipmen, to which I said, "Okay, fine. That's policy, then that's what we'll do."

Later on, at a Congressional hearing, I was berated very openly and very soundly by Senator Byrd from West Virginia. It was around the time of the cheating scandal, and he said, "That's why cheating scandals happen at the Naval Academy—because you allow that person and that book to be in there." And he continued "Obviously, Admiral Lynch, you weren't aware of that, because if you had been, you would have put a stop to it."

And I said, "No, sir, I was aware of that. It was brought to my attention and [it was permitted] because there was a policy of alum book signing, and the book had nothing to do with Iran-Gate. It was a love story, a novel. And we teach the issues that involved Iran and Contra-Gate; we teach the midshipmen the pros and cons of a lot of that issue, and Ollie North was very well known on the campus. And so I personally made the decision."

And with that he went off the rocker; he became livid and verbally attacked me personally for a good fifteen minutes.

Manatt, Charles: That's fairly common. I just emailed Tom Phelps, who would have a frame of reference. Kathy wouldn't. For some reason, when I started my own practice long, long ago, two or three guys did their best for as long as they could to make sure I never had happiness or succeeded. Not just in the law practice development, but also in anything I ever did. That's when you're especially confused when twenty-five years later, one of the guys, who has just passed on, surprised me and came into the office to apologize for his behavior and what he had done to me so erroneously twenty-five years earlier. The other two never did that. You know you pay the price in a variety of ways. You have to understand how it is when you're young and trying to start your own business. Sometimes you have the frame of reference of ten, fifteen, twenty years of experience before you started your own practice. I didn't. There were lots of adverse challenges.

When people gave you a little encouragement that was helpful. I don't know, if I'd had one mentor, if that would have been helpful. That's why with the younger lawyers, you try to be helpful. My dad was a farmer in Iowa; my brother was a professor at Iowa State. And I didn't have any relatives in California, etc. I didn't have one mentor, but I had a lot of men and women a bit older who gave me a little encouragement.

Santorum, Richard: Yeah, but it usually comes in combination with a vice leaked into the equation. Standing up for what you believe is right, but doing it in a way that could have been done better, or doing it in way that could have left a little bit of the puffery out, the arrogance out, the pride out. There's always an aspect to what you do, where you create the hook for someone to get you. The book that I wrote, *It Takes a Family*, I'm very proud of that book. There are some lines in there that I just left right out there to whack me with. I look back and I say, "Stupid! That was a little arrogant, trying to be a little cute, where you didn't take into consideration how someone might read that. On the abortion debate, you say things in a way that would just be a little bit rough. Were they not true?"

Everything I said I can defend as what I believe to be true, but when you are out there speaking the truth as you are called to do, you also want to take into consideration not how you mean it, but how people will hear it. That's a hard thing to do, considering the world is so broken; there are a lot of imperfect ears out there, so you can't twist yourself into a knot trying to say things that don't offend. That's not what I'm trying to say. You don't have to say them in a way that you know will be offensive.

Since good character is currently in short supply in politics today, where can it be found, and how can it be developed?

Black, Charlie: Part of our obligation, for those of us who have been around in politics and government for a long time, is teaching and training young people and the people with whom we work, sometimes even older people. I usually summarize it for young people in politics in that there are two essential things: that your word is good and that you are loyal to your friends. There are other things that they need to be taught, but if they get those two correct, then that's a pretty good path to character development.

The other thing, for those of us who are involved in campaigns and government and those of us involved in the spin-offs of campaigns and government, like public affairs—you have to make sure you are picking or supporting people of good character. Sometimes, somebody is very effective in politics or in a government job or in a private-sector job, whose character is marginal, and you need not reward those people.

Bliley, Tom: You know, I disagree with the premise of the question. Sometimes Washington gets a bad rap. Probably more often than not, it deserves it, but there are countless people that I have come to know and respect over several decades in public service that have genuine character and really do want to serve the people. Obviously I have a lot of Republicans on that list, but there are also Democrats. I may disagree with everything they have to say, but I know they are committed to their ideals and are not out for any personal gain.

I would add that our current process of redistricting does not help matters. State by state, the system is skewed to allow candidates of a particular political flavor to get elected—whether they've got character or not.

Bulger, William: I've always been grateful for this, and I fear it is becoming a little self-congratulatory: I was really blessed because I had people like Father Carl Thayer, my friend Dan Holland—Dan Holland had lived on the Jamaican Way next to James Michael Curley, and had worked for him as a secretary in his office when he was governor of the Commonwealth. [Dan is] an attorney and top-notch individual. Carl Thayer, he loved everything that was said about politics and the ancients. He would say to me, "If you know the ancient Greeks, you don't have to know anyone else."

I still remember when I was coming under some kind of fire; we were talking about the very first lines of one of the greatest speeches, Demosthenes's "The Crown Oration." And very briefly, here's Demosthenes addressing this audience of Greeks, and he says, "You sat here and listened as Aeschines said that I was not worthy of the crown." Demosthenes was being offered the crown because he had done such great public service. And Aeschines had said, "He's not worthy of it; don't give it to him!" He went on and on and on disparaging Demosthenes.

It falls to Demosthenes now to defend himself. Demosthenes notices something in his audience. They're increasingly inattentive. "Oh what intensity of intention you pay to Aeschines, but you don't want to hear from me. Because I am forced by the circumstances to tell you what a good person I am. And you're not interested. Why? Because men have always had an ear for gossip and invective." Of course, we can't get enough gossip! We can't get enough invective! We can't get enough of it, and we listen. Someone is being brought down. There is a huge appetite for it. It's human nature. And Thucydides says, "Human nature is the one constant through human history. It's always there." That's why he told us about these terrible wars; he wanted to warn people. We do read here and there about all these changes, but they're not differences in substance—we remain the same, despite what people say.

Cardin, Ben: That's a good question. The fact that [lack of integrity] is rewarded… We still need to increase integrity in politics. You've got to be true to your principles, and you've got to be true to the right moral compass. Let me give you one example from my life. I very much believe in organized labor; I very much believe in organized bargaining, and I believe in labor rights, but I also believe in free trade and fair trade. But there are conflicts there. So you have to be true to what you believe in, but then communicate.

When I voted for a trade agreement that labor didn't particularly like, I lost some support for a period of time. I think [it was] about pension reform in Maryland, and we had to get it done. But teachers didn't particularly like it, even though I'm very much in support of our educational system. So there are times you'll have these conflicts, yet you must stand up for what you believe in, explain it, and keep an open door so that people will understand what you are trying to do.

When I think about voting against the flag-burning amendment, which our veterans' groups very much wanted—and I believe very strongly in our veterans' groups, but they're wrong on that issue. You try to explain it, go to their meetings and listen to what they say. Stand up for what you believe in. Yes, there'll be some times that people will get upset and might vote against you in a given election or send you a nasty note. At the end of the day, they'll respect the fact that you're true to what you believe in and that you're open as to how you came about to your decision and that you're willing to listen.

I said that at the beginning, being willing to listen is important. You've got to listen. Listening is not just saying "I'm going to listen," and I won't have any impact on them. Listening means I'm going to disagree with them, but it'll have an impact, and it may change my view. It may not. But I really listen. So it could have impact in what I believe by listening to people. That is a very important part of character.

Carlson, Richard: I think our country abounds with people of basic good character. These are men and women who have a lot of practice at being honest; a lot of practice at being sincere; a lot of practice at being respectful of other people's views, opinions, and feelings. It is the repeated practice of those things, just like smooth ground strokes or a strong serve in tennis, which make the behavior second nature. The media culture in which we live, for people piling on at the top of the food chain, tends to wring some of these virtues out of them in their scramble to be noticed, to be quoted on TV—and to be politically correct in doing so. Political correctness, by the way, is a basic enemy of truth-telling, and the offering up of certain opinions or language, imposed upon us by political liberals and zealously maintained by "protected" special interest groups as a gainful lever for themselves through the mainstream media, which always serves as their advance guard. The further development of character in future leaders has to be through example at the top by our leaders.

Eckstein, Paul: Definitely. Why do we teach Bible tales and Bible stories to young children? Why do we have people go to religious school? We are trying to teach virtue and exemplary character. We learn through stories. I learned at a young age through stories of the Old Testament and biography. I was not a big reader of fiction until I went to college. I think I learned my lessons about character in reading biographies. I can still see the set of orange-covered biographies, maybe fifty of them. To the extent I am a reader, I read biographies.

My maternal grandmother was a great storyteller. She was German, came to the United States in her sixties. She knew enough English so we could communicate. She told Grimm's fairy tales. I particularly remember "Hansel and Gretel." I learned lessons from the fairy tales as well.

We haven't talked as much as we should have about how character is developed. We talked a little bit; maybe we talked around it. Start off by developing it with stories that one learns in Sunday school or religious school. The first lessons of your parents, you learn it by seeing what your parents do. You teach it by your role models, maybe grade school teachers, maybe high school teachers, your mentors. Long before you get to where a difficult decision has to be made, where character counts; you should have had many occasions to form your character by considering what good choices are available when faced with similar, if not identical, situations.

You may have considered the right choice in one situation and then had the crisis in another situation. You have to reach back in experience and by analogy, do the right thing. It's very easy to equivocate when called upon to make difficult decisions and rationalize, unless you have a clear view of what is right. To get off the tracks. I've seen it in political campaigns. I've never been in government, but I've seen people who don't have a clear view of what is right.

Here is a pretty good example of where maybe the end was right but not the means. When the Iraq War began, within a week or so of the war beginning, [Lori Piestawa became] the first Native American woman [serving in the U.S. armed forces] ever [to be] killed in combat, and our governor, Napolitano, rushed through a name change of a mountain in Phoenix, Squaw Peak, that is now called Piestewa Peak. The law says you are not supposed to change the name of anything until five years after someone dies. This was rushed through dishonestly. I think it cost Mario Lopez his job. There was no real sense that procedures matter. It was the end that mattered, and to "do something right" as opposed to "doing something right, in the right way." It hurt Napolitano early on. It certainly hurt Lopez. That is a good example of not understanding that procedures matter and trying to take advantage of a situation to do "the right thing." To take a name that many Native Americans didn't like and take advantage of a situation.

I want people who are generous. In a law firm environment, you have to be able to sublimate your ego so that other people take credit. Ronald Reagan gave the best advice when he advised, "There is no limit to what you can accomplish, so long as you don't care who gets the credit."

In our old iteration at Brown and Bain, we understood very well that the ratio between the highest paid partner and lowest paid partner was three-to-one, and we rewarded those at the lower end, the people who did the work, the *grinders*. In our new environment, the ratios can be as high as twenty-to-one and the *finders* are rewarded, and this is a reflection of what's happening in the legal market, the finders are disproportionately rewarded, and team production and team effort is not as rewarded.

Lynch, Tom: You have to start young, with accountability and responsibility. You have to foster praise and do what we can for those who have a selfless attitude. How is it that a Congressman can come to Washington and spend ten years or much less there and become a millionaire on a Congressional salary? I just don't understand how that happens. It never happened to anyone in the military on a military salary. We should expose and make examples of those who are greedy, unsavory characters.

We don't call it character [at the Naval Academy], but we call it "ethics development" and "leadership development." If you are going to be a good strong leader, lead men in combat, protect them, and be entrusted with their lives, you cannot be a cheat, a scoundrel, or a greedy person only out for yourself. So all of those values we cherish most—selflessness, courage, honesty, and trustworthiness—all these values that make good character and a good strong leader. They are all embodied in the leadership and ethics training conducted today at the service academies.

The Midshipmen and cadets are held accountable for their actions. You can go to any high school today and find most students with two or three false ID cards. If you're a midshipman at the Naval Academy and use a false ID card, that's a dismissible offense: false pretense. That is a lie. It is pretty hard when a Midshipman is on liberty with sandals and Bermuda shorts in Fort Lauderdale at 2 AM and wants to have a beer and impress his girlfriend, but he lied and will be dismissed.

[The Naval Academy teaches young men that they cannot be good lead-

ers without developing good character. So what Tom is saying is that Congress should be more like the Naval Academy!]

Manatt, Charles: Good character is in politics. As far as I understand it (universal principles), it definitely exists. It hasn't changed a whole lot over the period of time. You can go back two thousand years and talk about morality and democracy or lack thereof. And then flash forward and in the modern era, democracy started with us in 1776. So I mean we had pieces of it in England and other places, but not to any great extent. And then you go to these upheavals and convulsions and the campaigns of the 1830s, '40s, '70s, and '80s. Were the Muckrakers of good character at the Lincoln-Douglas debates when they took a goat and threw it right into the face of Douglas? By our standards today, this would be very harsh, very coarse. But by the morality of those times, that was a way to make a statement. And that was a very much harsher way than a pie in the face at the end of a program today.

I think the morality of the United States, for the vast majority of citizens, is very much in place. You are always going to have huge exceptions. You always look at Hollywood, which is also going toward whatever this center's specific morality is. You're going to go through a long convulsion now about Gordon Gecko and the greed on Wall Street and the fact that big money boys both fully understood (or didn't) the derivatives and insurance swaps. And all the rest of the people in the world are paying for it. Everyone is paying for his or her arrogance and deceit.

Fair and balanced. Keep family, health, politics, all of it balanced.

Santorum, Richard: One of my heroes in politics from the past was William Wilberforce. There was a movie made about him recently called *Amazing Grace*. Wilberforce was a Member of Parliament in England, a contemporary of William Pitt. His great objects were the abolition of the slave trade in England and the reformation of manners. I pattern myself after Wilberforce in many respects, because I see the struggle for the recognition of the rights of the unborn as a similar civil rights struggle as the recognition of the rights of Africans.

Josiah Wedgewood—founder of the Wedgewood Company—made a plate of a black man in chains in a block, and around the plate it said, "Am I not a man and a brother?" And that plate was sold to help finance the abolition movement in Great Britain. Wilberforce knew—and I know that eliminating abortion can't come without change in society as a whole and greater character. When he said reformation of manners, you think of manners as "please" and "thank you," and is the table setting right; but manners is really respect and civility toward each other. There are lots of ways of doing it. Civil society, civic organization, the family, and the church are the great shaping institutions that can provide and impart this kind of knowledge.

When I wrote the book *It Takes a Family*, I spent a lot of time on "social capital"—on trying to build trust and respect. In this society the avenues, the places that have done so have been family, faith, and civic organizations like the Boy Scouts. There are a lot of organizations that build character and civic responsibility—the military is another one. There is also a ton that tears down the popular culture. So one of the things I try to do since I left Congress is to enter the popular culture to create more character affirming content out there.

How can we reconcile the tension between principle and power politics in Washington?

Bingaman, Anne: The thing that takes the most character in these government jobs—and actually makes it easy—is if you don't want another job ... I thought I could honestly offer myself to the president of the United States, as a candidate for the job that I could do. I never thought I could do another job and I never wanted to do another job.

If someone had said to me, do you want to be Deputy Attorney General—I didn't know squat about that. I'm not being noble here. If you take a job, you should better be qualified to do that job from the first day, not eighteen months later, or your agency will suffer—your reputation suffer—and no way is that something I'd try to do.

Black, Charlie: Let me start this answer by saying that the great majority of people in Congress and who take high jobs in the Federal government are honest people of good intentions. And they enter their jobs wanting to do the right thing. But they're all human. And power is a great temptation and something that can corrupt some people and, if not corrupt them, make them self-centered more than they might naturally be. Most people who come to Congress have some basic principle, some basic philosophy they want to pursue. So what you want to do is appeal to them that this is in their interest because broadly, philosophically you agree with this, but explain how something is in their political interest.

Right now, given where we are as a country, and where we are in Washington, you hear it said by many people every day that the parties need to work together; leaders need to work together and compromise because that's what the people are demanding. Easier said than done. But back to my word "sacrifice": that requires everyone to sacrifice just a little bit to get things done, and it takes leadership by some people to really get out front and sacrifice. So, in 2006 and 2007, when there was a bipartisan effort to have comprehensive immigration reform, there were a lot of different views—detailed views that people held—but to get a bipartisan agreement it needed a leader like John McCain to come out and support a comprehensive plan, including parts of a plan that, if he had written it himself, he wouldn't have supported. But he did, knowing that he was going to be running for President and knowing that what he did in both '06 and '07 was going to hurt his political campaign.

So again that's an example of sacrificing to try to get things done, an example of compromise requiring sacrifice—at least in McCain's case on that issue—and there are a lot of other issues I could cite where he put that principle of getting things done ahead of power. Clearly, compromise and sacrifice work hand in hand to reconcile power and principle in politics.

Loyalty to your friends also involves being unselfish because sometimes your friends are up and sometimes they're down, but you don't discard them when they're down. And if you do, you won't succeed in politics in the long run, but we see a lot of that type of thing.

Bliley, Tom: Honesty and transparency. Let the American people know what Congress and the existing Presidential administration are up to. Thanks to technology, we've got the tools to do this, whether it's C-SPAN or the Internet. The more information we can provide, the better. Let a well-informed public decide the issues.

Bulger, William: First of all, every bit of this life is all temporary, including these wonderful assets we enjoy. Somebody somewhere has to have some kind of authority somewhere to implement a decision, to make a decision. If it falls to us, and frequently it does, it's because someone else out there trusted us. And when they don't even know what we're doing, that's the test. Again, Father Thayer, "when no one knows," and frequently, by the way, they cannot know what we are doing, it's totally the burden on ourselves. We have to say, "I know that this is an important moment. I want to walk away from this; they will never know." I think of Abigail Adams—of something she said to her husband: "Will they ever know of what kind of sacrifices we made for the good of this country?" She wouldn't begrudge, but she wondered aloud if they would ever come to understand what she and her husband had done for the good cause for which they had sacrificed.

If you know in advance there can't be a huge public gratitude for any public service rendered, we can contrive it; we can build it up. We can go out and get someone to give us a plaque or something like that. But, even then, we know it's artificial. It doesn't have any true meaning. The big reward comes in knowing you've done the best you could. And maybe even it's a purer gift if no one else knows. As long as you know it, what's the difference?

Carlson, Richard: I don't know how you reconcile it. Perhaps by indicting every second member of Congress for felonious ineptitude and sending those convicted to the new and empty Guantanamo Bay facility. Actually, there are many decent members of Congress, but there are more than a handful of dummies. If I could order them around, I would say, "Stand up and be true to yourself." That's what people of principle do—the ones who are few and far between, no matter whether on the left or the right. The ones who have strong principles take terrible hits, usually in this form: "Oh he's just an ideologue!" What does that mean? That he has a belief system and he sticks with it. That's a good thing, not a bad thing.

To thine own self be true. That seems the answer. But there are not a lot of people like that in politics. And if they're going to be principled, then they have to make some friends along the way to help support them in tough times because they will need it.

Lynch, Tom: Transparency! The American people understand the dynamics of politics, the temptations and pressures placed upon our elected representatives, and genuinely want them to be trustworthy and honorable Citizen Kanes. In this day and age, I think it would help a great deal to have every member disclose all campaign contributions, the rationale for each vote cast, [all] district or state projects he is championing with the reasons for them and how the funding is obtained (pork politics or departmental budget), any trips taken (where, why, who funded, cost), and any other pertinent facts the electorate should know. Only by total transparency will we ever relieve the tension between principle and power politics.

Eckstein, Paul: You have to have these values fixed and clear to know what to do. So going back to the Babbitt incident, I was sent by my client to go to Bruce Babbitt to get him to meet with my clients, as he was required by law, to either turn them down or to grant them the off-reservation gaming that they desired. I was a little uncomfortable in being put in a position of doing that, but I knew what my duties were to my client.

So I explained very clearly to Babbitt what I had been sent to do and what we wanted him to do. It was my duty to report to my client exactly what happened and I did, within minutes of leaving my office. It never occurred to me to tell my client anything other than exactly what Babbitt had told me because that's exactly what my client would want me to do. Would he meet? Why would he not want to meet?

Having that sense of responsibility to your client and later the issue of truthfulness, it was automatic. It was automatic that I would represent my client and Bruce Babbitt said a stupid thing, and he realized how much money these Indians had given to the Democratic Party and it was my responsibility to report that. I did. And my testimony reviewed that I don't think Babbitt made the decision based on that; maybe I'm naive. And I tried to put the best picture on my client. I told them exactly what had happened, and I think it was just automatic. I was on automatic pilot.

Life can change in a nanosecond. Things come at you fast. You see it in politics today when someone makes a misstatement. McCain had an opportunity to distinguish himself in the bailout, and what he did was play the political card, but to play it poorly. A different person like Mitt Romney would have played that a lot differently. You've got to be certain in public life where any misstatement will be used against you and played over and over again. You've got to be programmed to do the right thing instinctively.

Santorum, Richard: It comes down to people's decisions and people's motivations. But I'm not too sure I can answer that. I'm not too sure that the people who seek power and who want to use that power are necessarily doing so without principle. That's the problem I have with Washington— that there is an acceptance of legitimacy that you need the power to be able to enforce your principles that you believe are best for everyone.

I would argue that most people in Washington are not seeking power for the sake of power. It may have been the case back in the day that personal power was personal. The ability to do what Lyndon Johnson did. I don't think there are a lot of Johnsons around anymore, who crudely want to wield power for the sake of power. Most of the people are Waxman, who want to wield power because they have an ideology they want to impose on America and the world.

I don't want to wield the power, but I want the ability. And I don't look at Russ Feingold and Henry Waxman or John Dingle or people like that—maybe Dingle is more in line with people like Johnson—Barney Frank—most of these people want to wield power because they have a principled worldview that they believe is best for the country. I respect folks like Feingold. They are dangerous people. I respect them because they're believers. Let's use someone who just left—Ted Stevens. He just loved power. Why? Because his was a very simple game. Take care of my state. His principle was very simple: get as much for my state as I can. It was sort of Johnsonesque. Is that a principle? Yeah. Sure it is. But it is not a high principle or one that has an application around a broad variety of issues, whereas most of the guys who come to Washington right now—most, at least, during the time that I came—were folks where most of it is from a change in the parties from once was regional parties now to ideological parties. So you are getting more ideological people, which makes it harder to get things done in a bipartisan way because we really don't agree, which, by the way, isn't a bad thing.

Does how a person chooses to act under pressure reveal their character?

Black, Charlie: No one knows you have it until you are under pressure. It is easy to tell the truth, be unselfish, and be loyal to your friends when everything is going well. It is under pressure [that] you have to make the decision to do the right thing. Let's use that same example of the comprehensive immigration reform bill. There were Senators of both parties who cosponsored the bill and who agreed to compromise and sacrifice. When the pressure was on toward the end of the debate, they walked away from it. People from both parties. I'm not saying that they are of bad character, but some of them couldn't take the heat despite having committed to the effort.

Bliley, Tom: Sure. Pressure certainly reveals what a person's instincts are in how they act, and that reveals a great deal about his or her character.

Bulger, William: Oh, I think it does. It's what people do. What a man does. That's what counts. For example, a person who violates his oath, his bond of matrimony. He's made some kind of an understanding with a person. It seems as though he should take that very seriously. I understand it is very easy to slip and fall. A sustained period of infidelity seems to me a sign that the person doesn't know the meaning of honorable, virtuous behavior, doesn't know how important it is. And it must be done at every level, personal and public, if it is going to be true.

Cardin, Ben: It's already there. Pressure tests your character, but I'm not sure it *develops* your character. It's part of maturity, being able to handle difficult moments. There is nothing more difficult than to send soldiers into harm's way for a legislature. I've had several votes on that. It does test your maturity that you're prepared to allow the moment not to take control of you.

Carlson, Richard: Yes, it does. This is self-aggrandizing to say, but I have been better under pressure and more satisfied with my behavior than in any other mode. I reacted reasonably and intelligently as the pressure increased. I wouldn't have known that except for having been tested so many times. Maybe it's a matter of normally having too many choices available to you in calm, warm-water situations, whereas in a crisis you don't have any time to fiddle, so you make the right choice—or the moral one if that is called for—and do it. That's what occurred in my own life. How many times have you said to yourself, after hearing someone tell of an experience, I wonder how I would react if that happened to me? I have had many opportunities to find out, and I have never been disappointed in my responses in my own internal after-action report. I certainly can't say that about my behavior in noncritical circumstances. Too much time on your hands is the devil's work-shop, my mother used to say.

Eckstein, Paul: People build up through a lifetime choices and experience, and when confronted with a crisis call upon a lifetime of those choices and experience. They don't really have the time to strike down a different path. Life turns on a dime, and if you don't have a strong sense of ethics and responsibility, it is very easy to get off track. I've seen it, particularly in campaigns that are in lesser positions that do not have the wherewithal to strike out on their own and don't have the courage to stand up to say something is wrong. If you have principle, you have the experience to stand up to these issues. I had experience coming into the impeachment case because I had gone through something similar with the athletic director at ASU, which involved an awful lot of pressure. Having gone through that, seeing how I had reacted to that, helped me in the impeachment trial.

Lynch, Tom: Most definitely. They are at peace with themselves; they have confidence in the decisions they will make. They have a sense of responsibility that I cannot fold in this situation. I've got to show for my subordinates strength and courage under fire. No one likes a whiner.

In the military, because of the hierarchical structure, it's especially important for the most senior person to set the tone and provide the example. Because of the nature of the business—at sea with complex weapons and electronic systems coupled with the constant vagaries of the weather, operations, or breakdown in machinery or human error—there are frequent opportunities for things to go awry very quickly and for men of character to step forward.

Manatt, Charles: Starting a law practice reveals character. You don't panic, and you think it through. And if you're doing something you want to do and you think is right, and again you have some reasonable chance of pulling it off, then you go ahead with it. Adversity reveals character. For example, try hanging out your own shingle in LA with two Savings and Loans and two banks in formation at about $7500 each to start your law practice. And there you are in a city where there are a lot of law firms and big-time lawyers and you're twenty-seven years old. Well, many would consider that adversity … and strong character with courage was revealed when I opened Manatt Phelps.

Running for party office is adversity by definition, and it reveals character. Overall I have run twenty-four times, and I have won nineteen and lost five. And obviously you learn a lot, [even] more from the ones you lose. Adversity. I've learned a lot from the political races and how you win and don't win, and what you must do to win.

After Reagan got elected, my character was tested. The DNC was in the same shape as the embassy was in Saigon: the chairs were overturned and our word-processing machine was a 1957 robo-typer. And Pat Cadell had attached our only account to a debt the day I was elected party Chairman. Not only did we not have much money, but also a legal process attached. That was adversity on the political side. There was lots of adversity to be found on the business and the law firm side as well. One crowd was after one of my dearly beloved partners, trying to give him a criminal indictment. Perhaps I should or should not have come down to talk to a U.S. Attorney about that. But I did. And happily the partner is still alive and was never called to the bar of justice. But those kinds of adversities pretty substantially scare you. You just hang in there.

Santorum, Richard: Sure. Every time. There are a million examples. It reveals it. And conversely, adversity shows poor character, too. Bill Clinton is probably the best example of that. When he got in a tough spot, you saw the real Bill Clinton, which was at heart a phony, a fraud. I used to call him a sociopath.

What traits do you think enable a person to avoid misbehavior?

Black, Charlie: The devil is everywhere. We are all tempted all the time. Having faith and keeping current with the teachings of your faith, and having family with a certain priority helps you avoid a lot of temptation. I definitely want to put in a plug for having a sense of humor in the business of politics and government. For plenty of people, because they have a good sense of humor, it helps their relationships with people even when they disagree. And anger on an important issue or on a small issue never helps relationships or an ability to get along or an ability to get things done. So having a good sense of humor and knowing when to laugh at yourself are important attributes. Some people don't have it and are very serious about everything, but I think it would help them to have a sense of humor.

Bliley, Tom: Capitol Hill is well known for its humor. I think it got me through a lot of legislative ordeals. It doesn't replace faith and family, but it sure does help. And if you can laugh now and then while sticking to your core beliefs, you've got no reason to listen to that siren song.

Bulger, William: There is no guarantee. There is no guarantee anywhere that a person would not have his head turned, but I think the practice of good conduct, the day-to-day determination to be sober, to be industrious, to be true to very lofty principles, gives a far greater ability to remain steady and constant than little minor deviations here and there along the way. For example, if people violate maintaining a sober habit, one of sobriety, clearly if one is steady at that, there is a very good chance that other good things will follow. That is one of the places where if people falter in that regard, they much more easily misbehave in others in both public and private morality.

You have to try to acquire good habits. And also a person whose behavior is good, it comes to be known. I don't doubt fewer temptations are thrown his way. Who is going to be around to induce bad conduct if the person is never, ever inclined to behave badly?

There's a great thing to keep in mind: even with the press banging away, saying all these ugly things. Most people even at ground level understood that there is media perception, but the public knows a different perception. I'm back to the business of the media. Why would the public reelect you every two years if you were a crook, if you're the head of the mob—a professor from Harvard used to always call me the head of the mob. Then, of course, I'd give him a little needle. He told me he was going to report me to the Anti-Defamation League, and I told him I was going to report him to the Knights of Columbus. They're laying it on. Yet, why are these people still electing you? It's because they know.

Back to my friend, Demosthenes, you have to have some confidence in the public, too. They know. There is some sort of good instinct at work among the constituents. They might even enjoy seeing you get taken down a peg. They may see it as underserved. It'll keep you from getting too big a head. They know, too, it is an entertainment. It's a nasty entertainment, but it is an entertainment because if they believed one fraction of this stuff, they would never vote to keep you in office. You would not be worthy of it. So they must know that there is this sort of nonsense going on in the background. I was better off when for eighteen years there was no television. I didn't watch the television, I didn't have it, and I didn't own it. I'd hear in the morning, "you should have seen the thing last night."

Cardin, Ben: Humor is critically important: if you don't have a sense of humor, you can't survive. You've got to turn things around by humor. Humor is medicine, it's a weapon, and it's all of the above. If you don't have humor, you can't survive in my business, particularly in the United States Senate.

Carlson, Richard: Yes, but I don't know about the immune part. I consider a sense of humor one of the more important things you can have, and love and support of family is the other. Still, there are plenty of men who have gotten into trouble and they had both. The ability to laugh at yourself is more than just useful; it is necessary. Self-deprecation is a very important part of that humor. It keeps you from becoming too self-important.

Eckstein, Paul: Jack Brown thought that a sense of humor was a sign of intelligence, and I don't know if he's right or not. But I think he's mostly right. It's important to be smart and to be able to figure out who's after you and who's not. You can almost assume that everyone wants your position. I like the statement about what's the difference between Washington and New York. In New York, the coin of the realm is coin, and just because someone makes more money doesn't mean you'll make less money. In fact, your neighbor making more money helps you make more money, and your neighbor making less money means you'll make less money.

The coin of the realm in Washington is power, and everyone wants the position that is right above the position they have. Right up and above to the vice-president, who in this case, ran for president and would much rather be president than vice-president. Because people view the world in terms of power instead of money, and someone having more power does not translate into you having more power, Washington is a much meaner place than New York. You have to understand that to survive in Washington.

A self-deprecating sense of humor gets you over a lot of difficulties. I do think having a sense of humor helps a lot. It can't be mean and cutting. Jack Kennedy was a master of that, and that got him by an awful lot. The best line about Jack Kennedy and Bobby Kennedy: someone asked [Jack Kennedy] how was it that [he] wanted to announce that Bobby [his] brother was chosen as Attorney General. [His response was] "Here's how I'm going to do it; I'm going to get on my back porch in my house in Georgetown at two in the morning. I'm going to look down the alley one way and I'm going to look down the alley the other way, and I'm going to say, "It's Bobby" (in a whisper). He was able to deflect Bobby's lack of experience with the line that he wanted him to get a little experience before he went out on his own instead of trying to defend him. It worked. Plus Bobby was a pretty good Attorney General.

Lynch, Tom: With a sense of humor and a quick wit, you're more apt to not take yourself or life itself so seriously, and it helps you realize that we're here for a very short period of time and we are all in the same boat.

Regardless of your background, your religion, your rank, your status, or your financial position, we're all going to be back in the fetal position and then to ash in a relatively short period of time. Humor, therefore, provides an escape mechanism to better understand and realize that the irritants that occur in everyday life are not so serious and, when put in perspective, allows us to sit back and smile.

Santorum, Richard: I don't know if it is a sense of humor. I know some fairly clever and funny people who have gotten into a lot of trouble, particularly if you are really clever. Most of the people who get into trouble are smart and know they are. They know they can get away with more than other people. You would get into more trouble if you had less of a sense of humor. I will buy that. I'm not sure that humor is integral to staying out of trouble.

Intellect is a big part. Of all the gifts God gives you, the most troublesome is a brilliant mind. I look at my little Isabella and Brendan Kelly and all these little kids who are "simple," and in that simplicity is great virtue.

Do you believe there are common traits successful leaders display in political life?

Bingaman, Anne: The first thing that is crucial is a very strategic sense of what your goals are and how to achieve them. I mean substantively. Whatever your area of interest is, you have to set goals and you have to really work towards them because it's not simple up there. You have to work and get educated. I remember when Jeff got here. His campaign manager was a very smart guy, very unorthodox. You would never have picked this guy out to manage a campaign in a million years. But he was very smart and Jeff had the brains to see how smart he was. And we got back here and he said to this individual, Ken Richardly, well, we've got to pick the issues here that I am going to focus on back here. And this guy said to him, "Look, there are so many important things that it doesn't matter. What matters is how much you care about them. You have to have the passion for what you are doing. So figure out what you really care about and that will be what matters." And that was fantastically smart advice. And following that advice, Jeff picked education, health, and international trade.

You can't be something you're not. You are who you are. But I think success is being strategic about being back here. In other words, there is so much going. I went into the antitrust division, and I had a fifty-page agenda of what I wanted to accomplish by July 15. To come up with it, I interviewed about eighty people from the time in late April I got the job until I was sworn in on June 18, 1993. And I dictated this agenda and shared it with all the top staff. And we got all of it done and a lot more. But only afterwards did I realize how crucial that was because once you are in one of these government jobs, the incoming missiles start and you're reacting and you are fending of this and that. And unless you have your own very clear goals that you care about and have thought through—and keep thinking about and focusing and reviewing constantly—then you're going to react to everything, not act, and get dragged in a thousand different directions, and basically you'll get far less done.

Bliley, Tom: Honesty, integrity, and vision. Know what you want to do, make it clear, stick to it, and don't be afraid to make mistakes. It's an old phrase, but you only fail if you don't try. A warm manner doesn't hurt. I've never regretted not getting in a shouting match with one of my adversaries, though the temptations were always there.

Bulger, William: You have to see it as something worthwhile in and of itself. You have to be a person who does not need any adulation. Frequently, the only persons who can give you any satisfaction in that regard are people who want your attention. You have no right, really, to frequently give it.

Cardin, Ben: Honesty. Humility. I'm spoiled because I go home every night, so I get a dose of reality in my neighborhood and in my family every night. That's very important. It's a sense that regardless of what you've achieved lately, whether you're a Supreme Court Justice or a United States Senator, you're just like everyone else in your community. When you lose that, and you think that you're really something special, it will compromise your character.

Carlson, Richard: One trait common in political life, I am sorry to say, is an inability to loosen up. Here is my example.

I was asked if I would give Pete Wilson some training on how to appear on television in adversarial situations. Pete was mayor of San Diego at the time. He planned to run for governor, though later he switched it to the Senate. I consented, and I drove up to Los Angeles from La Jolla, where I lived. We taped five mock shows.

We finished about two o'clock. Pete was supposed to fly back to San Diego with Bob White, his horse holder, through Burbank Airport. The flight was cancelled. Pete had to be in a dinner in La Jolla with Helen Copley, who owned both San Diego newspapers. Bob asked if I'd mind driving Pete back.

It was hot that day. Traffic was terrible. It was stacking up to be a four-hour drive to La Jolla. Pete and I chatted superficially. Pete asked if I'd want a beer. I got off the freeway and drove into a strip mall liquor store. Pete ran in and got a six-pack of cold beer and a couple of small paper bags to hide the cans just like a homeboy on the corner. We drank three beers each. It could not have been colder or better, and the conversation perked up. We sat and talked about his dad, a retired advertising man who had had a great influence on his life. We talked about the Marine Corps, about women we had known, about annoying people in San Diego, about families, and our lives as kids. We had a great conversation.

Over the many years since that drive from LA, I have run into at least four people who have said, "Oh you're Dick Carlson! Pete Wilson once told me about you and that he had the best conversation with you, for hours, in a car in bumper-to-bumper traffic." And it was true. I think it was even better and maybe more memorable for Pete than me because he was a public figure, a politician—a decent and interesting man who could seldom, if ever, let himself go conversationally, even with people he knew.

Lynch, Tom: Ronald Reagan was admired and respected because he always made those around him feel comfortable. You knew that if you were going to suffer, he would be suffering with you, and if you were going to celebrate, he was going to be patting you on the back. Maybe not a trait, but a demeanor that is important for effective politicians and leaders.

Santorum, Richard: I try to look at success as Thomas More would: through the eyes of God as opposed to through the eyes of man. If you look at success through the eyes of God, then it is very easy to figure out the virtues that lead you to success. If you look at success through the eyes of man, you are caught with the reality, particularly today, of how fallen man really is. Worldly traits can bring worldly success. Barack Obama is a good example of this—cordial, talented at public speaking, but these are only worldly traits.

What stories or anecdotes might you share that teach good character?

Bliley, Tom: The New Testament certainly comes to mind!

If I were giving advice to my friends on Capitol Hill, it would be that, while you always want to stick to your principles, the most satisfying accomplishments you will ever have would be bipartisan ones. All of the major laws I have had the privilege of working on—the 1996 Telecom Act and Gramm-Leach-Bliley among them—were done on an overwhelmingly bipartisan basis. You may not get everything you want, but you get a result that can make you proud. Frankly, I think the same holds true in just about every workplace.

Eckstein, Paul: Look. One of the reasons that George W. Bush has had credibility problems is because of the way he lead us into the war; whether he lied deliberately or not, he clearly cut corners in presentation of the case. Once you lose credibility as a politician or as a lawyer, it's almost impossible to get it back. I just do not believe the man. There are millions and millions of other people who say that you lied to us once, and we are not going to be taken for fools again. It applies to LBJ, to a lot of people. A lot of politicians lie.

Sometimes one's principles come into a clash with one another. A lot of people thought that loyalty should have trumped truthfulness in the Babbitt affair, but it was the opposite: truthfulness always trumps.

Here's a good story. It's not one I've told you. I would not have been able to handle the pressures of the impeachment trial had I not represented a man by the name of Fred Miller in 1979. Fred Miller was the athletic director of Arizona State University. He and Frank Kush, who was the football coach, had been charged with violating the student's civil rights when the student who was a former football player lost his scholarship. The case was a ridiculous case, but the student claimed that Frank had grabbed him by the facemask and hit him during the Washington vs. ASU football game in 1978.

The kid files this lawsuit. I get hired to represent Fred Miller. On the day I get hired, Fred Miller terminates the football coach, Frank Kush, because he has evidence that Frank Kush lied. And more important than lying about the event, Kush was encouraging other people to lie on his behalf. And when Fred Miller went to him and confronted him and said, "Frank it's okay if you hit the football player. Don't worry about it, we'll deal with that." The football coach continued to maintain he hadn't hit him, and all this was made up.

Well there were six witnesses who said that they saw him hit him, but more importantly, there were three witnesses who came forward and said that Frank had told them that they all had to stick together, even if that meant that to do so they had to lie, cheat, and steal. So Fred Miller is faced with this situation of a football coach who is a God here. The field is now named after him. So what does he do? He terminates the guy, and he stands as a rock as people come after his scalp.

The day he did that, it is the night before the ASU-Washington football game a year later. I'm up in the skybox with him, and the fans are shaking their fists; they're stomping. I thought they were going to get up there and throw Fred Miller over the stadium edge and throw me along with him. I thought I was going to accompany him to a press conference to explain why Kush was terminated, but the college president was a coward and would not allow us to do that. So Fred did that, but he never really recovered from that because he lost his job.

I told Fred and I told a number of people that his was an act of incredible physical and moral courage. I learned how to deal with pressure, angry mobs, near violence. I also learned to follow your gut because my gut was to lay it out—why Kush was being suspended. Three days later we did that when I was representing Fred Miller and not the university. It just had to be done. I learned a lot of lessons in that. I went from October 9 to the end of the December when the president fired both Kush and Miller.

Jack was like Fred, a giant, this rock who not only took it. I remember one day in court, after the judge left, the judge's courtroom deputy comes up to Jack and Jack just lets loose on the deputy. And he said, "Now calm down, Jack; you don't want me to tell the judge that." Jack was so strong and showed so much leadership. People said I did the same thing during the

Mecham impeachment when Mecham was playing with me and pronouncing my name every which way. And I just stood there and took it. I don't think I could have if I had not seen Fred Miller and Jack Brown.

Manatt, Charles: Debates certainly are a good starting point for displaying good judgment, or lack thereof, in political types. I remember my first debate. I was the college Chairman of the Kennedy campaign, and my friend Bill Steiger and the future fine Republican congressman from Wisconsin who has since passed, well, we debated at a small, Catholic girls' school. Now I thought, my gracious I've got Kennedy and he's got Nixon—there's some real potential for fun debates. And the first debate of the actual candidates came along, and Kennedy looked like JFK always looked. And Nixon looked like he had a four or five o'clock shadow. Imagine. Forty-five years later, that's all people remember—that Dick Nixon had that shadow, like they remember in the '76 debate with Carter that President Ford proclaimed Poland as free. Then comes Governor Reagan very much, I think, like Obama-san. Whatever we get with these two, they make people feel comfortable in their skins as President Reagan did against Jimmy Carter. I will never forget in '88, when I was asked to raise the money for the Bush-Dukakis debates, the Democratic side in LA, and I did. So I've ARCO, Bank of America, Northrop, and Rocodine—many fine companies, most of which are gone now—Security Pacific, First Interstate Bank, and I'm looking at this TV, when this jerk was asked the question, "What would you do if your wife was murdered and raped?" And he says he would have a cup of tea. And I thought, God! We've got to have a better system for running these debates in the future.

Santorum, Richard: Yes, based on your last question, "what is success?" Go back to partial-birth abortion. We put that bill forward in 1995, '96, we lost. I looked at how we entered that debate and engaged in it. We did all the right things, but the other side lied. The other side deceived. It was just lies and deception, yet through those lies and deception they were able to convince enough people who weren't paying enough attention to vote with them, including the president of the United States. And we lost. Then we came back two years later and went through the same thing. Even though more things came out about how they had lied, how they had deceived, they still won. Then we came back two years later, and we were going to do the same thing, and the Supreme Court knocked us down. Then we came back three years later, and we were able to be successful.

Now, I would make the argument that all of those failures were in fact vital for a larger success—that had we not lost in '96, '98, and 2000, particularly in '96 and '98, the issue of partial-birth abortion would have been unknown to the American public. Had Bill Clinton just signed this bill on this strange and rare procedure, this would have never been an issue; no one would have known about it, and the public's perception of abortion would not have changed as it did over those years. We made more progress on the issue of abortion, particularly among young people, than anything else since 1972. So we had, on the face of it to the world, a humiliating defeat that in actuality was a huge success.

Look at things from the eyes of God not from the eyes of man. I lost my last election. I'll never forget. I told my wife; she was stunned. It was 8:30 PM, a half-hour after polls had closed, and they called my race. I had a smile on my face. "You're kidding," she said. "No. I lost. They just called it. I feel great. God's got something else planned for me." I went around and talked to my staff; I had a smile on my face. I went up, gave my concession speech. I felt nothing but gratitude for the people of Pennsylvania, even though I had gotten beaten worse than any incumbent senator had in thirty years. I felt nothing but gratitude, and even to this day, I feel nothing but gratitude. This state had given a kid whose dad was a first-generation American with nothing the opportunity to change my world and to change this world a little bit. I just thank you, thank you. On top of that, you've given me a platform where I can do things, and I can continue to do well. Why should I feel bad about this?

How might we move leaders to be touched by "the better angels of their nature"?

Black, Charlie: Again, it is leadership and leading by example. Everybody takes their cues from others around them, and especially people in politics and government take their cues from political leaders. Everybody in a position of responsibility has to understand that they are influencing people.

People are watching the people that they look up to. There is a responsibility to show character and integrity and truth telling, and you have to be also cognizant of the huge impact you have on people—a point that former President Clinton missed. He did a great many good things. He's a brilliant person. He is the greatest communicator of his generation in politics. We'll see if this new President is as good, but Clinton set some bad examples for millions of young Americans.

Bliley, Tom: Keep our leaders honest, and continue to make things transparent. In this day and age, we have the ability—whether through C-SPAN, the Internet, or otherwise—to make sure that the American people know exactly what their leaders are up to. How are they voting? Who are they meeting with? Who's donating to their campaigns? We have all the right laws on the books, it seems to me; we just need to be sure that there's accountability at the end of the day.

And unpopular as it may be, I think we need to really rethink how our leaders in Washington are compensated. For a young congressman with kids, holding down two homes, being away from family, and working long hours is a real strain. I'm not suggesting we make members rich in office, but removing financial difficulties will go a long way toward ensuring they can focus on their work and get things done for the country.

Bulger, William: I was very fortunate to have the influence of good teachers and good examples in my life on the part of those same teachers. They were good people. I really wanted to be just like them. I had good parents. I'd like to be like them. I wanted them to be proud of me. I wanted to please people. I think with young people it is worth encouraging them, praising them for some action, some behavior. The encouragement is very important because then they don't want to disappoint you. I would imagine very frequently there are people around who would have the opportunity to steal some small object and the prospect of punishment doesn't threaten them as much as the thought that they will disappoint someone. They don't want to do that. That is a powerful motivator. Someone trusts me. I don't want to be untrustworthy.

When people trust you, I think that's powerful. I remember a certain person telling me how he had to carry money from one part of a business to another in downtown Boston:

"It would be horrible to be stopped and robbed because the woman had such confidence in me; she thought I was the most reliable of all people. She would call upon me for these things. I would never want to disappoint her. If I lost the money, I'd rather make it up myself instead of disappoint her. "If they're trusted, then they're most trustworthy."

Carlson, Richard: I don't think that will happen until people demand it on the other end. Maybe that will happen; you see more discontent with politicians and their decisions these days than before. There has got to be a movement that pushes the funnel that brings good candidates to us. Think of Elliot Spitzer. That guy wanted to be President. He was a bully. He used the weight of his office to push people around. That is unacceptable in my world.

A good friend of mine was at a restaurant in New York before Elliot Spitzer got caught with the hookers. My friend is on television, and well known. He told me that Elliot Spitzer came over and said, "Hey ——, I'm Elliot Spitzer, how are you doing?" They had never met before but all celebrities know each other. My friend, an honest man, said, "I have no interest in talking with you! I know all of the things you've done as Attorney General and I don't approve of them!" My friend turned away and declined to shake hands with Spitzer because he dislikes bullies so thoroughly, particularly those who use the power of government to push people around, as Spitzer did multiple times and gloated over it. My friend said to me, "He was only sucking up to me because I'm on TV. Disgusting," As I have gotten older, I have grown to admire that attitude a lot.

Lynch, Tom: The Naval Academy is proud that we challenge our Midshipmen morally, mentally, and physically. There are many ways this is done over the four-year program, and it all begins with "Plebe Year." For most Midshipmen, the transition from high school to college, home to Annapolis, and civilian life to the military are all significant events in their lives. The added pressure during the freshman year is to cause them to perform under stress, and from it they evolve, mature, develop, and gain the confidence needed to be successful in the military. And they are taught the core values of honor, courage, and commitment as well as [receiving] indoctrination in the honor concept that a Midshipman shall not lie, cheat, or steal ... violations are punishable by dismissal.

Every year they teach leadership. Not only do you teach it, but also you practice it. For instance the brigade of Midshipmen is run by the Midshipmen "Stripe-per" organization. The senior, junior, and sophomore class each have different levels of responsibility throughout the brigade. Honor committee, "Stripe-per" organization—a plebe has no stripes; a sophomore has one stripe; a junior gets two stripes; and a senior has one horizontal stripe. If you're Company Commander, you have three; if you're a Battalion Commander, you have four; if you're a Brigade Captain, you have six. And then there is only one six-stripe-per. You have the Corresponding General, CEO, and staff filling in at the various stripe-per positions.

Santorum, Richard: To not look at things in the here and now so much. As Father Neuhaus said in his piece about death, "The mortality rate is still holding at 100 percent. We all have to look at things as the Church sees them: to be in the world but not of the world." That is as important a message to our leaders as any: To think of things not so much in the here and now, but in terms of the future of America and in terms of each one's own future in the hereafter.

Professional Questions

What is the measure of success in political life?

Do you believe there is a collapse of character in modern political life?

Could you cite examples of exemplary character and principled leadership amidst the corrupting culture of Washington?

What skills are necessary for political success?

How do you triage demands on your time? How do you remain focused upon what is right rather than what is expedient?

How do you navigate in a sea of power and corruption between the shoals of what is right and what is wrong?

Have you ever had to stand up to the "show business" of government?

Can you identify successful lobbying and political skills? Are these skills aligned with good character traits?

Can you share personal stories of character situations in your political life?

Imagine yourself in the political setting of your choice. What would it be?

What is the measure of success in political life?

Bingaman, Anne: That's a very good question. One measure is effectiveness—advancing of the issues you care about and choose to work on. A second measure is honesty. We've been talking about that throughout. People are rightly concerned about [it]. I am not close to the Hill at all, but the spate of corruption cases—you can almost look at that as an analogy to Wall Street and the focus on money. Too much focus on money! Obviously, honesty and effectiveness, effectiveness and honesty.

I would say as little demagoguery as possible. That is one of the biggest downsides—people demagogue everything. Just the posturing for the press. It's basically phony. You can see it ten times a day in the news and in the paper. You recognize it. If people would just knock that stuff off—it's a short-term sale, it gets them in the news. But ultimately it breeds cynicism and makes people lose respect for the people doing it—and therefore [creates] less trust in them and more ineptitude in our government. Maybe I'm just talking about Jeff here really. More focus on the substance and less on the form of politics. The press conferences. The PR. It's part of it. The public needs to know. I'm not saying there shouldn't be press conferences, but there is a line and it is often crossed. Just cheap shots. That's what I'm talking about, demagoguery. Just saying the popular or the newsworthy thing to get coverage.

It depends. There have been people who are true prototypes of successful politicians. Let's talk about Alan Cranston. That guy had less overt personality than anyone you can name. I had dinner with him a couple times. He was a machine. Cranston was amazing. And yet, he was elected in California. He was incredible. He didn't demagogue anything. He hardly talked. It took away from his efficiency. The guy was unbelievable. Inhuman, almost. In a state the size of California—and I'm not being critical—it is a huge task just to raise money to run in a state of that size. But what I am saying is that he is an example of not having to demagogue to be a successful politician. And there are plenty of other examples. Dick Durbin. He's the farthest thing in the world from a demagogue.

The problem is, people basically know. People are not stupid. Media does these issues of the moment, get-up for the publicity, and it serves as a cheap shot. It has bred cynicism—a lot of things have bred cynicism. People see it for what it is.

Black, Charlie: It's not always about winning. Success in political life is being a strong advocate for your agenda and the leaders who support your agenda, and doing the very best you can to win. If you went through a few decades and never won anything, you should re-examine your role or your agenda. One or the other. It's doing the best you can on behalf of the leaders and the agenda you are supporting.

When I did political consulting back in the '80s, I used to take on underdog candidates and tough races. I used to turn down safe incumbents who could win with relatively small effort. I could have made the money and had another win for my batting average. But I didn't care about my average; I cared about making a difference. And the best way was to pick people who weren't expected to win, and see if you could pull one or two of them through. So to me I was successful even though I didn't always win.

Let me refer back to another one of my former bosses, Jesse Helms, from whom I learned a lot about integrity and character. When Helms came to the Senate in 1973, there were sixty-three Democrats and thirty-seven Republicans. And even fewer conservatives than the thirty-seven. He would put in amendments that were right-to-life amendments, pro-gun amendments, anti-labor amendments, denying food stamps to strikers, those kinds of things, all the time. And he'd get a vote, and he'd get twelve or thirteen or fourteen votes, and people kept saying, "Well, Jesse, why do you keep doing this? Why don't you pick your spots instead of doing this every week?" And he said two things. First, a saying that he got from his father, that "The Lord does not require you to win. But he does require that you try." I wrote this in an article that I wrote in *Time* magazine upon Helms's death.

Second he said, "We've got to educate people, and maybe we'll get a few more votes next time." Well, a lot of those things that Helms would propose on the floor in the early '70s became law in the early '80s when Reagan was president, and we had a Republican majority in the Senate. Some of them might not have gotten done if he had not started them well ahead, just like Rick Santorum and the partial-birth abortion issue.

Bliley, Tom: Victory at the polls, whether it's in an election or the legislative process. Victory means that you're right on a public policy issue—or that an electorate trusts you to do the right thing on the issues.

Bulger, William: The measure is not poll results. I don't believe it's winning; that's not the measure. You could win elections, but if you had to do things that you deemed bad and not honorable, I think you've given up too much for it. For that reason, I was very fortunate that those conflicts didn't come to pass for me. I didn't have anyone out there that I had to behave badly against. There were no opponents who were that way. I was fortunate. I don't think there is anyone around that thinks that I told a lie about them. I hope not.

Your reputation is your success. It worked that way for me. The people had to have some confidence or trust in me. I think of the miles of slander and libel, the hours upon hours, years. But as I sit here and talk to you, something occurs to me, and I've alluded to it. People could not have believed it. They knew they were being put on and entertained. There's a lot of that.

Cardin, Ben: There are several. I point to things I have gotten done. I use the example of my first major victory in life as an elected official was getting a backstop in a high school field so that the Little League could have a place to play.

It just showed me the power I had in the Maryland General Assembly at ages twenty-two and twenty-three. It taught me a very valuable lesson that, first, I had power; second, I could get things done; and third, I should use it properly.

Little League was important to me growing up. I thought other children should have that opportunity. Since that time there are a lot of things that I've gotten done other than backstops for Little Leagues. I've gotten tax codes changed so that seniors could stay in their homes. I talked to seniors who have been able to take advantage of that. I changed our health care system so we don't have charity hospitals in Maryland. I'm proud of those accomplishments, and there are a lot of things over my career I've been able to accomplish, working with Republicans to get bills in preventative health care or Medicare, improving national savings and retirement savings. The list goes on and on and on. I look back at that, and I'm proud of the fact of being able to use that power, of being able to get someone on the phone who can make a decision at that moment or how I've been able to get a bill enacted into law, or how I've been able to get an agency to change the way they administer the law. That's one way you judge success: how you use the power and opportunity you've had.

The second is the reputation that you have, how people view what you've been able to accomplish. And that's a little more difficult to objectively judge, because people usually say nice things to you personally. It's that intangible.

Third is satisfaction: how well I feel I've used this opportunity. How satisfied I am. In all those respects I feel very satisfied that I've had a very successful career.

Lastly, how you set your own priorities. When I first started in the legislature, I saw a lot of marriages that were destroyed in Annapolis. I was just really worried about that. Maybe it's inconsistent, family life with public life, and it really challenged me in the beginning. But it was not at all inconsistent. Just go home at night. Pick your own priorities: if you want to go drinking every night you can; if you want to go home to your family every night, you can.

Carlson, Richard: That depends on who does the judging. If it is the media or political operatives, then winning is the measure. But that's only in the short term. People's names and reputations count for the long haul. A close friend says politicians invariably come either to a bad end or to a sad end; they never come to a graceful end. He is right. Look at how the media smears some political figures so terribly, at least the ones it doesn't like—hardly ever liberals—and the fallout destroys lives.

An example is my friend Scooter Libby. The liberal media and the leftist attack dogs wanted Dick Cheney and George Bush and Karl Rove. With the help of the lying Joe Wilson, Valerie Plame's husband, they tried mightily, but they couldn't get them, so they set fire to Scooter Libby instead. He was an honorable man, an honest and selfless pubic servant with small children whose life was destroyed by the media and partisan attack mutts. His reputation was crushed, and he lost his law license. It was a travesty of justice that riles me no end.

Ask the average person about Scooter Libby, and he will say something like, "Oh, that's the man who exposed a covert CIA agent. He put her life in danger and was convicted for it." That's all wrong! A total fabrication. He did no such thing. Scooter didn't give that phony woman's name to Bob Novak for his column, which is how this all started. Even Bob said later that he got it from Dick Armitage, Colin Powell's closest friend and his deputy at State. Armitage is a name the average American has never heard. Why is that? Because the media and the Democrats had no interest in tarnishing Colin Powell, whom they long ago decided was a saint. They wanted Karl Rove or Dick Cheney destroyed, and Scooter was Cheney's deputy. It was disgusting and unbelievable!

Eckstein, Paul: We had a governor in the 1990s by the name of Fyfe Symington, who was convicted of making misstatements on various financial [records]. Later the conviction was set aside, and he was given a pardon by Bill Clinton, who Fyfe had saved from drowning many years before. Fyfe is a big-time Republican. Symington and I, despite the fact we come from opposite political sides, respect one another, and I do work for him. I felt this way for a long time, and I finally had a chance to tell him in a dinner in late April this year that I thought he was one of the most successful governors we ever had, not because I agreed with him, but because he had a clear idea of what he wanted to do and he was able to accomplish it. His idea was to eliminate as many taxes as he possibly could; take as much out of the tax base as he could, and he did it. Now he had a vision, and he executed it, much the same way Ronald Reagan had that vision.

Success in political life is having a clear view or vision of what you want to accomplish, and having the skill and energy to do it, whether you ultimately lose an election or not or have other disappointments.

Lynch, Tom: It depends on your point of view. Whatever rank attained or political elections won are, in my opinion, immaterial to one's success. I consider the measure of success in any walk of life to be the person who has led a balanced life, was unconcerned by personal affirmation, always worked to the best of his or her abilities, displayed an empathy for his fellow man, and was known to be a person of character because he or she lived it.

Do you believe there is a collapse of character in modern political life?

Black, Charlie: There's two ways to look at that question. Everyone is a sinner. Some people were sinners in their public life and in their professional life as well as their private life. Every profession has bad apples in it: lawyers, doctors, and preachers as well as politicians. When you have someone of bad character and they get caught, it is a huge story, and everyone knows about it in public life. But I actually do not think that the percentage of people who would engage in Abramoff-type scandals is much higher in politics than in other professions.

Now the other way to look at this is, does our system corrupt or compromise people and make it tough for the people with the strongest character to succeed? Meaning, yes, you have to raise money to run for office, either in the House or in the Senate. And the people who are going to have interests before you make up the large proportion of people who are going to give money. Is that a conflict? Does the system cause the people to vote against their own principles? Or more accurately, does it put their time and attention toward public policy goals that wouldn't be their own priorities, because of campaign contributions? That is the big question. And I do think it is a problem, but I do not, however, have the solution. And I do not believe that most of the reforms that have been proposed are the solution, like public financing, which forces the taxpayers to pay for political campaigns that should be voluntarily funded. And there is not a way to design it so that it is not a huge advantage for incumbents, and reform should be for more competition in our democratic elections and not less.

Then the other way of looking at that is that a good person of good character is going to tell people, "I need your contribution, but I am not going to give you more time and priority than someone who doesn't contribute to me." And live up to that. And I think a lot of people do.

All of which leads to the notion that you not only have to act right, but you have to be really careful that you do not unintentionally err and get yourself into a position where you are unfairly presented as a bad example of character.

Bliley, Tom: It has always been there, due to man's nature. However, it is exacerbated today due to the 24/7 news cycle. We've had so many "gates" since 1974; it's not even funny anymore. But the important thing to remember is that scandal existed long before President Nixon—and it's never been confined to one party.

Bulger, William: Everyone talks about defective human nature. This world here, we describe it as attributable to original sin. Man has transgressed. Man is imperfect; it is his imperfect nature. And it's there. It's permanent. We're always going to be involved in a struggle, and it's the moral question each time. Not all of this is answered with legality and illegality; we're talking about the rightness and wrongness of some acts.

One time there was an effort to unseat me. It was in the early '90s, around 1993. It was a good effort. They never moved beyond five or six people. But one of them was reported to have been misbehaving with a young lady down in the garage. She said he was making comments to her. She went to the personnel people. And the personnel person came to me. The personnel person she told about it is now deceased. He said, "You know, Senator so and so, she's accusing him of such and such." Then he says, "I told someone on your staff about it, and they told me to tell you."

So I called the staff person. I said, "He is in the opposition. We don't know anything about the validity of this claim against him. I am charging you with this responsibility to say nothing about it. This is not the opportunity for us to pull the rug out, to give the business to someone who is against us, because he has a family, and for our wretched little game, it would be a catastrophic result for him."

Toward the end of the struggle, he came in to me and said, "When did you learn about this?"

And I said, "About two months ago. I don't even know if it is true."

He said, "Let me tell you that we were being instructed to find out something like that about you. We would have been out the door with it in ten minutes, if we could ever find any of that. I am so grateful because my poor wife and children…" and so on. That was the reason.

And why am I saying all of this? I wasn't giving up much. Truthfully, they only had five or six votes. But I would have been a shabby person if I had leaped on that, if I had foolishly undone him for a small political advantage.

Cardin, Ben: I'm not so sure I'll agree with that. There's weakness and collapsing at all times. I think back in the history of America, and there's been collapse of leadership at many times. There have been incredible people who have come forward throughout the history of our country in all forms of life, whether it is literary life or sports. I'm not so sure there's a collapse of character in sports when I see sports figures cheating today. I think they've always cheated. Look at what happened in Chicago in 1919. You've always had these problems. This is just human nature. This is part of life.

Then every once in a while things happen which really surprise you, like in Iran. The people are starting to speak up for what they believe in. Who thought you'd ever be able to do that, with the power of the clerics? Things happen. They really do surprise you about human nature. Doing things you never thought would happen. You see the collapse of South Africa without firing a bullet, and we all had something to do with that, the policies over the years. So that restores your belief in human nature. You see one of the worst things like the Holocaust and you say, "That'll never happen again," and then you see Bosnia and you see Rwanda and you see what's happening today in the Sudan, and unfortunately, this is always going to be with us. And we've got to overcome it as best we can, plant the seeds and speak out that this [mustn't] happen.

Carlson, Richard: I don't believe there has been a collapse of character in public life, particularly, no more so than is simply reflected by the changes in our cultural and social lives in America. Those changes have been monumental in my lifetime. They are the product of decades of work by the activist wing of the Democratic Party: The schoolteachers, the public service employees unions, the trial lawyers, the social workers, and the angry feminists… I associate the Democratic Party with the new liberals; they call themselves progressives now, since the term "liberal" became anathema to the public. These are serious left-wingers; don't kid yourself, of the George Soros/MoveOn.org ilk, people in whose collective chest beats a dark heart. These are the people who are behind the immigration problems in this country going back to the changes in the 1960s, who have caused the desecration of old standards that were proven to work so well. Long ago, but well within my lifetime, they captured the schools, from grade one through college. They dominate the administrations and faculties. They impose their political and social views on youngsters, and they do it daily, the changes in the academic world over the last fifty years are astounding, and not for America's good. Thanks to this group, all fifth graders can now put a condom on a banana, but few of them are functional in math or have reading interests in high school beyond *People* magazine.

In the main, these changes came about because of a relentless core of left-wing relativists who are primarily in the Democratic Party. There are some in the Republican Party, but the core is with the Democrats. With all due respect to my colleagues in this book—and one of the Democrats, Chuck Manatt, is a good friend of mine and a man whom I admire—but the committed leftists have changed America almost beyond recognition and may bring it down yet.

Eckstein, Paul: To a large extent, for elected political office, the handlers have gotten control instead of the party leaders. It's counterintuitive in a way: people would think that if you were beholden to county leaders and party leaders, the guys with the big cigars, you lacked character. But you were chosen because you were expected to win and because they thought you had certain characteristics and certain strength. Today most candidates are self-nominated for most positions and are molded by handlers and advisors, and they don't have party backing until the very end. And then it's not really the party acting but the handlers, marketing people, and the pollsters.

I don't know if it always worked that way, but there were instances where it did work that way. You had a guy like Truman who had a lot of character and came out of the Pendergast Machine, a corrupt operation that controlled elections and jobs in Missouri at the turn of the twentieth century. There may have been certain corrupt aspects about the machine, but they picked people often with character. They weren't molded to do the things the handlers and marketing folks told them to do. Polling wasn't nearly as sophisticated, so they couldn't take a poll and figure out where they should be.

Well, consider the Malcolm Gladwell view of the importance of hard work, ten thousand hours. Today, Obama is a good example of it: you can be known by no one, give a great speech in 2004, write a book, and within six months of no one knowing your name, you're considered Presidential timber. No ten thousand hours there. But Harry Truman put in ten thousand hours. Frank Roosevelt put in ten thousand hours. He ran for Vice-President in 1920. Even though he was struck by polio, he stayed active in politics. He ran for Governor. Even Dwight Eisenhower, what he did was very political. He was a very astute political General. He had that experience. It is a lot easier for people today to nominate themselves and, with a break or two, get that kind of publicity that is thrust into the top. Take Teddy Roosevelt, who is probably one of the youngest people to become President, even though he wasn't elected in his first term. He was a police commissioner, he was Governor of New York, he led a military commission; I don't know if he had his ten thousand hours.

Lynch, Tom: We are a different society than when I was growing up in Lima, Ohio. If you look at our whole culture, back when I was growing up I had a mother, father, three brothers and sisters, and a live-in grandparent. Every meal was together; Mom was always there for us, and with cookies three or four times a week in the oven. We played neighborhood sports until it was too dark to see the ball; we then came in to do our homework. We went to bed, attended school, and we went to church as a family on Sundays. It was a wonderful life; it was a very enjoyable life, and you spent a lot of time interacting with one another. TV was just coming in, and it wasn't predominating. We played checkers, cards, and quiz games at home with family and friends.

Compare that to society today; we have a very hedonistic society. We don't have the nuclear family in many situations. I would say too, when I left home and went to school; my teachers and coaches at school reinforced all the values taught at home, by our literature, by our music, and by our church. For the young people today, there are so many distractions. We didn't have a computer or a TV, Facebook, Twitter, the texting of messages, and now the "sexting" of messages as well. All these things are prevalent in our society. All the institutions we relied upon as the bedrock of our society such as government, church, or teachers have all been damaged or tarnished.

It seems there has been an erosion of the values we took for granted. There was osmosis through the environment. Today it's imperative for parents to sit down with their children and teach them these values, because they're not going to learn it from school, or from college, or from their literature, or from their music, and you see what is on TV. There are a lot of issues that we as a society have allowed to happen, and it has happened gradually.

Santorum, Richard: It's always been that way with all sorts of scoundrels. Politics is a reflection of society. We don't lead society; we reflect society. The more society is broken, the more its leaders are going to be broken. Today we see brokenness as a result of—and you can tell if you're conservative or liberal based on whether you thought the '60s were a good thing—the breakdown of sexual mores, which is just wreaking havoc in our society right now. There will be a reformation at some point, or there won't be an America. They'll be a revival of some sort; a Great Awakening that I hope will put this genie back in the bottle, but this is as hard as one we've ever faced. We're humans. We've had faults all along the way. The poor moral standards of current-day society may be the most difficult to overcome.

Could you cite examples of exemplary character and principled leadership amidst the corrupting culture of Washington?

Black, Charlie: There are a lot of good people in both parties. Joe Lieberman is probably one of the best examples of a person of integrity in everything he does every day. He almost sacrificed his Senate seat in order to do what he thinks is right in terms of the Iraq War. There are a lot of good people in both parties that aren't as well known. I could cite Ronald Reagan and others who are no longer on the scene, but in terms of pure integrity and trying to do the right thing, President Bush 41 comes to mind. He actually sacrificed the presidency by going back on a campaign pledge not to have a tax increase. The Democrats would not compromise on trying to balance the budget unless he did. And he agonized for weeks. And he asked people like me, "Will this hurt me politically?" And we said, "Yes." And he still said that getting reelected is not as important as doing something good for the sake of the country.

We were having lunch on the patio outside of the Oval Office in late May of 1990. And just after that lunch, I had a conversation with him [Bush] asking me about the political consequences if he broke the tax pledge. And I told him he probably wouldn't be reelected. I told him that nothing is impossible in politics if the economy really started booming over the next two years and if it was going so well, some people might attribute it to your decision to compromise on taxes. And maybe you could get reelected, but I wouldn't bet on it. But he doesn't get much credit.

Bliley, Tom: Oh, there are so many examples of exemplary character, and really on both sides of the aisle. President Ronald Reagan jumps immediately to mind, perhaps especially for me, because we both started our service in Washington at the same time. Reagan was of course a former union boss, but when the air traffic controllers' union posed a threat to airline safety, I do not think he hesitated for a second in firing them and moving on. Let me give you another example from the other side of the aisle: my old and very dear friend John Dingell, the dean of the House. During my six years as Chairman of the House Commerce Committee, he fought most of the Republican agenda tooth and nail. We had some very tough fights—fights that should have made us enemies even today. But I always knew that John was standing up for his principles and his caucus. His fifty-plus years of service is really admirable, a great American story.

Bulger, William: I don't know much about Chuck Grassley [R-Iowa]. I've never met him but I like him. I also like the things he's on top of, especially the pharmaceutical people. I think he's on to a lot of things that are damn good issues. I don't know him. I haven't met him. But it's instinctive. I like him.

Cardin, Ben: There are numerous examples I can think of over the years. I think of Jack Kemp, who just recently died, and what he did to help people who never knew he was there. I had several really good conversations with him over the years, and I admired him greatly, what he would do to help. There are a lot of people in the Helsinki Commission who work with me. Chris Smith [R-New Jersey] who really fought trafficking issues and made a difference in saving young women around the world. Now we have international policies to stop trafficking; it's not perfect, but it is certainly better than it was ten years ago.

Carlson, Richard: There are many of them, some of whom I've known well enough to judge. A couple of White House counsels come to mind. Leonard Garment, my dear friend, now retired in New York. He was a bright and balancing force in the Nixon White House, respected by everyone for his wisdom and quiet wit. Another is Fred Fielding, a White House counsel to a couple of presidents, and a great fellow.

Joe DiGenova, who used to be U.S. Attorney in Washington and was known for his aggressive probity and real fairness, Joe is dynamic, very smart, and uncorrupted.

I had another old friend, gone now, William Hundley, who was unaffected by any corruption but did a lot for America. Bill was chief of the organized crime section of the Justice Department under Henry Peterson in the '60s. An effective public servant in the days of a powerful Mafia in America. It was Bill and the FBI who flipped the greatest mob informant ever, and the first of substance, Joe Valacchi. Bill went on to great success in private practice, for many years with Plato Cacheris, later with Edward Bennett Williams.

Judges Bill Webster and Louis Freeh, both friends of mine, were extraordinary and very principled public servants of the highest order. Both ran the FBI; Bill also ran the CIA. These are very tough jobs demanding remarkable integrity and judgment.

On the subject of judges, three other men who had an impact on our country, all also federal judges, come to mind. Larry Silberman, a very powerful and thoughtful U.S. Appeals Court judge who once ran the Justice Department; Stan Sporkin, who was the longtime general counsel for the CIA and a man of impeccable reputation; and Judge Gene Sullivan, chief of the U.S. Military Appeals Court, a former Army Ranger, and now a retired and successful novelist—a wonderful man.

It just occurred to me that every person I chose here is a lawyer, a group I sometimes have antipathy towards for the bad things their profession has done to this country, but who, as individual friends, are the very best—and thank God for them as a balance for societal good against the abuses of other members of the bar.

Eckstein, Paul: Truman. Pendergast chose him. He totally escapes the Pendergast Machine, but he is not afraid to go to the Pendergast funeral. But when it comes time to look at the government contracts at the beginning of World War II and look at the corruption, he exposed a lot of the corruption. I don't know if that's what leads to him being nominated in 1944. He had a lot of powerful friends in the Democratic Party, including the father of one of my friends, Ed Pawley. They saw something in him. They were fearful of Wallace. He was hardly a successful businessman. He had this haberdashery shop with a Jewish partner and it failed, but he went on to great things.

There aren't any characters in politicians today. They're all in the same mold. Their hair is trim, combed the same. They all look the same. Tim Pawlenty is a good example. Charlie Crist. John Edwards. That may be one reason why Sarah Palin attracted so much attention—she wasn't of the mold. McCain is not of the mold, and neither is Obama. It is hard for people. I don't know how Barry Goldwater could get to first base today. He was a character; he was a person not afraid to speak out. Any day you do that in this world, the slightest mistake, slightest misstep gets you in the news.

Lynch, Tom: As the navy's chief of legislative affairs, I met and worked closely with many politicians on both sides of the aisle. Two stand out. The late Senator John Stennis of Mississippi was a true gentleman in any discussion or debate. He was beloved by the people of Mississippi and anyone who had the privilege of knowing and working with him. The other is my friend Dan Lungren, the Representative from California. Dan is the most sincere and hardest working member I've known. Bright, energetic, always on top of the issues, and unwavering in his positions. His logic is always indisputable, and he is a public servant in the finest meaning of the term. He will debate the merits of an issue without ever demeaning the opposition and works tirelessly for his constituency. He and his close friend the late Jack Kemp have both lived their character.

Santorum, Richard: The most principled leadership I see out there is one you don't see much of. If you've reached the level of, say, a McCain or Coburn. Those two guys, there is an analogy. Both are really bullheaded, tough, stubborn SOBs. I like Tom a lot, but he can be really difficult. He has the curse of brilliant physician: the doctor that knows everything. There is a wonderful side to Tom, but there is a tough side to him. It's more personal-based than policy-based in many cases. It's being able to wave that flag.

I look at a guy like Jim DeMint, and there I see a man quietly laboring in the vineyard on principle and not getting a whole lot of publicity about it, but that's not why he's doing it. Phil Gramm was another. Phil probably balanced the huge intellect with maintaining principle and not letting his ego get out of control. It did on occasion. He did it as well as anybody. Of the guys I served with in the Senate, the best senator I served with was Phil Gramm. He was an amazing senator because he had the powerful intellect; a strong, principled worldview; a great sense of humor; and awareness of his huge ego, and he made fun of it. That doesn't mean that his ego still didn't get him into trouble. It did many, many, many times; but it didn't get out of control.

What skills are necessary for political success?

Bingaman, Anne: It is real long-term success, as opposed to flash in the pan. The trouble is that it ultimately breeds distrust and cynicism, and we have too much of that. I think Obama himself is a good example of this. By and large he does not take cheap shots. I think people trust him more because of it. People pick up when guys are doing cheap-shot sort of stuff over time. Over time, it doesn't take a lot of time. He's cautious. He's not flip. He's not zinging people. It breeds confidence in our elected officials, and that's what we are sorely lacking. That's a big part of Obama's success. People just feel that he is different. They desperately want it. They want to feel like someone is telling them the truth as that person sees it. They started out with that hope from Bush, but over time, he disabused them of that. And they came out at the end not trusting him. People want to believe in their government, but basically, in the end, they were hurt.

It is important not just for the success of the individual politician but also for the success of politics and the government. People need it, they want it. They want to believe the government. They have a hunger for it. But it is hard for them when people are spouting off.

Black, Charlie: Communication skills. Not all leaders have to be great speakers or great on television, although that helps. But the ability to communicate effectively, make arguments, organize your position, and marshal the facts well. There is a premium on brevity in all that we do, whether it is in government, or lobbying, or designing a campaign. In a political campaign, a thirty-second commercial has about forty words, and it could be as few as thirty words, depending on the rhythm of the speaker. The ability to communicate effectively, succinctly, and efficiently is essential.

Bliley, Tom: A firm faith in God, a good marriage, and an ability to work with others who may not share one's views. Those are most important, without question. But let me add another notion: damn the torpedoes! The Republican success in 1994, for instance, didn't come about because of dumb luck or just a shaky presidency. It happened because we shot for the moon and the stars. We had our policies and our facts straight. We knew which direction we wanted to take America. There's nothing wrong with being bold.

Bulger, William: There has to be some sort of an ability to communicate. I didn't use the press very much or at all. But at some level, inside the building, inside the Senate, there had to be an even greater understanding of what it was I was trying to do. We would have a caucus, and I would say, "If someone has a better idea of what it is we ought to do, I need to know. We need direction." And ultimately, if you don't have it … so they had to know pretty much what it was I was doing. They had to be sure of me. They were the people to whom I would go at the end of two years looking for their vote. I worked with them every day. That mattered a great deal to me. It meant that they had confidence. I know they are going to know me for my failings as well as my virtues. I want the positive to outweigh the negative. So someplace, the skill to communicate had to be there. I think it was.

Carlson, Richard: Obama has some of the skills that are so very effective in the media and on the campaign trail these days. It is a talent at articulation, but it addresses generalities in a simplistic way, idiocies like "hope and change" come to mind. I call them idiotic, but obviously they weren't seen that way by many of millions of people to whom they appealed, though they were designed to be intellectually meaningless.

Eckstein, Paul: The most important skill a successful politician has to have is to figure out who are the right people to have around you. It may be that when you are a congressman, a senator, a city councilman, it may be the person you need around you to get elected is not the right person you would need if you were the president of the United States. At all levels you need to pick and choose the right advisor but understand that the person who got you there might not be the right person for the next level. I don't know that McCain did a good job of that. He's had the same people around him forever. As Obama was going through the campaign, he was adding people who were much better equipped to advise him. Maybe it is that they saw a winner, so they were more attracted to him than that he persuaded them.

Harry Truman had a lot of great statements, but one of his greatest was that "with every appointment I make, I make one ingrate and twenty enemies." Every time you pick someone to a position, that person will to some extent be a sycophant or an ingrate and you'll have a lot of people upset they didn't get the position. To use the horse metaphor, it's very important to be a good judge of horseflesh. Horseflesh changes, and the kind of horseflesh you need changes according to the position you have.

George W. Bush is very loyal, and he was loyal to Rumsfeld to a fault. Harriet Miers. You can go the other way, and a good example of someone who went the other way is Bruce Babbitt, who had no loyalty to anyone, and I think he's the most extreme example of anyone I've seen in politics, and it caught up to him. He didn't understand that politics is reciprocal.

Lynch, Tom: You have to be able to communicate your thoughts and ideas. You can be handsome and intelligent, which are helpful, but you can have the best of ideas and not be successful if you cannot communicate. You need to articulate and defend your position and then, in order to convince others, you must be a trustworthy person. It all interplays whether it is in the political process, the military life, or the corporate world. We have something called "service reputation" in the military. It's something that you don't put a grade on, but everyone has a service reputation. It's a very close-knit society, so whatever happens, others hear about it, and people know. So your service reputation is very important. In the political process, your political reputation is very important. In corporate life, your corporate reputation is very important. In essence, a positive reputation means I can trust you.

Manatt, Charles: *[Chuck answered this question with several hypothetical questions.]*

Success in political life starts with asking yourself a few key questions. Are you going to have a normal life? Are you going to have a wife and children? Are you going to be a decent father? Are you going to be a decent husband? Far from a perfect father, far from a perfect husband, but a decent one. On a scale of one to ten, if you got real lucky, a seven or eight. Are you going to have the financial capacity to do things with your time other than to support your family? That's a very key part of the discussion that is often missed. Are you going to be able to have the financial capacity to support your family to the degree that then you'll have additional time to devote to politics, public office, party office, the different stylistic offerings that the body politic offers? That's why it is fairly unusual to be involved unless you are wealthy and have the luxury to allocate time and effort and have sufficient financial independence so that you can support your family and still do your political activity. It's fairly unusual.

Santorum, Richard: Communication. You have to be able to communicate. You can get by without it. George W. Bush did for a long time. George W. Bush had a lot of great speeches, a lot of great words, but he didn't deliver them particularly well. The ability to be able to connect with people through television, with the masses, is essential.

How do you triage demands on your time? How do you remain focused upon what is right rather than what is expedient?

Bingaman, Anne: Well, hopefully, you are always trying to do what is right. Honestly, I'm pretty bad at relationships. I honestly am. I don't focus on them. They're almost accidents with people who are great to me, who are dear to me. I don't call people enough. I don't take them to lunch enough. I've always been so manic about the work; I've always felt I don't have time to go to lunch three or four times a week. That's eight hours out of my week. I don't have the time. I've got to get home and see Jeff and John. So, truthfully, relationships—it's not very Washington and it's not very smart. I was just always more focused on the urgent, the immediate task before me and trying to do it to my very utmost. And it takes a long time to get to know people. It's not one or two lunches. A lot of people are great at it. I was never very good at it. Honestly, how often do I call you to go to lunch? I love you dearly but I don't do it. I don't call anybody. People call me and I say, "Okay, great." But I am always caught up in my little thing. It's a weakness of mine.

Black, Charlie: Bob Dole when he was leader—and he used to do this before—he used to have two or three negotiations going on in different conference rooms with other people in charge of them, and he'd just sit there for ten minutes, make a point, and then go down the hall and participate in another conference room. And when the negotiation was ripe, they knew they'd get him. And he'd help finalize it.

Time is the most valuable asset any of us have, and managing your time is very, very important. And what I have learned is that it is always a balancing act between not wasting time, spending your time on the right things that someone else can't do, but also not being stingy with the time.

For example, if a twenty-four-year-old kid who was working the McCain campaign is now working for low wages and out looking for a job, I may not be able to find him a job right now, but I can sure counsel him. People did that for me when I was young.

Bliley, Tom: Great question. Life is all about priorities. Mine are my faith, my family, and my community. Too often, I think, people come to Washington and get carried away with the trappings of office. Stick with what got you here.

Bulger, William: Every day you are not confronted with a huge moral question. Usually, if it's a tax question, we had members of the Senate who voted against every tax and for every expenditure. You can do that. It's a very popular role. I remember being in a caucus and saying, "Look, we have to have the revenue to do this. Everyone agrees. Is there anyone who thinks we can do this without the revenue? Okay, we have a dozen here who think they can't vote for any tax. So, ultimately this is what I'm asking you: those of you, who think we are doing the right thing, take the hard vote for the tax, don't wax demagogue against us. We're going to have a whole batch of Republican opponents who are going to be doing a good enough job of us. Vote as you wish, but simply refrain from seeing us as a political opportunity to exploit the situation because you know better. That would be something dumb." So they all sit there. There are guys sitting there who can't say anything, but they're voting against the tax and hoping it goes through because then they can repair the bridge.

Cardin, Ben: You've got to do both in life. You've got to be expedient. Being pragmatic, being popular is not a bad thing. I want to make that clear. I do a very good job at politics. I haven't lost an election yet. I'm getting to the point where I think I'm pretty good at being a good politician, which I think is an important characteristic to have. I am very pragmatic. I like to get things done. I really don't like to leave things on the table, incomplete. I don't think that's a bad trait to have. If you're compromising your principles and all you're doing is trying to get things accomplished and you are not terribly concerned if it solves a problem or not, then that's not a very good characteristic to have.

Carlson, Richard: It's changed for me over the years. My kids were always important to me, but I also always had live-in help. They don't call them "help" by accident. Their presences freed up my wife and me to spend more quality time with the kids. I've had a full-time houseman and a maid, sometimes a cook, too, for more than forty years, an old-fashioned style of living now pretty much out of date. My wife and I once had a very active social life. We were out almost every night, sometimes after the kids were in bed. Or we had dinner parties at home. I'm much less interested now in any social events. There are seasons for things, and that season is over. It was nice while it lasted, but I've said bye-bye without a regret. I find I have more interest in my boat, in reading, in playing with my dogs, or talking with my wife. I still spend a little time with my kids, but they have their own happy lives. I do see my sons for an occasional meal. I saw Buckley for dinner last night. I had lunch with Tucker at the Metropolitan Club today. I thank God regularly for giving me those boys. My two boys and their children have made for a fuller life for me than I ever imagined.

Eckstein, Paul: It's hard to keep your own sense of who you are and where you came from, once you have the trappings of power. I admire people who are direct, dissembled to a minimum amount, and enjoy getting into the details of the policy and being around people. President Richard Nixon didn't really enjoy being around people, although it appears that he enjoyed foreign relations.

Being able to be disciplined in your own life in terms of how you use time in whatever high position you are involved in is exceedingly important. I think we saw that in Obama. He was just a machine in how he regulated his schedule. Clinton was notoriously undisciplined in how he kept his time and kept his appointments. And I think it showed. You need people around you like Rahm Emanuel who will help you manage your time well. If you don't have that skill, you need people around you to help you.

Clearly, choosing your priorities. Everyone uses this hundred-day statement because that's what Roosevelt did, because in a hundred days, he got a lot of legislation passed because he needed it. Going in he had a good idea of what he needed, and the economy was deteriorating, and he took office four months after he was elected. If you don't have a pretty good idea of what needs to be done by the time you are elected, you'll be in trouble. Clinton's Presidency got off to a bad start because he didn't have key people appointed until about Christmas, and he didn't have his White House staff until January. He didn't feel any pressure. Obama feels a lot of pressure but he came in and was elected knowing what he had to do. And he had his agenda.

Lynch, Tom: "Where principle is involved, be deaf to expediency." A famous naval officer said that in the 1800s and it's come back to me many times. When the heat is on and you're pressed to make a decision or take an action, it's helpful to relax, look at the broad view, and hopefully make the correct move. Another piece of this is always focus on what is important, but maintain that balance in your life so that no single issue is overwhelming. When you're rushed or you need to get a letter out right away, you think about it. If that's not the right way to go, we have to redo it or reengineer it.

Santorum, Richard: I would say I had my schedule: when constituents wanted to meet with me—people who were important for my state, important politically, important for the community, we would try to rank and rate. We would meet with everybody; we had an open-door policy. I had two conference rooms, my office, and a hallway conference room. Those were the four places where meetings would be going on and I would just rotate, and when I was finished with the rotation, the one I had started with was usually the conference room, where I would start with another one. So we cranked those out. People would meet with my staff for twenty or twenty-five minutes, and at some point in the meeting, I would come in, and I would say to get to the nub of what you need, what you want, why you are here. I would put my two cents in and task the staff in attendance to follow through. That's how I did things.

Things that I felt like I was really there to do—and by the way, I was there to meet with constituents, too, those are obligations. For those we developed a system to attend to those obligations with the most minimal demand on my time. I was there for decision-making, so summary, make a decision, and move on; revisit if necessary at a staff meeting. When there were things that I was called to do, I would block larger amounts of time to do that. And that was always a challenge.

Things included: legislative initiatives; press conferences; speeches both on and off the Hill, in and out of Washington, for that matter; meetings and decisions on strategy and tactics; communications strategy; leadership issues. A lot of planning.

How do you navigate in a sea of power and corruption between the shoals of what is right and what is wrong?

Black, Charlie: Everybody has a code of right and wrong, whether they are Christian, another religion, or purely secular. Everyone has a code of right and wrong. You have to measure everything you do against that. It does require you to walk away from things: to walk away from money, a client, and a friend who otherwise is not doing the right thing. You have to be willing to do it. Temptation gets people if they let their guard down.

Bliley, Tom: Well, the Ten Commandments are a pretty good start. I hope with a clear vision based on faith—that's what certainly guided me. Success in Washington is only as good as your word, so I would put honesty very high on the list. I've never lost sleep because I've lied to somebody on the Hill, because I never have.

Bulger, William: If it's clearly right or wrong, the question is pretty easy. Most people want to be right. I don't think that's a frequent thing. The rhetoric will exploit and make it seem like it's so wrong from the other side. But usually it is not a moral question.

Cardin, Ben: You've got to be true your own beliefs. And this may seem obvious, but you've got to be honest. That's a prerequisite. You have to be honest. There are people who are not honest. I am not talking about politically corrupt or legally corrupt. You have to be honest. So the rule of the road number one is to be honest. I think to a certain degree, you have to have openness. You have to be willing to let people to come in. I said that earlier, but listening for me is a very important virtue to have. You have to have some form of transparency in the process and allow people to become part of it. If you don't, then you really are abusing power and are compromising character and ethics if you're not open.

One thing is clear: going into public life is not good for making money. Fortunately, I was in a very good situation. I had a family that had developed a fairly substantial business. They sold the business. I was able to generate a fairly substantial income and wealth out of that, which was enough to send my children and grandchildren through private schools and college. Otherwise I would not be able to afford that. So I was able to do that, thankfully. That to me is a small price to pay.

The biggest price you pay is privacy. Something you have to be willing to give up. If I had my choice, I'd rather have privacy than people recognizing me in the streets as much as they do. I don't mind engaging people; that's part of my life. I once didn't like parades, but even now I enjoy parades. I enjoy going out to a political event. You have to. Some of it is conditioning; some of it is humor. It's convincing yourself that you enjoy it, although I'm not sure how much of it I really enjoy. But privacy is something that my family likes. My daughter, my son-in-law, and my grandchildren, they prefer privacy.

No. It's like two different countries. It's hard to describe it until you have been there. The Senate is just a totally different animal from the House. Totally different rules, different employment agencies. We have the exact same ethics rules, but the ethics rules are enforced differently in the Senate than they are in the House. The rules are totally different in actuality. It's really a totally, totally different situation. It's really hard to describe, until you've been there. My friend Hoyer thinks I've been co-opted! I love it.

Carlson, Richard: Keep your hand on the tiller and ask God to place his hand on top of yours. Also, learn to read the navigational maps. I haven't been corrupted and I don't find it difficult. It's a slow development of values that keeps you from being corrupted. I don't want to sound like I couldn't be bought off, but I don't think I could be. I knew Jack Abramoff, knew him reasonably well. I first met him at Tony Blankley's house at an all-day party given by a congressman who was a friend of Jack, Tony, and me. Jack was a very likable guy. Kind of thoughtful, obviously smart. He had a lot of interesting things to say. We sat on Tony's porch and talked for a couple of hours. Later, he had me over to his law firm for lunch a few times. Who would have thought he would get involved in what he did? It seems to have been the money and the lack of a moral compass. He was exposed by virtue of his law practice to lucrative opportunities.

Eckstein, Paul: That is one of the most difficult things a politician has to do: to have a philosophy and agenda in the sense of what he or she would want to do, but understand the importance of pragmatism, being able to get it done and when events change, the agenda has got to change. But principle, you have to have a set of principles. A good example of that was Richard Nixon. He had a set of principles in terms of opening up discussion with China and bringing China into the world of nations. He was pragmatic in how he did it. He didn't do it right away. But he was working at it right away. He had to get the Vietnam War resolved before he did it.

Nixon—very few people would say he was charismatic, but in part because he was linked with Eisenhower and Kennedy. Eisenhower was charismatic in his way and certainly as a general. Eisenhower didn't come across as charismatic, certainly in comparison to Kennedy. Charisma will help, but it won't get you all the way, and we've had charismatic people. Huey Long is an example of someone who was charismatic.

Lynch, Tom: Watch for the expedient thing. The higher the rank, the greater the seniority, the more one is put in a position to be lionized, much like a professional athlete. They become targets for corruption. The higher you get, the bigger target you become. Politicians should forever be guarding against this, as in any walk of life, by keeping yourself grounded and remembering your basic principles.

Santorum, Richard: Don't go near the shoals! And when you do, one of things I firmly believe in, when you screw up, just step up and admit it immediately. Just take the hit. Don't cover it up. It's hard sometimes. I've found in a couple cases that it is hard to grapple with what is a mistake and to grapple with what people think is a mistake but what you in your heart don't really think is. Those are the hard things.

The easy ones are like when I stood up on the floor of the Senate and used an analogy about Hitler and referred to Bob Byrd about something. Now, I wasn't comparing Byrd to Hitler, but I put him in the same phrase, but in this silly world of politics, I issued an apology immediately. I said it was a stupid phrase and I shouldn't have said it that way. Fall on your sword and move on. I got hammered and moved on. But Alan Combs still brings it up when I am on his show. I said something in-artfully, and I admit it.

You do things you shouldn't do. You've got to stand up and say, "I shouldn't have said it. I shouldn't have done it." The hard part is—and Mc-Cain does this where he didn't do anything wrong, but the perception is he did, and he still apologizes. And we have a lot of politicians running around apologizing for everything even though it wasn't necessarily wrong. I remember when I said the famous line about the *Lawrence v. Texas* case in an interview. I don't know if you remember this, but this is what got the gay community in rabid opposition to me forever. I got up and said, "If you have the right to gay consensual sex under the Constitution, then you have the right to bestiality and incest and all these other things." And I just got creamed.

The point is you have to know when *not to* apologize for things you must do and are willing to take heat for having done.

Have you ever had to stand up to the "show business" of government?

Bingaman, Anne: I would put that in the demagogue category I was talking about; a more advanced form of demagoguery. Basically, that is what it is. It is a two-hour form of it instead of ten minutes. A member of Congress or a senator has the power to call a hearing and they are using it to beat up on someone to make the evening news. Ultimately, I don't think it is good for the government. I think it breeds distrust. People pick up on it over time and often right then.

Black, Charlie: It is part of the game, if you will, and you have to be prepared to make sure your clients and your candidates can succeed at it. Not that they are compromising their integrity, but that they are good at it and that they do not do things that demagogue up issues for the sake of the nightly news. But as for oneself, make sure you have a purpose when you go into the center ring of the circus. I have done hundreds of television interviews always as an advocate for someone else, not for myself, or so I like to think. There are certain days I have gone on *Crossfire* and been very proud of myself for beating up James Carville or winning on the issues. But I was there for my cause or my side of the argument, not to promote myself. I don't need promoting.

You have a purpose. I had to go a year ago this month in front of a lot of reporters, including television, to fight the *New York Times* on behalf of John McCain. We were honest and we were tough on the *New York Times* and on a lot of reporters. No one likes to do it. In our business no one wants the *New York Times* as an enemy for the rest of your life, but I did it because they were unfair to John McCain, and he needed to be defended.

Bliley, Tom: Were there times that I would have preferred spending time with my family rather than going to a black-tie fundraiser? Sure. But my family and I understood the greater purpose in my work. In the grand scheme of things, I've never compromised.

Bulger, William: When I was called to testify before Congress. I felt very bad about that because I thought they should have known better. This is an unfortunate biological relationship. There is nothing I can do to undo that. It's not of my doing. Half of it, I don't know the answer to it. I didn't know even at that time. But I asked Congressman Richard Neal, why do I have to go there? They have the Governor and the rest of them there bearing down on me. I know the Talk Master was behind me at the hearing. People up here were telling me that in order to watch me on television without distraction, they actually took pieces of cardboard to cover him because he'd be reacting to my testimony. The lawyers asked the committee Chairman to stop him. And I think they were afraid of him. It's ancient history now. The fact is they shouldn't have done it. If Congressman Moakley were there, it wouldn't have happened. If he were there, he'd say, why should he be answering questions? It's not his doing. That was just a bad break. But again, it was sensation. It was the fellow from Indiana, Congressman Burton.

Cardin, Ben: That's humor. Show business is you have to give people what they want to a certain degree. Show business is part of the game; it's what you do. It's part of politics. If it becomes all encompassing, you've lost your way. But if you totally ignore the public and what they want, then you're sort of putting yourself on a shelf and not allowing the process, the American political system to work. I don't want to be a showman; I don't think I am. But I do want to respect the fact that people's attention spans are based upon giving them what they want. Part of it is the town hall meetings and the one-liners. A lot has been accomplished by one-liners in life.

One of the things that I do not like about modern politics is the pollster. It's a way of life; we're not going to get rid of it. We're going to poll every day. And they are very effective. And they can really help you in trying to understand how you will achieve an objective. But I think we've gotten overly sensitive to the popularity of the moment.

As for representing my district versus my conscience, there is no one answer to that. That's one of the questions I pose in my ethics class. We talk about that for hours—to represent what you believe in or what your constituents believe in. Do you represent what's important for the country or what's important for your state? Do you represent what's important for Democrats, or what's important for your contributors, or what's important to the editorial people in the paper because they might endorse you or not? These are all the pressures that come to bear, and the truth is that all are important. If you ignore everything, then you won't be an effective legislator. If you want to get things done, you've got to be effective without compromising. Really, it's all a balancing act. How you balance it is how effective you are as a legislator, as a justice, as a lobbyist, or as an attorney.

Carlson, Richard: Not personally. The theatricality of political life annoys me, but then again, TV annoys me, too, so it's not surprising. I try not to watch TV even though I made my living from it for so long. Too time consuming, too little information in exchange for the investment.

Eckstein, Paul: Let me talk a little bit about the impeachment trial. There were plenty of opportunities for interviews and to get publicity. The other lawyer and I who were trying the case decided this was a trial that we would handle professionally. We would let our actions in court stand for themselves. I would talk about cameras in the courtroom because there were cameras in the courtroom there and people had objected to them, saying that lawyers would act differently and worse if there were no cameras. Cameras were there from the beginning, but I think after about thirty seconds I didn't pay any attention to cameras. There is so much going on in the courtroom that if you are trying to primp for the cameras, you're going to miss a lot of what's going on. As a lawyer if you have a witness on the stand, you are asking a question, you're listening to the answers, you're thinking of the next question, then how the answer fits into the points you're trying to make. That's a lot of stuff going on. Then you want to keep an eye on the jury, in the case of the impeachment trial, that was one eye on the thirty members of the Senate. That's a lot to take in before you can do things for the camera.

The people who were most reticent in the beginning to participate in the trial were just as happy to have Mecham twisting in the wind. There were some Republicans, like Brewer, who thought he was getting a raw deal. At least half, if not three-quarters, of those who voted against impeachment were Mormons, LDS, as was Mecham. So there was a religious element to that. Brewer is not Mormon, but from some fundamentalist sect of some sort.

Bill French was selected by the Speaker of the House to conduct an investigation to see if there were grounds to support impeachment. French was a former superior court judge and a Democrat by party registration. He did his investigation; he was scheduled to give his report on January 15, 1998, at 1:30 PM. I was sitting in my office around noon, and I got a call from Art Hamilton, who was the Democratic majority leader in the House who said that Democrats were skeptical as to whether there were grounds for impeachment and they wanted my advice.

So he wanted me to go to the House, and he'd get a ticket for me to sit in the galley. He wanted me to listen to French's report, get a copy of it, analyze it and report back to them over the weekend. For whatever work you do on this, I can't guarantee you're going to get paid.

I came down; I listened; I got the report, and I got seven or eight lawyers looking at various aspects of impeachment. We wrote this report. We handed it out to the Democrats on Monday. It was deliberately leaked because the Democrats were so happy with it and thought it was a superior work product that had been produced that they gave it to the Republicans. And the Republicans liked it. I was then retained as a result of that to represent the Democrat minority in the impeachment hearings.

When the articles of impeachment went over to the Senate, the tradition is that the Board of Managers will walk across the hall and hand the articles to the President and Majority Leader in the Senate, and then they formally accept them—the President and the Majority Leader said, "We can accept them, but you can't have Eckstein as one of the two lawyers because he's too partisan." But the Board of Managers said, "We get to choose our lawyers, not you." Three Republicans, two Democrats. The Republicans had a majority. That's how it happened. I did get paid, but it was considerably less than my hourly rate, even then.

Lynch, Tom: Again, it gets back to all the things we were saying before and how you got to where you got: selflessness. You've got to be a selfless person. These things come because of the rank, because of position, because of where you came to be, but they don't contaminate you, because that's part of the trappings of the office but not the essence of the office. You understand that, but you do some of the things you've got to do, like parades and things like that. It's just the necessity of what needs to be done.

Can you identify successful lobbying and political skills? Are these skills aligned with good character traits?

Bingaman, Anne: Again, I go back to honesty. You've got to be as good as your word. Always. My dad used to always say that you've got to live by the code of the Old West, "My word is my bond." If you say something, you do it. I don't know any political person who can't be taken at his or her word by other political people and then seen as trustworthy.

You've got to have that person's trust. These people are smart.

Actually, I think having great legal and strategic skills. It is very hard to be a good lawyer. It is very, very hard. There actually aren't that many great lawyers. There are some. And I've been privileged to know a number. But they are one in a hundred or one in a thousand. Great lawyer skills include understanding the case, the issue, the bill, and whatever it is you are doing, inside and out. Then you can present it honestly, but in a way that advances your goals, by not misstating anything. There are just so many ways in laws to present something. That is just one of the endlessly interesting things about practicing law. Give any ten lawyers the same set of facts, they can come up with ten different cases to present, and only one or two of them are going to be clear winners.

It matters a lot what your strategy is and how you see … and to do that it is very complicated. You've got to think who is your opposition, who are the interest groups against you, what are they going to be saying. To actually do this well takes a lot of legal ability. Whether or not you are a lawyer is subsidiary to it. And strategic ability. So you have to be honest, but you have to put your side of it forward in the best light, because the other side is going to do that, and presumably your goals are worthy goals.

Black, Charlie: The political skills get down to communication and people skills. I throw in work ethic and discipline. Some of them are character traits that you develop like work ethic, discipline, and honesty. You are not successful in politics if you are not honest and your word is not good. So there is some overlap if there is not complete alignment of political skills with character traits. And for some people their strongest political skill is their integrity, like Joe Lieberman. With John McCain, you can't say it's his strongest political trait, because of his service in war and his support of his country. His integrity and his reputation for integrity is a strong sell.

Bliley, Tom: Always be truthful. Make sure that the people you're seeking to influence know exactly why you're at the table. Never mislead or be untruthful. And always respect your opponents, particularly the other side of the aisle.

Cardin, Ben: First of all, you really have to be knowledgeable as to how the process works—you have to know the issues, you have to know the players, you have to have a sense of political reality, and you have to make good political judgments. I go back to Bill Clinton in his first term: his skills needed some maturity when he started taking up the health-care issue, and he was unable to get it completed. Barack Obama is trying to understand history. So the skills part of it understands where you are and how much energy you are going to need to get it done. Realize there is a limit to your political energy and how much you can get done. Set your priorities.

Every issue is important. One of the skills is judgment—whether you put forward ending discrimination against gays versus solving the health care crisis versus energy independence versus ending the war in Iraq and Afghanistan. You're president of the United States. How do these line up in importance? If you're a person being discriminated against because you are gay, that issue means the world to you. Whereas peace between the Israelis and Palestinians could have an enormous impact in terms of world security.

It's these types of choices you have to make every day. I have to make those choices every day. I have a lineup of issues that we face every day, and I might be able to offer an amendment, so what issue am I going to pick? That's judgment. The skill you need is good judgment, but you have to have the right information to make those judgments, and you have to understand the political system, so you can make the right type of decision as to what you *can* get done.

Carlson, Dick: Know what you are talking about and deliver that impression to the person you are talking to with controlled enthusiasm and in simple language. Take a cue from LBJ and always touch the person you are trying to persuade, more than once if possible.

Eckstein, Paul: Good character skills may assure defeat in politics. There are a lot of people who believe that people with sterling character can't get elected because there is a fair amount of deception that's required to succeed in politics. Once you are honest about doubts that you may have about a certain course of action, or you're too revealing in your personal thoughts about a position, you can be dead, stillborn before you get started. It is important to appear to be genuine but not be genuine. The secret in Washington: appear to be truthful and genuine; as long as you can fake that, you've got it made. It leaves us with the hope that some of the fakers do have principles and know where to draw the line. It's pretty rare to have that kind of person.

Calmness. They have a certain sense of serenity. When it is important, they have to be able to turn on the passion to show that there things that you care about. In most cases, you have to be reasonably articulate; we've seen cases where people are not articulate. You have to be likable, or at least appear to be likable. One of the reasons Al Gore and John Kerry lost was that they did not appear to be likable compared with George W. Bush. Likability is one of the most important—if you went back and did a poll of which candidate you would rather have a beer with, have dinner with, which is more likable, I bet 95 percent of the time, the person who scored higher on the likability score would be successful.

Likability. Calmness. Articulateness. Organization. Ability to control your time. Discipline is terribly important. Certainly discipline in being able to get elected, and discipline in being able to convey a message in today's world. Certainly in the old days it was more important to be perceived by the powerbrokers as competent and trustworthy and be perceived by them as electable.

Good lobbyists and legislators and people in the executive will tell you that the most important thing for a lobbyist to have is knowledge in the area they are talking about and absolute honesty. Everything has to be laid out. Lobbyists perform a valuable service in that they're the experts on their particular issue. Yes, they are presenting a view, but a legislator ought to seek out contrary views, and you want people who are knowledgeable and thoroughly honest.

Candidates look to lobbyists to raise money, but if a lobbyist is unreliable—Jack Abramoff—you not only can suffer, you can go to jail. You absolutely need people who are totally honest with you and you can rely on. Truth is the first casualty of war, and maybe the first casualty of politics. A version of the truth comes out in campaigns and the best you can say is that version is an abbreviated version of what is true, and that in the abbreviation, truth is left out where half-truths are told. But for politicians to succeed, they need people telling them the truth.

Lynch, Tom: In the political world, in the military world, in any world, you must be genuine, honest, and trustworthy. You can be counted upon, and you don't go to the person every time you want something. You are there for the person when they need something, and you try to help them in any circumstance.

We have children, we all have grandchildren, they have needs—and many times people have come to me and asked, "Could you be a reference for my son or daughter?" "Could you introduce them to this company?" "Could you talk to them about going to the Naval Academy?" "Could you talk to them about the service or a military career?" "Could you talk to them about the venture-capital life?" I always make time for a person who makes a request of me [on behalf] of their son or daughter. I always respond to such a request because that really is the essence of friendship, and really, you get to know a person when they come to you with their most precious asset, his or her child, and they believe you can assist in some way, or help the child to think differently about a subject.

Manatt, Charles: Start with listening to other people. Start with trying to line up and link their goals and motivations with some things that are similar to yours. If it can be pulled off, it certainly would be a good achievement, a positive nature in the good of the order. Timing helps. Part of this is a time warp. The organizational skills encompassing Martha Lane Collins and Lynn Cutler and Diane Feinstein and Nancy Pelosi and on and on, just at the cusp of the time when the women were really moving up and moving out from the volunteer assignments to the elected official assignments. I was about ten years ahead of the curve on that one. And it has proven to be very helpful.

So it is a matter of fundraising, having empathy with the other people you are working with in the political realm, and it is a matter of being able to speak and present your causes.

Santorum, Richard: Political lobbying skills are not necessarily aligned with good character skills. Bill Clinton was a great communicator but not a great character. That's something we see in our society: things that make you successful today are not necessarily things that reflect on your character and on your skills.

Can you share personal stories of character situations in your political life?

Bliley, Tom: I remember attending a meeting in the Committee when someone came up to me and said "I have supported you on every vote for ten years, but you voted for some issue and I will never support you again." I said, "Sir, if you only disagreed with one vote, I think I have served you well. By the way, I see you have a wedding band. Have you agreed with your wife on everything for ten years?"

Cardin, Ben: For the past fifteen years I have lectured at the Institute for Public Policy Studies at Johns Hopkins. Most of them have been three two-hour lectures. The first usually talks about the individual: the character of the individual as far as ethics is concerned and the dilemma the individual has very much goes towards whether you follow your constituents or your own views. The second goes to institutional problems we have such as how we finance elections, seniority, those types of problems, which confront ethics: how committees are organized, how committees work, how we deal with special interests and how leadership works. And the third deals with our country as a whole, fighting wars, choosing to deal with environmental issues.

Today it is much more issue specific: how we deal with health care, how we deal with energy, how we deal with the wars in Iraq and Afghanistan, and how we deal with those types of issues. It's evolved over time, but [the course] has a strong dose of ethics.

No one is pure here. Most people do have a sense, a purpose, of ethics. It's hard for us to understand that. It's hard for us to take a terrorist and think a terrorist has ethics, but a terrorist is focused on a specific objective and thinks that this is critically important for society. They have clearly lost their way in terms of what is accepted. I think this is another important point. Ethics is not what you think is right, although what you think is important in a lot of ways. Character is not what you think you'd like to do. If there was ever a poster child for why that is wrong, it is Dick Cheney and perhaps George W. Bush, where they imposed their own views and were not prepared to listen to a broader audience. Ethics is very much a more universal value. And you have to be able to open up.

Ethics is not what you say is right; ethics is not personal. It has to be broader than that, but it does involve that you do things right. So I guess the challenge here is how personal it is to do what you think is right, but also understand there are principles here that are broader, and [you] have to recognize that we are all susceptible to a basic international view of human rights. War crimes in Nuremburg pointed that out pretty clearly. Just as what is happening right now in The Hague points that out very clearly.

This is just like one of the issues we are facing right now as a society: are the lawyers who drafted the memos allowing torture criminally or ethically responsible for those documents? They did that under the best of intentions to keep them safe. I don't think it is ex post facto. There is no question that what they thought they were doing was important for national security. They knew what the laws were and I think some of them, if you read some of the books, they understood the risk factors of what they were doing. They understood that they might be judged as war criminals. And in fact, there were Department of Justice and FBI who refused to go along. And they said it was wrong. They pulled out and wouldn't let anyone get involved in the interrogation. To people's credit, there were people questioning at the time.

It is an interesting thing about character. A lot of people think strength is character. Strength is clearly part of character, being willing to stand up and not be intimidated and get the mission accomplished. But if that turns into blindness about the moral direction in which you are going, and blindness to what is acceptable process, or blindness to changes in circumstances to which you should be able to take consideration, then that's a weakness. That strength becomes a weakness. Nothing is absolute in this. Nothing is absolute at all. Certainly I want a president who is going to be strong on the attack to our country and root out the terrorists. Everyone wanted that. That's why we gave the President all the powers he needed to go after the Taliban and go after Al Qaeda. But circumstances changed. What he did in Iraq required a different strategy. And yet the strength of our leader was a single focus on a common strategy, and it was a weakness here.

Is there an absolute in character? There is certainly honesty. Honesty is always an absolute. You have to be honest. You have to be focused in strength and results-oriented. They are all important things that must be done. But they are not absolute. It's a challenge. There is no one formula.

Carlson, Dick: Let me take you back to San Francisco in the mid 1960s when my news partner, Lance Brisson, and I, covered frequently unusual events for the ABC-owned TV station, and tell you two stories, unrelated directly to politics but quite related to character, or again, lack thereof.

One late night, while we were working from a surveillance truck filming for a documentary on prostitution, we tailed two drunken lawyers, both of them large, athletic men in their early thirties, Deputy AGs from the California Attorney General's office. We had recognized them from seeing them in a bar across from our TV station. Now we were watching them as they wandered in and out of Tenderloin hot-sheet hotels trying to buy dope and girls, or so said the hotel clerks we spoke with as the pair stumbled in tandem from fleabag to fleabag spot, and we came in behind them.

We shot film of their antics from our surveillance truck, including the two of them urinating against the side of a bowling alley on Eddy Street. We wrapped up the project with a shot of them zipping their pants in the middle of the sidewalk, slapping each other on the back, and staggering away past a huddle of curious drug dealers, pimps, and hookers.

Like many of our investigative news efforts, it seemed like a sterling idea at the time but we ended up killing it after KGO-TV's general manager, Dave Sacks, a friend of California's Attorney General, sent word through our news director Roger Grimsby that this story would run on his TV station only over his dead body. We offered to cut the urination scene, but Mr. Sacks was having no part of it.

Lance and I were firm believers in doing all we could to profit from spent time and effort, so we made appointments with the two AGs at the state building on Golden Gate Avenue. They had no idea what we wanted.

We met in the Attorney General's own large conference room and entertained the pair, Don and Carl were their names, in great detail about the surveillance and the film. Entertained may be the wrong word. Their emotions ran immediately from incredulity to misery to boiling anger. We provoked them in the extreme. Carl, by reputation a former Olympic discus thrower, had to be physically restrained by his friend Don after Lance described him on film as "trying to write your name in urine" on the bowling alley's wall. "Or was it some other message? We couldn't make it out." We considered it unlikely at the time that we would be beaten to death in the Attorney General's conference room.

When Carl and Don seemed to reach the apex of joint emotion, we told them not to worry, we planned to kill the story since it would obviously destroy their careers. They instantly dropped off their high horses. No, sorry, we couldn't turn the film over to them, we said. We did have some standards and news ethics at KGO, even if they were a bit low. Our news director would keep the film in his safe and nobody would ever see it. That safe was already loaded with filmed peccadilloes of plenty of others—like Assemblyman George Moscone, notorious for unsavory behavior—and none had seen the light of day, not too worry.

We didn't mention that Dave Saks had killed the story—no sense in mitigating the intensity of their gratitude, and we modestly accepted credit for saving their careers. Later, after they had become frequent and useful confidential sources—and we had shared a few drinks with them at the Federal Reserve Lounge, situated midway between their offices and ours, they tried to enlist our help in planting a bug and a transmitter in a classroom at San Francisco State College used by the radical Black Student's Union. Those Deputy AGs were reckless boys, but we already knew that. We declined.

Eckstein, Paul: We talked about this certainly in the Babbitt imbroglio. It was never any doubt in my mind that I would say exactly what happened, and that I would report to my client exactly what happened. I think there are a lot of other people who in my situation would have done things differently.

I'll go back to the Fred Miller situation in 1979. I had just turned thirty-nine and Miller came to me the day before he suspended Kush and told me he was going to do it. Several people including a professor of Law at the Law School, John Morris, recommended to him that he needed an independent lawyer, and he hired me. What I experienced helped me with the impeachment trial because I didn't stand up to the President of Arizona State University at the time: either he should have taken the heat or allowed Fred Miller to explain fully what he was doing. When Fred Miller gave that first press conference, he was dead meat after that because he wasn't allowed by order of the University President to tell why he was suspending Kush. Meanwhile, Kush was threatening players and coaches that if they didn't stick together with him, they were going to be in trouble. Two or three days later, after the damage had been done, I made the decision, to hell with it! Fred Miller was going to stand up and explain why he did what he did. We knew it would cost him his job, and it did eventually, but it was the right thing to do even if it did mean being unemployed.

It was a tense period. I remember listening to sports' talk radio all the time and people just wanted to lynch Miller. I wasn't someone they cared about at all. Flo and I were in the Athletic Director's box on the night of the final game that Fred Miller fired Frank Kush, and Kush won that game. Fans were down below, and I thought they were going to come up and rip Fred Miller's throat out. They were shaking their fists. It was a very mean situation.

Football is king in many states, it was king then; it's not king now. Frank Kush was king. Miller realized that he had kind of let Kush get out of control and he was probably to blame for this cult of the coach's personality.

We talked about the Fred Miller experience. We listened to the President of the University, and there was a good reason to do that because he was the boss of the University and Fred Miller's supervisor. But it was a huge mistake. If Miller was going to go down, he should have gone down on his terms, which he did eventually. But I sure learned as a lawyer that my duty and responsibility was to my client and not to make the President happy. I thought that by making the President happy, I'd be representing the best interests of my client. That turned out not to be the case.

Lynch, Tom: Coach Bobby Knight was at the Academy in March '92 in the middle of March Madness. His Hoosiers had played at the Capital Center the night before, and he called our coach and athletic director for permission to use our facility for practice. As it happened, Senator John McCain and his family were visiting that weekend as my guests and, after watching a Saturday morning lacrosse game, John suggested we go over and watch the Indiana practice. I had never met Coach Knight but I'm thinking that when we walk into the gym, he's going to say, "Hey, this is a closed practice. You, out of here!" And I know I'm going to say, "Hey you, out of here, this is my gym!" I'm concerned that this is going to be an embarrassing moment all around. We entered a side door and no one was there other than assistant coaches and the team conducting practice. I'm looking around for Bobby Knight when all of sudden he comes from behind me and puts his arm around me and says, "Admiral Lynch, I've been looking forward to meeting you!" He had coached at West Point and has always followed the service academies. "You're doing a terrific job here..." and I don't remember all that he said but it was very laudatory. And I said, "Thank you coach, it's very nice to meet you. I'd like for you to meet Senator McCain" He says, "Oh, hi Senator...Admiral, will you take a picture with me?" He later sent me the photo inscribed and I have it in my study. Bobby Knight is my hero!

Another humorous incident occurred at the Academy. The Brigade of Midshipmen hosts an annual Foreign Affairs conference and invites college students from across the land. When I inquired who the keynote speakers would be, I was unimpressed by the lineup and suggested that we get a noteworthy speaker, such as Charles Krauthammer. Charles was invited and accepted to give the keynote address. I had never met Charles, but his speaking and his writing skills impressed me. I was unaware that he was a paraplegic. The plan was for me to host a luncheon in his honor at my quarters with selected Midshipmen, professors, and a number of our civilian college guests.

The day before, unknown to me, our Public Works Department built what I called a "Bridge on the River Kwai" from the road to my quarters. When I saw it the night before the luncheon, I was flabbergasted and was concerned that this was waste of the highest order and would even be an embarrassment to our guest. Needless to say, I had a few words with the Public Works Officer and hardly heard his explanation that Charles does not want anyone touching his wheelchair, and that the Bridge was engineered with the correct slope so that Charles could easily navigate the ramp, and of course, it needed to have the sides so that he wouldn't fall and injure himself. I was unconvinced, but it was too late to do anything about it.

I waited anxiously for his arrival at noon. He came in a white van, and with the help of a young man, he exited and looked at the ramp for a moment, and then came up all the way from the street to the house— *Vrrrrroooooommm*. Kathy and I met him, had a very nice luncheon, and afterwards all the students and professors in attendance retired to the auditorium to prepare for his keynote address. He and I were left together alone in the foyer, and he looked up from his chair with a twinkle in his eye and said, "By the way, Admiral, as you might suspect, I'm a connoisseur of ramps, and yours is one of the finest I've ever seen!" We both had a good laugh, and whenever I've seen him since, we both get a chuckle remembering the Bridge on the River Kwai.

Manatt, Charles: I will always remember my first race for state Chairman, having just run for county commission in Los Angeles and lost. And I thought, well, let's skip over LA County and run for state. And everyone was for Congressman Brown, who had just left Congress because he had just been whipped in the primary and happily—with me whipping him in '71—he got back into Congress in '72 and died in office twenty-seven years later. And that was kind of tough. There were the Burtons and Willie Brown and all those who were skilled and professional supporting a well-known senior congressman, a well-known four-term congressman, against a young kid lawyer who most people didn't know all that well.

Imagine yourself in the political setting of your choice. What would it be?

Bingaman, Anne: I had the best job for me, quite frankly, because antitrust is a great job. The White House doesn't have anything to say. As far as antitrust cases, nothing. Up above, Janet Reno was there, the woman was a phenomenal lawyer, and she didn't get enough credit for that. She was a prosecutor for fifteen years in Miami. You can present a case to Reno in about five minutes, and boom, she is right on it. She is asking the right questions. She was so sharp. And I didn't have to report to her except on very large cases. She has about a million other things to do to hear about small cases. John Schmidt from Chicago, I reported to directly. He knew everything we were doing.

But by and large, assuming you have good judgment you call it as you see it, live and die with the result, and hopefully your judgment is good and you do the right thing. So for me, I would not be good at traditional politics. I don't have the personality for it, I don't suffer fools gladly enough, and I'm not good at keeping my mouth shut. Really, I wouldn't be any good. I wouldn't have any friends. It would take about three months before people said, "This woman is nuts. I couldn't take any more from her." Not my thing.

Bliley, Tom: As chapter three of Ecclesiastes says, "For everything, there is a season, and a time for every purpose under heaven." A time to come and a time to go. The best political setting I can imagine right now is being with my family on election night in November 1994 watching Republicans take back the House. I'd like to think I had something to do with that and firmly believe we did a lot of good for the American people. I think victories in 2010 will mark another changing of the guard, and I can't wait to watch more victories in 2012.

Cardin, Ben: For a while I thought I wanted to be Governor, but it's not where I wanted to be. No, I'm really where I want to be. Now, I'm going to tell you something because I've been accused of not wanting to be very ambitious, but the only thing I've wanted to be other than a legislator was Governor, and I couldn't get that, but I recognized it. I never wanted to be in Congress. I never wanted to be in the United States Senate. I am not terribly ambitious. I think everyone is somewhat ambitious, but I am not focused on a specific ladder that I want to get to in life. Where I am now, I am extremely happy, and have no desire to seek anything other than being a United States Senator.

I never ever thought I'd run for Congress. That was the furthest thing from my mind. It only happened because of happenstance. I couldn't win governor. McCloskey had decided to drop off to run for Senate. There just happen to be an opening at the time, convenient to where I was, it was the only reason I decided to go for it. I knew that it was convenient at the time, that it was the right time to leave the legislature, and I better leave now, or else I'll be there a long time. And I know it was right for the institution and for me, and I needed to move on from being Speaker. If the power is what you want, you can be Speaker for all your life. The power of this position is incredible. I'll never have a more powerful position than being Speaker of the Maryland House of Delegates. Well, being a United States Senator in many respects will have more of an impact than being Speaker. I didn't plan for it.

Carlson, Richard: I ran for office, for mayor of San Diego in the early 1980s. I'm grateful now that I didn't win. For one thing, I would have spent so many years dealing with issues like Mexican sewage from Tijuana and Baja California, which was always washing up on our beaches. And I wouldn't have become the VOA director and come to Washington, where I have lived so long and so happily. In San Diego, I ran against Roger Hedgecock who was the Mayor. We were the two top vote getters in a busy primary with a lot of candidates. You had to get 50 per cent of the vote plus one. We were both Republicans, although all municipal races in California, by law, are nonpartisan. So we couldn't use party affiliation. We had a run-off. I spent $1.2 million; he spent $1.3 million. We were restricted to $250 per person with no political action committee money, no union money, and no corporate money. This was a San Diego law that had come on the heels of Watergate. Like many laws, it had completely unintended consequences. In this case, it favored the incumbent because he could use the power of his office to solicit more donations than his challenger could. To raise something like a million dollars in $250 increments or less is overwhelmingly difficult. How many friends and relatives do you have that will give you $250? Ten, twenty, even fifty? I raised about $700,000 that way, it was tough, but I couldn't raise any more. To keep up with Roger, I had to put in $500,000 of my own money. Part of San Diego's post-Watergate law was that you couldn't run up unpaid campaign debt. It had to be paid within thirty days of incurrence. So when I lost, I had about $70,000 in debt that I had to pay immediately. If I had won, I could have held a fundraiser right away to eliminate my debt. As it was, I gambled and lost. I got burned. I hate to waste money, but it was a great experience anyway.

Eckstein, Paul: In the Mecham impeachment trial, there was plenty of opportunities for interviews and to get publicity. The other lawyer and I who were trying the case decided this was a trial that we would handle professionally. We would let our actions in court stand for themselves. I would talk about cameras in the courtroom because there were cameras in the courtroom there, and people had objected to it, saying that lawyers would act differently and worse if there were no cameras. My experience with the impeachment trial was a very good experience. Cameras were there from the beginning, but I think after about thirty seconds, I didn't pay any attention to cameras. There is so much going on in the courtroom that if you are trying to primp for the cameras you're going to miss a lot of what's going on.

Lynch, Tom: Again, it gets back to all the things we were saying before and how you got to where you got: selflessness. You've got to be a selfless person. These things come because of the rank, because of position, because of where you came to be, but they don't contaminate you because that's part of the trappings of the office, but not the essence of the office. You understand that, but you do some of the things you've got to do like parades and things like that. It's just the necessity of what needs to be done.

I could see myself as a city mayor or state governor. Both are appealing to me because of the opportunity each would provide to have hands-on immediate impact in the lives of your constituents. I supported Mayor Nutter here in Philadelphia, and I admire his work ethic, his openness, and his zeal to do his best for the city as he battles overwhelming issues which confront most major cities today.

Ten Characters with Character

Their Virtues

"Excellence is an art won by training and habituation. We do not act rightly because we have virtue or excellence, but we rather have those because we have acted rightly. We are what we repeatedly do. Excellence, then, is not an act but a habit."

—Aristotle

This chapter will examine the particular virtues that belie the good character exhibited by the principled politicians in this book. For each character interviewed, several virtues exhibited in their lives will be highlighted. Historical or literary figures that share similar virtues will then be discussed. The juxtaposition of the book's characters with historical figures exhibiting similar virtues reinforces the enlightened worldview of "Diogenes the Realist": namely, in each generation, when good character persists in a few, society remains elevated above selfishness and depravity.

The Honorable Anne K. Bingaman

Wat virtues most mark Anne Bingaman? Remember that Anne is one of the early successful lawyers, from the small town of Jerome, Arizona, and she was a trailblazer in law for her gender. Hard work, family, and a sense of place were important to her. Anne recalls values instilled in her in the small town, in particular being genuine. "Everybody in the town knows everything about you," Anne explains. "You get called out if you talk too big and look too smart. Kids will beat you up on the playground if you put on airs." It sounds a lot like Shakespeare's perennial advice, "To thine own self be true." Perhaps, too, it reminds us, as Anne said, of the code of the Old West, "My word is my bond." Anne demonstrates the virtue of honesty.

It is this foundation of being genuine, straightforward, and honest that generates an interesting comparison of Anne to Eleanor Roosevelt. Like Mrs. Roosevelt, Anne is "her own woman." Her husband's most illustrious run as President could have easily overshadowed Eleanor, but it did not. Despite her own husband being a U.S. Senator, Anne's personal relationship with him does not professionally define her. Anne, like Eleanor, has her own vision, integrity, and drive, which help to define everything she does.

Anne also demonstrates the virtue of diligence. When she arrived in New Mexico, she knew no one. She was one of the few women even admitted to practice law during that time. When she left a tenured law professorship to start her own practice, she took an enormous risk. But what made that risk possible? Her virtues of diligence and caring. As Anne says:

> What it really comes down to is that you've got to care, really care, and
> if you do, you'll focus on it, think about it, work at it, stay ahead of the

curve. As long as you care, it'll eventually be okay. One way or another, you'll make it.

Eleanor Roosevelt also cared. She saw the suffering caused by the Depression. Harvard Professor Mary Ann Glendon points out in her book, *A World Made New,* that this experience spurred Eleanor to make sure that the world would never forget the dignity and compassion that each person deserved. For this reason, after World War II, she spent years drafting the Universal Declaration of Human Rights. Today this declaration is a well-known document on fundamental human rights.

Diligence, the virtue that Eleanor and Anne share, stems from caring. It enables one to stay focused against all odds. It was precisely this value that her family drove into her by example: think of how many of her relatives were willing to take risks and start their own businesses. Why? Simply because they cared to live life in their own way, notwithstanding the risks. Eleanor took a risk trying to draft the Universal Declaration of Human Rights. She had accomplished "enough" in life; but she never stopped caring. A person without persistence looks past the present moment to an unrealistic future; but a person with persistence concerns themselves with the present moment because they know, come what may, the future will be fine. Anne calls it chance, serendipity. Others might call it practicing the virtues of honesty and persistence.

Charlie R. Black, Esquire

Charlie Black resembles two men from two different eras. The first is a name perhaps not known to many of you, the Roman philosopher Seneca. The second is a more familiar name, Reverend Billy Graham. Seneca knew how to persevere. Billy Graham knew this as well. Charlie is a reflection of that virtue.

Lucius Annaeus Seneca, sometimes known as Seneca the Younger, was a philosopher, statesman, and author. He is considered one of the greatest poets of Rome's Silver Age of literature. Unfortunately, during Seneca's time some of the most corrupt emperors were in power, including Nero. This didn't seem to trouble Seneca at all; he knew that sometimes fortune required a good man to persevere despite the evil men around him, and he cheered himself along: "Behold a worthy sight, to which the God, turning his attention to his own work, may direct his gaze … a brave man matched in conflict with evil fortune."

Perseverance means to stay on task. One doesn't look at what can be done, but one asks what must be done. Like Seneca, Billy Graham showed exceptional perseverance to build up his ministry.

Charlie is also a man of perseverance. In his political life he has been part of many campaigns when victory was far from certain, but he pushed through anyway. Campaigning for Governor Ronald Reagan in 1976, he knew that Reagan was the right man for the job. When Reagan lost to Gerald Ford, Charlie could have given up on the campaign, but he didn't. He came back to be a key player in Reagan's 1980 campaign. In a sense, perseverance is more than just tenacity. A dog can be tenacious by holding on hard to a rope or bone and not letting it go, but the dog doesn't know why he does it.

By practicing the virtue of perseverance, Charlie stays focused upon what is important. Charlie learned this virtue from mentors like Jesse Helms, who often reminded others, "The Lord does not require you to win, but He does require that you try." Together with the virtue of perseverance goes the virtue of diligence. Strange as it sounds, the virtue of diligence is linked with the virtue of love, because work is love made visible. The diligent person works hard in every little detail because he loves a great cause and knows that a great project is made up of many smaller details. Diligence is a virtue that takes time to acquire. Perhaps Charlie did not set out to acquire this virtue, but through each new job he had, through each new experience, this virtue, grew stronger.

In modern America, no one was better at diligence than Billy Graham. He started as a small-town preacher, but through his experience, he soon learned how to use the many tools available to him—including radio, magazines, television, and gatherings—to spread the message of his gospel. Billy Graham could have just settled in his life at being a preacher at a small church, but he didn't. Aware of his own diligence, he announced: "I am going to preach a gospel not of despair, but of hope—hope for the individual, for society and for the world."

Over time Billy Graham became the advisor to ten presidents, the author of numerous books, and the reformer of many lives. Billy Graham and Charlie certainly share the same passion for their Christian faith. But on a personal level, they share the virtue of diligence. Charlie and Billy Graham both show that diligence can accomplish great things for great causes.

The Honorable Thomas J. Bliley

I n his long and distinguished public career, Tom Bliley has often been described as a gentlemen's Representative. He is known by his Southern stature, manner, and charm. When in the House of Representatives, he stood out with his trademark bow ties. But the most enduring qualities that distinguished Tom were his sense of responsibility and his strong faith.

Bliley is much like the "Patron Saint" of Representatives, Edmund Burke. I have already quoted Burke's admonition to Members of Parliament about the virtue of responsibility: "Your Representative owes you, not his industry only, but his judgment; and he betrays instead of serving you if he sacrifices it to your opinion." There is irony here. Tom followed Burke's advice. Burke lost his seat in Parliament, but Tom did not lose his seat in the House of Representatives. Was that a bad thing? No, because Burke was a man who took a long view of history. Burke believed that:

> All government, indeed, every human benefit and enjoyment, every virtue, and every prudent act, is founded on compromise and barter... Sometimes, to achieve that compromise and barter means paying a personal price, but if it is for the betterment of society, then it is worth it.

In the moment of battle—legislative battle in the case of Burke and Bliley—perspective is often lost. Bliley was involved with many of the fights against so-called big tobacco in the 1980s and 1990s. He shouldered the derisive nickname "The Representative from Phillip-Morris." That sort of misperception was something that Burke saw as part and parcel of the public life, and Bliley bore it in order to responsibly serve his constituents. "Circumstances give reality to every political principle, its distinguishing color and discriminating effect," said Burke. "The circumstances are what render every civil and political scheme beneficial or noxious to mankind." That is to say, sometimes it is difficult to draw absolute lines in representative government. That is why it is so important for representatives like Bliley and Burke to practice the virtue of responsibility.

Responsibility is a funny word. When we are young, as kids, we do whatever we like to do; that is the hallmark of infancy. However when we get older, we hopefully learn, if we mature, to do what we have to do. The virtue of responsibility helps us stick to our duties and priorities even when it is difficult. It recognizes that other people are counting on us to get the job done. That is exactly what Tom did in working across the aisle with Henry Waxman.

Sometimes responsibility is thrust upon us, and we have little choice. Other times, perhaps more virtuously, we seek that responsibility for a greater good. The latter is exactly what Tom did. Tom could have been quite content running his family's funeral business. Instead, he ran for Vice Mayor of Richmond. That was not an easy job for a city still in transition from segregation, but he continued stepping up to more responsibility. Next he served as Mayor, and then he became a U.S. Congressman. The virtue of responsibility sometimes calls one to take a job because it has to be done well. That is something that Burke and Bliley understood.

But Tom is also like another character, Cicero. Recall that Cicero was a Senator in Ancient Rome who stood against corruption. He also articulated the necessity of cultivating virtue while in the pursuit of truth. As Cicero describes in his work entitled *On a Life Well Spent*:

> The best amour of old age is a well spent life preceding it; a life employed in the pursuit of useful knowledge, in honorable Actions and the Practice of Virtue; in which he who labors to improve himself from his youth, will in old age reap the happiest fruits ...

For Tom Bliley, practicing his Catholic faith has consequence in all aspects of his life, including his actions as a legislator. This can be tough to do as a representative. Like Cicero, Bliley's pursuit of truth points to his role as steward of laws in society that have God as their original author:

> True law is right reason in agreement with nature; it is of universal application, unchanging and everlasting; it summons to duty by its commands, and averts from wrongdoing by its prohibitions ... It is a sin to try to alter

this law, nor is it allowable to repeal any part of it, and it is impossible to abolish entirely. We cannot be freed from its obligations by senate or people, and we need not look outside ourselves for an expounder or interpreter of it. And there will not be different laws at Rome and Athens, or different laws now and in the future, but one eternal and unchangeable law will be valid for all nations and all times, and there will be one master and ruler, that is God, over us all, for he is the author of this law, its promulgator, and its enforcing judge. Whoever is disobedient is fleeing from himself and denying his human nature, and by reason of this very fact he will suffer the worst punishment.

His reverence for the truth compelled him to constantly work for honesty and transparency concerning the business of Congress. Bliley wanted to let the American people know what his colleagues and the Administration in power were doing. He was willing to compromise where possible, but anything that could bring harm to faith or family was non-negotiable for him. He stood up on more than one occasion for what he thought was right. Even though much of his legislative district supported abortion, Tom worked tirelessly to educate all who would listen on the issue, and, in Congress, he staunchly defended the dignity of the unborn little ones and their right to be protected from death in the womb. Tom worked as part of the minority on this issue for the first half of his legislative career before his party came into power and he was able to make some progress. Congressman Bliley exemplifies the virtues of responsibility, truth seeking, and faith. He is a true Southern gentleman.

The Honorable William M. Bulger

Bill Bulger is a politician steeped in the wisdom of the Classical Age of Greece. He epitomizes two classical virtues: integrity and wisdom. Bill even acknowledges that he modeled himself after an ancient Greek politician, Demosthenes, and a contemporary politician in Boston, James Michael Curley.

Bulger took to heart the Crown Oration, where Demosthenes defines a statesman:

> Of what a statesman may be responsible for, I allow the utmost scrutiny; I depreciate it not. What are his functions? To observe things in the beginning, to foresee and foretell them to others—this I have done: again, wherever he finds delays, backwardness, ignorance, jealousies, vices inherent and unavoidable in all communities, to contract them into the narrowest compass, and on the other hand to promote unanimity and friendship and zeal in the discharge of duty. All this, too, I have performed; and no one can discover the least neglect on my part.

Asking what exactly makes a statesman, he discovered the virtue of wisdom. Wisdom is what we might call a super virtue. It needs several other virtues in order to function. Indeed, wisdom might be called the virtue that we develop only after we have developed the four cardinal virtues of prudence, justice, fortitude, and temperance to their fullest.

One can never have too much wisdom. Why? Wisdom is a combination of our experiences—of the good we have done, of the bad we have recognized and corrected in our lives, and of the evil deeds of others we have endured. Wise men understand these experiences against a balanced sense of right and wrong. They use fortitude to endure; they use temperance to take in these experiences in the right measure; they use justice to react correctly and fairly to others. In short, wisdom is the final product of a lifetime of learning and experience. That is why the virtue of wisdom is acquired slowly, over time, with one's own effort and the help of others.

Bill studies those who have gone before us precisely to gain wisdom. Look at Bill's life: he has accomplished much as a legislator, passing wise laws and unraveling the difficult issues that confront a university president. Bill has lived by the aphorism that example is always more efficacious than precept, again showing his wisdom. He has endured the insults of others, in particular in reference to his brother. He has been able to apply to his own life the lessons learned from his mentor, Father Thayer. Bill remembers Thayer's observation and works to be the same man whether alone or in the company of others: "Show me what a man does when no one else is around, when no one knows what he is doing," he would say, "and I'll tell you what a person he is, what kind of a person he is."

This leads into the interesting comparison of Bill with James Michael Curley. Curley was an extraordinarily popular politician in Boston. He served both as a Representative in the U.S. House for Massachusetts, as Governor, and four times as Mayor of Boston. His last term as mayor was interrupted with charges of corruption, political charges that ended up placing Curley in jail. President Truman eventually pardoned Curley. Curley never went off course, and he knew what he had to do: he always kept to his duty. In many respects, Curley's description of how to serve in public life is applicable today. One would be wise to take his advice:

> Expect no gratitude for it. Do it and do your best. And if you know it, and no one else knows it, even though they would dispute it … the fact is, if you know otherwise and you are true to yourself in your effort to give your very best public service humanly possible, then you will have something that many people don't have.

Doing one's duty not without expecting reward—and even perhaps enduring punishment for helping others in politics—requires the virtue of altruism. That virtue pushes us to serve others and to neither weigh nor count the cost.

Bill's most powerful example of altruism, one that formed him greatly, was of a woman named Mrs. Pryor, a widow who in Bill's youth lived in the apartment upstairs from him. Mrs. Pryor had five children and a meager income. Yet Bill cannot recall a time when Mrs. Pryor was not kind, patient, and generous with all those in need around her. This was true whether she was out on the street or in her own home. That selfless concern for others, despite all the adversity, was a virtue for Bill to emulate. He has tried to practice the virtues of wisdom and integrity in his own life.

The Honorable Benjamin L. Cardin

Ben Cardin has led a life of public service. He was one of the youngest members of the Maryland House of Delegates; he quickly rose to become its Speaker, and he then served in Congress, first representing Maryland in the House and now in the Senate. Ben describes his ability to commit himself to both public service and his family by practicing the virtues of temperance and prudence:

> When I first started in the legislature, I saw a lot of marriages that were destroyed in Annapolis. I was just really worried about that. Maybe it's inconsistent, family life with public life, and it really challenged me in the beginning. It was not at all inconsistent. Pick your own priorities: if you want to go drinking every night, you can; if you want to go home to your family every night, you can. And the person who goes drinking every night doesn't get any more bills passed than the person who goes home at night. That's true. I got more bills passed than a lot of the drinkers. I became speaker; they didn't. And I went home every night to my family. I felt that was the right thing to do, and I wanted to do that. I married in 1964, so it's been forty-five happy years.

Temperance helps us learn how to feed our appetites in moderation: not too much food or drink but just enough. Ben has taken it to the next level. Temperance is an enabling virtue. Ben displays temperance to give the proper priorities to his life, and the right amount of time that they need. It is tough to deny that because Ben knows when to call it a night, his life produces fruit. This is seen in the numerous bills he has passed; all the people he has helped, from kids to seniors, and the fact that to this day he enjoys a beautiful family and healthy marriage. Because of the balance he shows in all aspects of his life, he is able to be the model legislator.

These achievements are admirable. Sadly, they're also rare. It is a cliché that if we wish to be successful, we must seize the day. Some politicians take this cliché too far and go to lengths too great—stretch themselves too thin—to make sure they've seized the day. A "carpe diem" attitude cares little for temperance; it wants everything a career can give right here and right now. Ben's life shows us that not every moment must be spent to further one's career. He has balanced his priorities of family and of committed public service in order to squeeze the most out of every moment; but he hasn't let the moment squeeze everything out of his life.

Ben's temperance echoes the figure of Isaiah from the Hebrew and Christian scriptures. Isaiah was a prophet. Like Ben, Isaiah had a great deal of temperance: he focused his energy on the mission of helping the people of Israel turn away from their evils and return to the Lord God. Isaiah worked and prophesized over the reign of three different kings of Israel. His message was always consistent because in many respects, his life was always consistent in its focus and in its priorities. Isaiah wanted nothing more than to return Israel to the Lord.

Like Isaiah, Ben shows that temperance is the root of consistency and stability. Great things often take much time to accomplish, and things that are worth doing are often not finished in our lifetimes. Temperance enables one generation to pass along a difficult task to the next with some progress made. Think of all the work on human rights that Ben is doing with the Helsinki Commission. He began his work on the commission precisely because of his priorities, not because it accrued any political advantage for his reelection. But more to the point, Steny Hoyer, Ben's close friend, introduced him to the importance of this work.

Part of what temperance enables is another important virtue that Ben displays: stability. It does seem strange at first to call stability a virtue, but it is. Stability cultivates a sense of historical memory of facts that are truly critical to our civilization. Ben tries to pass on knowledge of the achievements of those who came before us. That is why working on human rights is so important to him: so that mankind never forgets. That's also the echo of Holocaust survivor Elie Wiesel. In his Nobel Prize-winning speech, Wiesel spoke of the necessity of remembering the past in order to safeguard the future:

The call of memory, the call to memory, reaches us from the very dawn of history. No commandment figures so frequently, so insistently, in the Bible. It is incumbent upon us to remember the good we have received, and the evil we have suffered. New Year's Day, Rosh Hashanah, is also called Yom Hazikaron, the Day of Memory. On that day, the day of universal judgment, man appeals to God to remember: our salvation deepens on it. If God wishes to remember our suffering, all will be well; if He refuses, all will be lost. Thus, the rejection of memory becomes a divine curse, one that would doom us to repeat past disasters, past wars.

Ben treasures the virtue of stability. The enduring peace that stability can bring requires that every generation refresh their historical memory of the horrors of the past. We should never forget what occurred before us. In fact, we should cultivate the type of memory recommended by Elie Wiesel—the type that secures a better world. Wiesel explains further:

> My goal is always the same: to invoke the past as a shield for the future, to show the invisible world of yesterday and through it, perhaps on it, erect a moral world where men are not victims and children never starve and never run in fear.

Recall that Ben has all of his staffers call him by his first name at the office. This act itself will make sure that Ben is being reminded of his past. It stems from practicing the virtue of stability. He wants all to remember that our founders believed no one citizen should hold a special title or privilege over another. Ben's first-name policy is a daily reminder to Ben of his place in history.

Ambassador Richard Carlson (Ret.)

Dick Carlson has led a complex, eclectic life. His diverse interests drive everything he does. As his son Tucker said, his dad told him never to pass up an interesting opportunity after a quick cost-benefit analysis. Dick was able to do this because of his intellect, his self-mastery, and his mannerly and ebullient personality.

What do I mean about self-mastery? Dick is one of the most well educated individuals I know. This isn't because he has a string of lettered degrees after his name. It's because he reads, reads, and reads some more.

Like Dick, Abraham Lincoln was a self-educated man. Lincoln was a man of self-mastery. He knew how to stay disciplined and focused in order to better himself. Part of this was out of necessity. Lincoln did not come from money or any sort of privileged establishment. He had to work for everything he needed or wanted, and there were many times he was simply unsuccessful; his first victory in national election was to the presidency. That takes a man who is both confident and able to practice self-mastery so as not to give into any insecurities or fears.

His son Tucker says that his father reads a book a day. Wherever he goes he takes a book with him. The similarities with Lincoln only begin there. At the start of his career, Dick read for the bar in California, teaching himself the law as he worked for a famous lawyer. Like Lincoln, Dick came from quite a difficult background. He was orphaned by teenage parents, he spent his first couple of years in foster care, and by age twelve his adoptive father had passed away, leaving Dick to fend for himself and for his adoptive mother. Both Lincoln and Dick had adverse circumstance. Like many people they could have simply said, "Well, forget it! Life has dealt me a crummy hand, and that's that. What can I make of it?"

Neither Lincoln nor Carlson did that. They both committed themselves to working hard and constantly bettering themselves. Dick's self-mastery is particularly important because of his strong sense of curiosity. Dick wants to try everything, but his self-mastery gives him the ability to follow through with things until the end. He takes what could be a fatal vice—inordinate curiosity—and turns it into his strongest virtue.

Self-mastery is easy to see with Lincoln. He stayed the course on the Civil War because he knew it was his duty to pressure the Union. Never had Americans seen such losses, and certainly not at the hands of other Americans. But Lincoln persevered precisely because he had learned through a lifetime of difficulty to be in control of himself.

Self-mastery helps Dick channel his curiosity and makes him interesting, and his practice of the virtue of gentility makes him charming. Tucker recalls his father's admonition to him to always have good manners; manners are what a person is known for and are what make the most lasting of impressions on others. Dick's manners are not about knowing how to use the right fork. Rather they are an expression of his self-mastery. They are a clear understanding that it is absolutely important and essential to treat others as one would want to be treated.

Manners are something that many great leaders have understood are always needed. George Washington spent a great deal of his youth studying, categorizing, and memorizing the most important of manners. He copied and studied *Rules of Civility & Decent Behavior in Company and Conversation* before he turned sixteen. At first, the manners seem somewhat silly, if not completely obvious: don't hum to yourself when others are in the room; don't ever come out half dressed; cover your mouth when you cough. Yes, these seem like the basic needs of decorum for society.

Washington goes on to offer more wisdom:

> Don't be glad at another's misfortune. Stand when someone comes to speak with you if you are sitting. Do not be arrogant and lecture those who are your equal in an art. Associate yourself with men of good quality.

Gentility was evident in Washington, for he is often remembered as a figure "above the fray." In fact, in his farewell address Washington warned that partisanship—championing your own political cause—can run contrary to a spirit of manners that seeks to treat all as an equal.

Dick often laments with de Tocqueville (specifically his book *Democracy in America*) that "There are many men of principle in both parties in

America, but there is no party of principle." His commitment to manners might be part of the solution. Washington's wisdom aside, political parties are essentially here to stay in America. They are not going anywhere anytime soon. But it is possible to practice gentility on both sides of the aisle. For Dick, learning manners makes one a gentleman with whom people are willing to work; they are willing to look past differences when dealing with a gentleman.

Dick has known many interesting people in his life, including movie stars, businessmen, mob bosses, singers, and politicians. These connections exist because Dick's extraordinary personality, knowledge, and good manners made such a positive impression on the people around him. Dick is a man of principle, but more to the point, he knows that good principle is nothing if you do not know how to treat others with respect. Dick, like Washington, demonstrates the force multiplier that a virtue like gentility enables.

Paul F. Eckstein, Esquire

When you talk about the great lawyers in American history, one name comes to my mind: Atticus Finch. Intelligent, full of strength and integrity, committed—Atticus is the lawyer every counsel at the bar should want to be. He is prepared for every case and has a highly developed sense of justice. There is just one problem: Atticus isn't real. The fact that Atticus is a creation of Harper Lee further adds to the growing cynicism in America about lawyers. Do lawyers as dedicated as Atticus exist? Of course they do! There are many and many of them. Would that more people knew Paul Eckstein. He is the embodiment of Atticus Finch. Paul is more dedicated to the practice of the law than any attorney I know. This isn't by accident. Paul made a conscious decision to practice the law and to practice it well. He learned from the very best, Jack Brown, about the level of dedication it takes to complete the job and to make sure one gives one's client not just a fair and adequate representation, but the very best.

Paul is very sensitive to this fact; he is very keen at fostering the virtue of dedication to work and the service of his fellow man. Why else would he, a Jew, dress up as Santa Claus every Christmas for the poor children of Mexico, if he wasn't dedicated to making life better for them? Why does he keep helping his alma mater time and again if not for dedication to keeping education high caliber? Why is Paul known as one of the country's top lawyers, if not for the fact that he'll never settle for merely doing the work? To be dedicated means precisely to give not just when it hurts, but when you have no more to give—and when you don't want to give any more.

As a lawyer Paul has had enough moments where giving less than he gave would have been enough. Think of when he represented the university athletic director who was ousting a popular and winning football coach. Paul could have just given him advice and called it a day. Instead, he went the extra mile, even going to watch the coach's last football game with the outgoing athletic director, when they both knew it would be at the very least uncomfortable for both. Recall how Paul undertook the prosecution and the impeachment of the governor of Arizona, even when he was being paid little to try the difficult case. Just his advice would have been more than enough, but Paul went the extra mile and secured impeachment of the sitting governor.

Several traits spur on Paul's extraordinary dedication. There is, of course, the reality of the Golden Rule, by which Paul tries to live: "Do unto others as you would have them do unto you." But it is a deeper motivation that drives Paul. It is a love of truth. "To be a person of truth," says Rabbi Nockmen of Breslaff, "be swayed neither by approval or disapproval. Work not needing approval from anyone; then you'll be free to be who you really are." The dedicated person doesn't care what others think or say; he just does what has to be done.

Paul is also dedicated to justice. In many respects, Paul is like a figure from scriptures; Abraham in that neither of them saw themselves called to the cause of justice at an early age. Paul never thought he'd practice law his entire career. Abraham was just an itinerant herder. In the scriptures, God calls Abraham to a contract, a covenant with God. If Abraham promises to be faithful to God, God will be faithful to Abraham.

Abraham may be thought of as the first lobbyist. He petitioned God to relent from destroying Sodom and Gomorrah even though they broke their covenant with God. But why did he do this? According to the Bible, these cities Sodom and Gomorrah were two cities overrun by depravity, from their sky-high crime rates to rampant sexual deviancy and a general disregard for the people around them.

Like Paul, Abraham had dedication to justice and to his fellow man. He hoped that a few men who practiced virtue could be enough to spare the cities from God's wrath. He was able to find nine even amid the corruption. Similarly, even if some lawyers are corrupt, as long as men like Paul are around—men dedicated to justice and their fellow man—we know that somehow the whole profession can be saved.

This is not easy. The temptations for the lawyer to cut corners and to go through the motions are many. Paul talks to young lawyers time and again about this. Yet Paul knows that the key to cultivating a sense of justice for the lawyer is cultivating a strong work ethic. Practicing the law, like any profession, is hard. A dedication to justice can only be achieved by truly committing oneself to the difficulty of the task and by not cutting corners. Thus, this type of dedication is not in the heroism of winning a great case, but in the willingness to commit oneself again and again to the mundane and grueling.

Dedication to work, to his fellowman, and to justice is the reason people wanted to hire Atticus Finch. All had a sense that he'd get the job done. That's the same reason why people turn to Paul Eckstein. These same dedications make Paul an excellent lawyer and a special person.

Admiral Thomas C. Lynch (Ret.)

A lifetime in the navy with a myriad of responsibilities shows two things about Tom. He is a man with a classical sense of the virtue of doing one's duty, which encompasses the sub-virtues of courage and magnanimity. Back in classical Greece, there was a man known as Pericles. He was a great military and political leader with a strong sense of right and wrong. More important, he had the necessary fortitude to know when to do and to say the right thing. In a funeral oration for the soldiers of Athens, Pericles identifies the fusion between courage and thought that the Athenians alone possessed among their fellow Greeks:

> Then, again, our military training is in many respects superior to that of our adversaries... We rely not upon management or trickery, but upon our own hearts and hands. And in the matter of education, whereas they from early youth are always undergoing laborious exercises which are to make them brave, we live at ease, and yet are equally ready to face the perils which they face ... we go alone into a neighbor's country; and although our opponents are fighting for their homes, and we on a foreign soil, we have seldom any difficulty in overcoming them... If then we prefer to meet danger with a light heart but without laborious training, and with a courage, which is gained by habit and not enforced by law, are we not greatly the better for it? Since we do not anticipate the pain, although, when the hour comes, we can be as brave as those who never allow themselves to rest; thus our city is equally admirable in peace and in war. For we have a peculiar power of thinking before we act, and of acting, too, whereas other men are courageous from ignorance but hesitate upon reflection.

Like the Athenians, Tom practices the virtues of courage and magnanimity as part of doing his duty because he has gained them by habit over a lifetime. Tom was trained at the Naval Academy not only to think before acting, but also to practice the virtue of courage and act after the thinking was done. Perhaps the first place this manifested itself was his position as captain of the 1963 "almost" National Championship football team, which included the great quarterback Roger Staubach, Tom's close personal friend. But that was also the football team that, composed of young sailors, had to carry the burden of a nation deep in the fall of 1963 after the assassination of President Kennedy. This was a duty that Tom thoughtfully executed with courage. That was a team with a "can do" attitude, despite all the odds.

Fast forward in Tom's career to his first command. His mantra while in command was, "Ship. Shipmates. Self." Tom's sense of duty allowed him to discover the secret to greatness: serving, giving, and forgetting himself.

Tom's strong sense of duty led him to practicing the virtues of courage and magnanimity. In this regard, Tom is not unlike the ancient figure of Cincinnatus. He was the farmer who took up arms and absolute power in Rome for a short period to get the empire through a crisis. Unlike notable dictators, Cincinnatus laid down his power at the end of the emergency and returned to farming. He knew when to do his duty. He knew when his duty was over.

Admiral Lynch spent a naval career doing his duty. He stuck with the Navy even during the difficult times after Vietnam in the 1970s, when suicide and alcoholism and attrition were rampant. That is duty. He returned to the Naval Academy as Superintendent. When the opportunity came to become a three-star admiral, an opportunity presented to only a few, Tom said no thanks. He was Cincinnatus. He knew his duty was over and it was time to return to life as a private citizen.

Ambassador Charles T. Manatt (Ret.)

Chuck Manatt has cultivated himself as he cultivated his Iowa farmland, and from this self-improvement, he has put himself in a position of power. He now can use his power to help others with efficacy, as his selfless disposition inclines him to do. Chuck's practice of the virtue of generosity comes first and foremost from his connection to the farmlands of Iowa. Growing up, Chuck learned to practice that very simple creed of the Future Farmers of America: learn to earn, earn to live, and live to serve. Think about how straightforward that makes life. Learn a useful skill. Why? So you can provide for yourself. Why is that important? So that you can help others.

Like some of the other virtues mentioned, Citizenship seems strange to discuss. If most people were asked, "What does citizenship mean?" they would probably answer that it is being from a particular country. "I'm American, so I have an American passport. I salute the red, white, and blue. I watch fireworks on the Fourth of July; I eat apple pie on Thanksgiving." What virtue is in that?

As Chuck has shown us, citizenship is more than that. It is a commitment to practicing the virtue of generosity. In particular it is using our talents and our abilities to serve our fellow citizens for the common good. From the outside looking in, many people look at politics and a long-time political operative like Chuck and say, "Well, he just wants his guy in power." That's a crude and quite cynical oversimplification. If one looks at a guy like Chuck—who has committed a lifetime to law, farming, banking, democracy building, and party politics—one sees that the virtue of citizenship is precisely about serving others. And most fundamentally, it is

about leaving the country and the world in better shape for future generations.

Perhaps no figures in our nation's history stand out more in the quality of citizenship than Virginia's Thomas Jefferson. Like Chuck, Jefferson
was intelligent, well educated, and committed to public service. Both were
agrarians, Jefferson running his plantation at Monticello and Chuck raising
hogs in Iowa. Jefferson was a party man, the founder of the Anti-Federalists
(later the Democratic Party that Chuck served as the National Party Chairman).

Indeed, like Chuck's great love of farming, Jefferson had a great love
of cultivation. Jefferson helped save the worldwide wine industry in the
eighteenth century when he discovered how to graft grapes onto a grape-
stock that was resistant to a pestilence destroying crops around the world.
Although not as dramatic, Chuck has on many occasions stepped in to save
farms and help farmers in need throughout Iowa.

Jefferson knew that a commitment to America meant a commitment to
the virtue of citizenship. Both men served in whatever capacity was asked
or required of them. It seems that Chuck understands this same quality of
being ready, willing, and able to serve whatever and however it is necessary.
This is an important tradition begun by the likes of Jefferson and continued
through Chuck today.

Practicing the virtue of good citizenship requires another virtue: generosity. For Jefferson and Chuck, the virtue of generosity is simply a facet of
selfless citizenry. Both men would never turn down someone in need. Like
Jefferson, Chuck has spent a lifetime helping those less fortunate, from back
in the farmlands in Iowa to his time in California, to Native America on the
Red Cloud Reservation, to folks in Latin America, where he continues to
be helpful even though his term has ended as the U.S. ambassador to the
Dominican Republic.

The virtue of generosity should not be confused with the idea of largesse. Possessing much and giving it away was something that the so-called
robber barons did, as did the aristocracy before them. We call that largesse,
not so much because it is a virtue, but merely because it is the ability to
extend power and influence.

The virtue of generosity requires a giving of self. It means caring for
others not because it makes you look good, but precisely because it helps
others in whatever needs they happen to have. Chuck's life demonstrates
that virtue. He doesn't help merely because he has the resources to do so,

or because it will make him look good. He does it because, as the creed of the Future Farmers of America taught him, it is the right thing to do. That is precisely what it means to be generous. Chuck, like Jefferson, is that generous citizen. His life can simply be summed up with wise words from Winston Churchill: "We make a living by what we get; we make a life by what we give."

The Honorable Rick J. Santorum

Rick Santorum has many admirable qualities, but above all he is staunchly principled. It is for good reason that during his time in Congress, Rick was often referred to as the conscience of the Senate. His principles and conviction were always clear. Rick always took his responsibility seriously; he always had a clear vision based upon hope.

Among historical figures, it's hard not to think of an easy comparison between Rick and Saint Thomas More: Both were men of principle. Both valued faith and family as first in their lives. Both were willing to take responsibility for their actions and their principles, even if that meant sacrificing career in Rick's case, and in More's case his very life.

Thomas More lived in England during a tumultuous time. Henry VIII was King, and before his break with the Roman Catholic Church, he was considered a great Defender of the Catholic Faith. Some say that More even penned the treatise that won Henry VIII accolades from the Pope in Rome. In any case, because of faith and because of his wisdom, Henry VIII drew More close to his inner counsel. He eventually conferred upon More, the Chancellor, the functional equivalent of the President's Chief of Staff, or the Prime Minister in present-day Great Britain.

More took his responsibility seriously. His last words before being beheaded were, "I am the king's good servant, but I am God's first." He knew where his duties and loyalties lied.

Rick, like Thomas More, displays a similar hierarchy of values. Think of Rick's fight to pass legislation banning partial-birth abortion. Despite the electoral peril the issue of abortion always holds, Rick never backed down, through two vetoes and one Supreme Court reversal, to pass a law that he felt was necessary. Rick saw that law bear fruit even before it was enacted.

Recall that young couple that saw Rick's plea on television and repented of the abortion they were contemplating.

Rick paid a price for being principled, just like More. Henry VIII wanted More, the skilled lawyer and intellect, to navigate his divorce with Rome. When More refused, Henry VIII attempted to force More to swear an oath that Henry VIII and the Crown were supreme over More's Catholic faith. More's sense of responsibility and principles stood firm; he said no. Rick commented that sometimes you have to speak the truth, and when you take the hit, you take the hit. Like More, such a firm perspective on responsibility is only based on a long-term view of how to conduct oneself. He realized that this life, though short, counts and that people must make it count. *Tempus Fugit. Momento Mori.* Time passes quickly. Remember death.

More literally gave his life to fulfill what he believed was his responsibility. Rick stuck to his guns and suffered one of the more lopsided defeats for an incumbent senator. Rick was neither deterred nor distraught. Like the catchphrase of the fictional president Josiah Bartlett on *The West Wing*, Rick simply asked, "What's next?" Rick embodies this motto. Think of how he conducted his meetings in the Senate: he went from one office to the next, popping in for the important moments. He knew what his responsibility was, and he also knew to trust those working for him to be responsible and do their duty.

Rick's practice of the virtue of responsibility becomes a very expansive and social virtue because it is grounded in a sense of priority. Like More, Rick has a sense of priorities in his responsibility. One of the most famous portraits is the Hans Holbein portrait of More praying with his family. More, in the center wearing his chancellor's chain with a prayer book in his lap, leads his family in nightly prayer. Family prayer was a habit that formed both More's and Rick's character. Rick places leading his family in faith at the center of everything he does. Rick knows that this starts with placing his wife first among his relationships.

For a legislator, perspective and responsibility mean little without vision. For vision, Rick looks to another Englishman and legislator, William Wilberforce, for inspiration. Wilberforce thought big. He had vision. He knew that England could never be the country it was supposed to be unless it ended the injustice of the slave trade. England was both responsible for evil and perpetuating that evil around the world. Likewise, Wilberforce knew that the people of England lacked compassion for their fellow men. The changes of the industrial revolution were creating a new society, one that at times was hostile to the weakest. Wilberforce dedicated his thirty-plus years in parliament to help the weakest, even when it cost him friendships and health.

Like Wilberforce, Rick thinks big. He has committed himself truly to two great causes in our society: to defending the unborn child, whom Rick sees as deserving the right to life, and to strengthening the family. Rick has definitely suffered for the commitment to his vision. But his vision is not deterred. Rick keeps on going. This combination of vision with responsibility, the melding of More and Wilberforce, has made Rick a formidable character, even when he is seemingly out of the game.

Lessons Learned

The Thinker sculpture by Auguste Rodin, Musée Rodin, Paris, depicts a man in sober meditation, attempting to choose wisely.

Good character is important to politics. That has been the central theme in this book. Hopefully, through the interviews, our ten characters have shown that principle and power can interact properly in politics to achieve great things for the common good. The integrity of all of our characters has remained intact, persevering through difficulties. They came to crossroads and chose a path—the right path, the path of principle.

Our nation counts on these ten people of good character—and thousands of others like them who work day in and day out in our government—to provide essential services necessary for our life. Their good character isn't a convenience or luxury; it is an essential element.

When considered collectively, our characters display several habits in common. All of our characters value continuous learning and are voracious readers. All know the value of storytelling; they tell stories to their children to pass along values. They communicate to help inform others with their stories from campaigns, court trials, and travels. All are, as Aristotle says, "social animals," serving others through the political arena.

But there is more. Many had key defining moments. Marriage and good families are important to all ten. Hard work and perseverance are values of all because their respective mentors nurtured these traits through good example. Each character values integrity. While they are skilled at the art of compromise, they also know when to stick to their principles in political exchanges, even when doing so requires taking a hit. Each character values humor as a means to stay above the fray, which is essential for public service. Conversely, each character recognizes when politics ceases and show business begins. All the characters reject that type of demagoguery. They caution others about trying to be too clever. Because our characters have had strong mentors, they generously mentor others. Several of the characters, because of their party loyalty, have supported candidates that were not their first or second choices. However, if a principle is important enough to our characters, they are willing to oppose even party leaders, or in Senator Cardin's case, his President. Even when they have had to pay a price for maintaining their integrity, they do so.

The interviews reveal some differences that are also worth considering. One important distinction involves the contrasting worldviews held by the Democrats versus the Republican characters interviewed. Democratic characters seem to be visionaries about the human condition. Like Robert F. Kennedy, they see things that never were and say, "Why not?" The Democrats are inspired by an idealism that seeks a better world. They think that generally people desire to be good and to make themselves and the world a better place. They also see government as the primary agent for change that can make these dreams come true.

The Republican characters tend to hold a slightly more cautious view of human nature. Their worldview is not far from that of Kenneth Hobbes, who saw life as "nasty, brutish, and short." The Republican view is also close to that of St. Augustine, who realized that while men were created good, they have fallen and have a natural proclivity toward evil. For the Republicans, the first role of government—its dominant role—is to protect and hedge against the evil potential in all men's hearts. Senator Santorum's fight against partial birth abortion is a good example of this mindset.

Another important distinction arises around party-line approaches to compassion. The Democrats, for the most part, seem to adopt compassion as the foundation for building a just society. This makes them adept practitioners of the "politics of pathos." The Republicans do not always share this view of compassion as a virtue. They see it as emotion—not a virtue, only a fleeting feeling that can yield to self-interest. This may seem like a cold-hearted view, but when adversity strikes, the Republicans have the advantage of appearing less surprised and more capable of promptly confronting the evil acts of others.

There is also an area of agreement across party lines. Both sides of the political aisle share their trust in government. Few of the characters see their roles as restraining government. Both Republican and Democratic members are more concerned about how to play the game of politics ethically as opposed to the expediency of winning elections or passing particular pieces of legislation. Of course, they want to win at the polls and be effective public servants, but they are more concerned about acting rightly and having their careers come to a graceful end.

Let us take a last look at the role models for good character presented in this book. Like those in civilization's past, they have acted based upon the good example and values that were handed to them from their families, teachers, and mentors. By studying the lives and conversations of the characters in *Politics with Principle*, we can identify some of the guiding principles that enabled them to preserve virtue while working in politics. We can pass them on to the next generation of political leaders.

Guiding Principles for Aspiring Public Servants

Make the best decision you can from where you stand and don't look back.

🪶

Be prepared to resign your position or fire your client when asked to participate in, or condone, unjustifiable conduct.

🪶

Be prepared to take principled stands, even against what is perceived as popular wisdom.

🪶

Disagree with others when necessary, but do it in a civil and agreeable manner.

🪶

Master humility.

✥

When you come to Washington, don't get carried away with the trappings of office. Stick with what got you here.

✥

Realize that it will have to be enough that you alone know what good you have done.

✥

Have a clear and grand vision, but master the details as well.

✥

Never stop learning, seek out and learn from great people.

✥

Always practice good manners and think about others first.

✥

Be selfless. Practice the Judeo-Christian Golden Rule: "Do unto others as you would have them do unto you." No one can do it perfectly, but try to sacrifice for the greater good.

✥

Be honest with yourself about yourself and with others in all things.

✥

Never lie, cheat, or steal.

❧

Be trustworthy to all and loyal to your friends.

❧

Treasure the blessing of a good and lasting marriage and the family it produces.

❧

Go home at night. Establish your own priorities and remember them.

❧

You owe not just your industry to your constituents, but your judgment.

❧

Stand for what you believe in, even though it may not be popular.

❧

Keep yourself on a short leash. Focus every hour of every day on what you ought to be doing, not want you might want to be doing.

❧

Do not to be the first to adopt the new—nor the last to throw away the old.

❦

Never compromise your principles. It's a fallacy to say that compromising compromises what you believe in. It does not. It's being able to effectively carry out what you believe in by being willing to sit down and make concessions in other areas.

❦

You've got to listen. Listening is not just saying, "I'm going to listen, but you won't have any impact." Listening means I may disagree with you, but by listening, you may have an impact, and I may change my view. I may not. But I will really listen.

❦

Standing up for what you believe is right, but do it in a good way, leave out a little bit of the puffery, the arrogance, the pride.

❦

Mothers, fathers, aunts, uncles, and grandparents all work hard. You just watch them. You see it. You understand. No one has to tell you to work hard.

❦

Strength is clearly part of character, being willing to stand up and not be intimidated and get the mission accomplished. But if that turns into blindness about the moral direction in which you are going, and blindness to what is an acceptable process, or blindness to changes in circumstances, then that's a weakness.

❧

The end does not justify the means. You have to have a sense of morality.

❧

Develop and obey a moral compass and have a clear view of the "right."

❧

Seek the Truth, and, when found, live it.

❧

Look at success through the eyes of God, then it is very easy to figure out the virtues that lead you to success.

❧

Always work as hard as you can, pray as hard as you can, and leave the rest up to God.

❧ ❧ ❧

Abraham Lincoln called America "the last best hope" for the world. From these interviews, we have learned how ten good characters have worked to secure that hope for our present generation. The question remains: Will we continue their good work by supporting character development in our rising generation of political players? Or will we, quite simply, drop the ball?

Our government is important, but it is only a means and not the end. No government can make its people good. No laws can make its people moral. It is up to each of us grow another generation of characters with character.

There is work to be done. Developing and mentoring principled be-havior in our young citizens—whether through family, church, school, or formative organizations like the Boy and Girl Scouts or Future Farmers of America—is the task ahead. This task is critically important to our future because it will secure and protect the liberties necessary for the pursuit of happiness.

Our ten characters now hand off unfinished business. In his second inaugural address, Abraham Lincoln offers fitting words as the unfinished task is passed:

With malice toward none, with charity for all, with firmness in the right as God gives us to see the right, let us strive on to finish the work we are in, to bind up the nation's wounds, to care for him who shall have borne the battle and for his widow and his orphan, to do all which may achieve and cherish a just and lasting peace among ourselves and with all nations.

It is for us, the *vox populi*, to try to guide aspiring young politicians, to make sure they understand the importance of cultivating virtue and developing good character as they prepare for public life, and to reinforce good character when and where we see it in our present leaders.

We must reclaim Lincoln's spirit of virtue (charity) over vice (malice) by building the character of our elected officials long before they take office. Hopefully, this will help to bind up our nation's present wounds of partisan rancor and replace them with politics of virtue.

About the Author

I am a blessed man, husband to a loving wife of forty-two years, and proud father of three UVA lawyers. All my children survived my parenting, married well, albeit to more lawyers, and graced our ever-expanding clan with eleven beautiful and talented grandchildren.

My career has not always been as idyllic as my family life. I have labored in the tough advocacy business, lobbying in Washington and in the states. The first half of my career included work representing tobacco. Through that time, like Diogenes, I wondered if an honest man could be found among the assertive legislators, lawyers, and lobbyists who shape and prod what emerges from our Congress and our state legislatures. I even questioned whether, if Diogenes were successful, would I be among the "found"? My soul-searching found me falling back upon my Catholic upbringing and firmly committing, in spite of secular challenges, to "know, love, and serve God in this world." I preached the priorities of "God, family, country" to my children because I believed them myself.

In the advocacy business, I would defend the right of all sides of any argument to be heard, but I would neither cross the line to murky conduct, nor personally yield to expediency. My growing conviction about the necessity of seeking the "greater good" and avoiding evil led me to meet others in politics that seemed to share this goal; it enabled me to make many sincere friends in the halls of power. My friendships with them have been, and continue to be, based on a shared pursuit of "God, family, country," coupled with the simple enjoyment of a good pal ... nothing more, nothing less.

As I transition from lobbying for commercial clients to advocating character building, I feel an urgency to pass on the "God, family, country" priorities to my grandchildren and to the rising generation of Americans. Keeping these three in focus allowed me to grow in virtue and keep a healthy balance in an arena fraught with temptations. I hope to share my approach with others who plan a career in politics. I intend to raise awareness among all who will listen about the importance of cultivating in their daily lives, something as old as Greece and Rome, the Aristotelian habit of good conduct called virtue. By again passing on the need for virtue, the capstone of our Judeo-Greco-Roman-Christian heritage, I hope to inspire the next generation of public servants to seek both the "greater good" and personal virtue.

Politics with Principle is my contribution toward raising virtue literacy in our country. It is proof-of-principle that virtue and politics need not, and must not, be severed from one another. I intend to assemble from this first step a comprehensive Character Building Project (http://www.characters-with-character.com). Please visit the Web site and join my virtue literacy campaign.